Karl Marx

MARX
ENGELS

The
Socialist
Revolution

PROGRESS Publishers

Moscow

Compilers: F. TEPLOV and V. DAVYDOV

Preface by F. TEPLOV

Маркс
Энгельс

О СОЦИАЛИСТИЧЕСКОЙ РЕВОЛЮЦИИ
(Сборник)

На английском языке

First printing 1978

English translation © Progress Publishers 1978

Printed in the Union of Soviet Socialist Republics

М/Э $\dfrac{10101-633}{014(01)-78}$ 12—78

Contents

The theory of socialist revolution is one of the most important sections of Marxist-Leninist science. Its basic principles were formulated in the 19th century by Karl Marx and Frederick Engels.

The general philosophical basis underlying the Marxist theory of revolution is the *materialist conception of history*. In contrast to their predecessors, Marx and Engels extended philosophical materialism and the dialectic—the theory of development—to the sphere of history. They showed that the production and reproduction of material life is the basis of the life of society and the historical process. History is the natural process of development and change of socio-economic formations. The movement of social forms depends ultimately on the development of the productive forces, to the level of which the relations of production and of property must invariably adapt themselves. The relations of production thus form the basis of society upon which the superstructure is erected, that is, political, juridical and other relations and the institutions corresponding to them, forms of social consciousness and ideology, etc. The objective contradiction between the productive forces and the relations of production, between the mode of production of a given society and its forms, leads at a certain stage of development to radical changes in the life of society, to social revolution. This contradiction constitutes the *material basis* of revolution. Revolution completes the process whereby the preconditions for a new system gradually mature within the old, resolves the contradiction between new productive forces and old relations of production, smashes obsolete relations

---

a) English translation © Progress Publishers 1978

of production and the political superstructure securing them and provides room for further growth of the productive forces.

The classic formulation of the materialist conception of history is to be found in Marx's "Preface to *A Contribution to the Critique of Political Economy.*" Marx emphasises that the essence of social revolution lies in resolving the conflict between the productive forces and the relations of production and in the transition from one socio-economic system to another, noting that "no social order ever perishes before all the productive forces for which there is room in it have developed; and new, higher relations of production never appear before the material conditions of their existence have matured in the womb of the old society itself" (see p. 117 of this book).

While underlining the objective character of the historical process, Marxism also attaches great importance to the conscious actions of classes, parties, groups and individuals, emphasising the immense role of advanced revolutionary theory. The fundamental principles of Marxism concerning the role of the people in history were already formulated in *The Holy Family*, the first joint work of Marx and Engels. Recognition of the decisive role of the people is one of the most important principles of the materialist conception of history. The masses, the working people, workers and peasants, constitute the most important productive force in society. By their labour they create all material wealth and are true creators of history:"Of all the instruments of production, the greatest productive power is the revolutionary class itself" (see p. 46 of this book). In the course of the progressive development of history the importance of the decisive role of the people is steadily growing. The broader and deeper the upheaval which takes place in society, the more numerous are the masses which carry it out. "Together with the thoroughness of the historical action, the size of the mass whose action it is will therefore increase" (Marx and Engels, *Collected Works*, Vol. 4, Moscow, 1975, p. 82). Social revolutions are accomplished by the people. "Where it is a question of a complete transformation of the social organisation, the masses themselves must also be in it, must themselves already have grasped what is at stake, what they are going in for, body and soul", Engels noted in 1895, reviewing some of the results of the class battles in the second half of the 19 th century (see p. 318 of this book).

Investigating the laws of material production and the dialectic of the productive forces and the relations of production, Marx and

Engels demonstrated that the source of development, the motive force of all societies which are divided into classes is the class struggle. Marxism teaches us to see the struggle between classes, the struggle between exploited and exploiters, as the principal factor behind every political, social and other change in the life of society. Social revolutions represent the culmination points of this struggle in antagonistic formations. "The history of all hitherto existing society is the history of class struggles... oppressor and oppressed stood in constant opposition to one another, carried on an uninterrupted, now hidden, now opén fight, a fight that each time ended, either in a revolutionary re-constitution of society at large, or in the common ruin of the contending classes" (Marx and Engels, *Collected Works*, Vol. 6, Moscow, 1976, p. 482). The class struggle of the proletariat against the bourgeoisie inevitably leads to the social revolution of the working class, to socialist revolution, which is the highest type of social revolution.

Marx and Engels also showed that the great historical significance of social revolutions consists not only in the fact that they advance society to a higher stage of development, to a new socio-economic system, but also in the fact that they are powerful accelerators of social and political progress. In *The Class Struggles in France* Marx graphically termed revolutions "the locomotives of history" which greatly speed up the pace of development and unleash the powerful creative forces of the people (Marx and Engels, *Selected Works*, Vol. 1, Moscow, 1976, p. 277). Revolutions make it possible to accomplish in months or years what, under ordinary conditions, would require many decades or even centuries to carry out. They are a festival of the oppressed and exploited. The mass of the people are never more active in creating social orders than during revolutions.

In analysing the necessary material preconditions for a revolutionary upheaval in *The German Ideology*, Marx and Engels noted that there must be present for this "....on the one hand the existing productive forces, on the other the formation of a revolutionary mass, which revolts not only against separate conditions of the existing society, but against the existing 'production of life' itself, the 'total activity' on which it was based" (Marx and Engels, *Collected Works*, Vol. 5, Moscow, 1976, p. 54).

These ideas are developed in more detail in the *Manifesto of the Communist Party*. Capitalism is a natural stage in the development of mankind; it is progressive by comparison with feudalism, but is an historically transient stage, which will give way to more highly organised social relations. In creating colossal productive forces, bourgeois society has thereby paved the way for its own downfall; it has given birth to its own grave-digger—the proletariat. The struggle between labour and capital is universal, it has a world-wide character. At a certain stage of development private ownership of the means of production becomes a fetter on the productive forces, making the destruction of capitalism by socialist revolution inevitable. The conflict between the developing productive forces and the obsolete bourgeois relations of production is the economic basis of the socialist revolution. The irreconcilable contradiction between the proletariat, the chief productive force of capitalist society, and the bourgeoisie, which appropriates the greater part of the product created by wage-labour, constitutes its social, class basis.

Revolution by the proletariat is the only possible means of transforming bourgeois society. Its purpose is to bring the relations of production into conformity with the gigantic productive forces developed by capitalism, thereby creating conditions for the further advance of society—the achievement of mastery over the forces of nature, the flowering of the individual and the harmonious combination of the interests of the individual and society. No previous revolution has done away with exploitation of man by man: only its forms have been changed. The proletarian revolution eradicates all exploitation and establishes public ownership of the means of production—in this lies its essential difference from all other revolutions.

Marx's *Capital*, his major work and the labour of his entire life, gives the most fundamental economic proof of the inevitability of socialist revolution. "Along with the constantly diminishing number of the magnates of capital ... grows the mass of misery, oppression, slavery, degradation, exploitation; but with this too grows the revolt of the working class, a class always increasing in numbers, and disciplined, united, organised by the very mechanism of the process of capitalist production itself. The monopoly of capital becomes a fetter upon the mode of production, which has sprung up and flourished along with, and under it. Centralisation of the means of production and socialisation of labour at last reach a point where they become incompatible with their capitalist integument. Thus integument is burst asunder. The knell of capitalist private property sounds. The expropriators are expropriated" (Karl Marx, *Capital*, Vol. 1, Moscow, 1974, p. 715).

Marx emphasises that, in establishing public ownership of the basic means of production, the socialist revolution transforms the whole of society. The spontaneous, blind action of objective economic laws is replaced by their conscious utilisation: by the planned regulation of social production for the good of each member of society and of society as a whole.

The scientific proof of the inevitability of the collapse of capitalism does not, of course, mean that this will take place of itself, automatically. In addition to objective preconditions, which do not depend on the consciousness or will of men, conscious revolutionary mass actions are also necessary. In order to abolish the outmoded capitalist relations of production the power of the ruling classes defending this basis of their domination, must be broken and for this revolutionary power is needed. Marx and Engels not only demonstrated the necessity for socialist revolution, but they also revealed the social force to which history has assigned this most revolutionary task. This force is the proletariat, the working class, in whose hands, as Marx put it, lies "the renaissance of mankind".

The *Manifesto of the Communist Party* reveals the world-wide historic mission of the proletariat with exceptional power and depth. The working class is given birth to by capitalism itself and grows, develops, unites and organises itself in direct proportion to the progress of industrial development. The objective position of the proletariat as wage-labour of capital in itself makes it the irreconcilable enemy of the entire system of wage-slavery. Constantly growing while other oppressed classes split and become fragmented, this class is the only unwaveringly consistent and uncompromising opponent of all forms of exploitation and every kind of oppression.

The working class's struggle against capitalism is not aimed at its own emancipation alone: its interests coincide with those of the broadest sections of the working people. Capitalism leaves the peasantry and the urban petty bourgeoisie no alternative to decline and ruin; for them the only solution is to join the proletariat in the struggle to overthrow the rule of capital. The proletariat cannot emancipate itself without eradicating forever all forms of social and national enslavement and thereby emancipating the whole of society. That is why it is this class, lacking private property, concentrated in the key centres of bourgeois society, united and organised and conscious of its fundamental interests, that forms the vanguard and leader of all working people in the struggle for full social emancipation, socialism and communism. This has now been demonstrated many times in practice, as history shows. "It is to the great historic merit of Marx and Engels that they indicated to the workers of the world their role, their task, their mission, namely, to be the first to rise in the revolutionary struggle against capital and to rally around themselves in this struggle *all* working and exploited people," Lenin wrote (V. I. Lenin, *Collected Works*, Vol. 28, p. 165).

The world-wide scale of the struggle between labour and capital determines the international character of the proletarian movement. One of the most important conditions for the victory of the proletariat is the internationalism of its revolutionary actions. In setting up the International Working Men's Association, Marx and Engels saw its object in "combining and generalising the till now disconnected efforts for emancipation by the working classes in different countries", in working consistently to put the principles of proletarian internationalism into practice (Marx and Engels, *Selected Works,* Vol. 2, Moscow, 1976, p. 77). National narrow-mindedness, neglect or violation of these principles harm not only the international labour movement but, above all, its separate national detachments. "Past experience has shown how disregard of that bond of brotherhood which ought to exist between the workmen of different countries, and incite them to stand firmly by each other in all their struggle for emancipation, will be chastised by the common discomfiture of their incoherent efforts," Marx wrote in the "Inaugural Address of the International Working Men's Association" (Marx and Engels, *Selected Works*, Vol. 2, Moscow, 1976, p. 17). The international power of capital and the united efforts directed by the bourgeoisie of various countries against the proletariat must be opposed by the international unity and solidarity of the working class. It is a necessary condition for its victory. "Nothing but an international bond of the working classes can ever ensure the definite triumph" (Marx/Engels, *Werke*, Bd. 16, Berlin, 1968, S. 322).

Marx and Engels laid the foundations for the theory of the Communist Party as the revolutionary conscious vanguard of the proletariat, its organiser and leader. They demonstrated that leadership of such a party is an indispensable condition for the implementation of the world-wide historical mission of the working class. Without this leadership there can be neither victory for socialist revolution nor the building of a new society. "For the proletariat to be strong enough to win on the decisive day it must—and Marx and I have advocated this ever since 1847—

16

form a separate party distinct from all others and opposed to them, a conscious class party," Engels wrote in 1889 (see p. 274 of this book). In order to win in the revolution the working class must be properly organised. The proletariat begins to move spontaneously, unaware of what will be the ultimate goals of its struggle. In the course of this struggle various forms of organisation of the proletariat are worked out: trade unions, for example, which uphold its economic interests, and others. The highest form of class organisation is a revolutionary party, able to lead the working class forward together with those social strata which follow it—the peasantry, the intellectuals and other non-proletarian strata of the working people. The party brings a scientific world outlook into the labour movement, thus making it the leading social force, conscious of its great historical mission. Only the party is capable of leading the class struggle, the revolution and the building of a new society.

The fundamental principles of the theory of the proletarian party were formulated in the *Manifesto of the Communist Party*. The *Manifesto*'s authors looked upon the party as "the most advanced and resolute" part of the working class "which pushes forward all others" (see p. 68 of this book), thereby revealing the correlation between the party and the class and characterising the party's aims and tasks. The party must be inseparably linked to the working class and armed with the most advanced theory; it must understand the conditions and course of the movement, see further than other workers and be the most conscious and active part of its class. At different stages Communists "also uphold the movement's future" in the struggle for the immediate goals and interests of the proletariat. They express the most general interests of the entire working class, the interests of the movement as a whole. Without the party, the *Manifesto* concludes, the working class can neither win power nor fundamentally transform society. Subsequent events fully confirmed this. One of the main reasons for the defeat of the Paris Commune was the lack of a proletarian party as the guiding force of the movement.

From 1847 onwards many works by Marx and Engels were devoted to working out the programmatic and organisational principles of the proletarian party. The Communist League, the first international organisation of the proletariat, which proclaimed scientific communism to be its ideological banner; the International Working Men's Association (the 1st International), which ideologically prepared the working class for the Paris

17

Commune, the first attempt in history to establish a proletarian state; the foundation of workers' parties on the principles of Marxism in a number of countries; Engels' participation in the creation of the 2nd International (1889)—these are the principal landmarks in the work carried out by Marx and Engels to establish parties of the working class. Socialist revolution, Marx wrote, summing up accumulated experience in the Introduction to the Programme of the French Workers' Party (1880), "... can only result from revolutionary action by the class of producers—the proletariat—organised into an independent political party; ... it is necessary to strive to achieve such an organisation by all means at the disposal of the proletariat" (see p. 252 of this book).

Marx and Engels exposed the reformist notions on class collaboration between the bourgeoisie and the proletariat and the peaceful development of capitalism into socialism, viewing them as a distortion by opportunists of the revolutionary theory of class struggle, substituting the false for the true. Only socialist revolution and the conquest of political power by the working class, irrespective of the form this takes, whether peaceful or non-peaceful, can create conditions for the building of a new society in which there are no classes and no exploitation of man by man.

The dictatorship of the proletariat is central to the theory of socialist revolution. Proletarian dictatorship is necessary in order to defend the revolution, uphold its achievements and rebuff attempts by the overthrown classes to restore capitalism. Without the dictatorship of the proletariat it is impossible to smash the resistance of the exploiting classes and carry out the social and economic measures necessary to build a new society. Dictatorship of the proletariat means that the principal issue of revolution—that of power—is resolved in favour of the working class and the working people. The theory of the dictatorship of the proletariat represents the further elaboration in concrete terms of the theory of the world-wide historical mission of the working class.

The necessity for the working class to conquer power, the idea of the dictatorship of the proletariat was first put forward in *The German Ideology*: "... every class which is aiming at domination, even when its domination, as is the case with the proletariat, leads to the abolition of the old form of society in its entirety and of domination in general, must first conquer political power" (Marx and Engels, *Collected Works*, Vol. 5, Moscow, 1976, p. 47). This idea runs through the entire *Manifesto of the Communist Party*. The term "dictatorship of the proletariat" did not yet exist (Marx

18

introduced it later, in 1850, in *The Class Struggles in France*), but this fundamental programmatic principle was itself clearly and positively formulated: "The first step in the revolution by the working class is to raise the proletariat to the position of ruling class, to win the battle of democracy" (Marx and Engels, *Collected Works*, Vol. 6, Moscow, 1976, p. 504). It is this political supremacy of the working class which, in Engels' apt phrase, is "the only door to the new society" (Marx and Engels, *Selected Correspondence*, Moscow, 1975, p. 386).

Political power in the hands of the working class and the working people is necessary to rebuild social relations on socialist principles. In explaining the role dictatorship of the proletariat should play, Marx and Engels wrote: "The proletariat will use its political supremacy to wrest, by degrees, all capital from the bourgeoisie, to centralise all instruments of production in the hands of the state, *i. e.,* of the proletariat organised as the ruling class; and to increase the total of productive forces as rapidly as possible" (see p. 75 of this book). Establishment of proletarian dictatorship also means, as Marx and Engels wrote, "the winning of the battle of democracy". The dictatorship of the proletariat uses force against the enemies of socialism, the exploiters, who seek to reverse the course of history and restore capitalism which is hated by the people. But for the overwhelming majority of the people, for the broad masses of the working people, dictatorship of the proletariat is the most complete and broadest democracy, real, not formal democracy.

Marx and Engels gave a brilliant critique of bourgeois democracy and of parliamentarism. This democracy represents limited, curtailed, formal democracy for the minority. Bourgeois parliamentarism is only a form of bourgeois dictatorship. Under the conditions of parliamentarism the working people possess only one right—to choose which of the bourgeois parties will rule for a certain period. It is not until power is taken by the workers that the main sections of the population acquire democratic freedom. Then democracy for the working people, for the majority of the people—democracy of the highest type, true democracy—comes into being.

Marx's *The Eighteenth Brumaire of Louis Bonaparte* holds an important place in the elaboration of the theory of socialist revolution. After analysing the revolutions of 1848-49 and other bourgeois revolutions, Marx established that all of them had failed to smash the military-bureaucratic centralised state machine of

19

the ruling classes, which had later been utilised by counter-revolution to crush the revolutionary working masses. "All revolutions perfected this machine instead of smashing it. The parties that contended in turn for domination regarded the possession of this huge state edifice as the principal spoils of the victor" (Marx and Engels, *Selected Works*, Vol. 1, Moscow, 1976, p. 477). The task of proletarian revolution, in contrast to bourgeois revolution, is to smash the state machine of the bourgeoisie. Marxism counterposes this conclusion, which has been fully confirmed by the practical experience of all the socialist revolutions of the 20th century, to the profoundly mistaken notions of reformists on the possibility of making use of the bourgeois state for the purpose of socialist reforms.

The Paris Commune of 1871 was a great new step forward. Marx was the first chronicler and historian of the Commune. In *The Civil War in France* and other works the reader will find a detailed exposition of the history and experience of the Commune and a thorough, profoundly penetrating critical analysis of the reasons for the mistakes and the defeat of the Communards. Marx saw in the heroic Commune, which existed for only 72 days, the prototype for a state of a completely new historical type. The Paris Commune, born of the revolutionary creativity of the masses, showed that the working class must not only smash the state machine of the bourgeoisie, but must also replace it by the dictatorship of the proletariat. The Commune, Marx pointed out, "was ... a working-class government ... the political form at last discovered under which to work out the economic emancipation of labour" (Marx and Engels, *Selected Works*, Vol. 2, Moscow, 1975, p. 223). Its main social measures were directed specifically towards this end. The Commune was to serve as "a lever for uprooting the economical foundation upon which rests the existence of classes, and therefore of class rule" (Marx and Engels, *Selected Works*, Vol. 2, Moscow, 1975, p. 223). However, in view of the Commune's short life, "its special measures could but betoken the tendency of a government of the people by the people" (Marx and Engels, *Selected Works*, Vol. 2, Moscow, 1975, p. 227). The world-wide historic significance of the Paris Commune lies in the fact that it was the first state, the first experience of the dictatorship of the proletariat.

The revolution of the proletariat, socialist revolution, is a prolonged and complex process, Marx noted in *The Eighteenth Brumaire*. Unlike a bourgeois revolution, it does not end when power is transferred to the revolutionary class and the barriers to the political and economic domination of that class are removed. The conquest of power serves only as a starting point for the revolutionary reshaping of society. Realisation of the creative tasks of the revolution begins with the establishment of proletarian dictatorship, which is the condition and instrument of their implementation. Later, in analysing the experience of the Commune, Marx emphasised that the winning of political power by the working class does not in itself eliminate class struggle: it does no more than create a favourable situation for the working class in which this struggle continues and "can run through its different phases in the most rational and humane way" (Marx and Engels, *On the Paris Commune*, Moscow, 1971, p. 156).

These ideas were further developed in the *Critique of the Gotha Programme*, which set down the programme of scientific communism. In this work Marx formulated the highly important principle that a separate transitional period between capitalism and socialism, the first phase of communism, was historically inevitable: "Between capitalist and communist society lies the period of the revolutionary transformation of the one into the other. Corresponding to this is also a political transition period in which the state can be nothing but *the revolutionary dictatorship of the proletariat*" (Marx and Engels, *Selected Works*, Vol. 3, Moscow, 1975, p. 26).

Marx established that communist society passes through two phases in its development: the first is socialism and the second, higher phase, is communism proper.

One of the most characteristic features of socialism, the first phase, is the distribution of material wealth on the basis of the principle "from each according to his abilities, to each according to his work", that is, according to the quantity and quality of labour of each member of society. Man is no longer exploited by man but a certain inequality among people in respect to the material reward received from society still exists. This shortcoming, Marx noted, is inevitable "in the first phase of communist society as it is when it has just emerged after prolonged birth pangs from capitalist society" (Marx and Engels, *Selected Works*, Vol. 3, Moscow, 1975, p. 19). Socialism is not a short-lived stage but an entire historical epoch. The economic, social and other advantages of the new system are revealed most fully in a developed socialist society, and the complete and comprehensive development of socialism naturally ensures gradual transition to a higher phase.

21

Touching on the future of the state, Marx showed that a socialist state is necessary for the building of socialist society. After it has achieved its goals, eliminated exploitation and exploiters and ensured the building of communism, the socialist state begins to wither away. Only under communism does it wither away completely.

The second, higher phase of communist society ensues as a result of the era of socialism, following upon a prolonged process of creating the necessary economic, social and spiritual preconditions. Marx wrote that "in a higher phase of communist society, after the enslaving subordination of the individual to the division of labour, and therewith also the antithesis between mental and physical labour, has vanished; after labour has become not only a means of life but life's prime want; after the productive forces have also increased with the all-round development of the individual, and all the springs of co-operative wealth flow more abundantly—only then can the narrow horizon of bourgeois right be crossed in its entirety and society inscribe on its banners: From each according to his ability, to each according to his needs!" (Marx and Engels, *Selected Works*, Vol. 3, Moscow, 1975, p. 19).

The revolutionary transformation of society is an exceptionally complex, prolonged and many-sided process. The views of the founders of scientific communism on the actual course of its development have an imperishable theoretical and practical significance.

In the "Address of the Central Committee to the Communist League", as well as in a number of other works (*The Class Struggles in France* and *The Eighteenth Brumaire of Louis Bonaparte* by Marx, *Revolution and Counter-revolution in Germany* by Engels, etc.) Marx and Engels develop the idea of continuous revolution. They point out that, where the stage of bourgeois reform has not yet been passed, socialist revolution will be preceded by a bourgeois-democratic revolution. The fundamental role of this is to clear the future battle-ground between the working class and the bourgeoisie of the detritus of feudal institutions. While actively participating in the bourgeois revolution, the working class must fight under its own banner. Remembering its ultimate goals, it cannot limit itself to a bourgeois-democratic revolution, but must strive to make revolution continuous, that is, to advance it as far as possible. The proletariat must not allow itself to be lured by trifling concessions from the bourgeoisie, which seeks to deceive the proletariat and itself enjoy the fruits of the revolution which has been won by the people. The revolution must not stop halfway, but continue until all the propertied classes are removed, one by one, from positions of domination and state power is conquered by the proletariat. In examining the overall democratic struggle and the socialist revolution as different stages in a single revolutionary process, Marx and Engels warned against attempts to by-pass the necessary stages of development. They taught the proletariat not to be apathetic towards bourgeois revolution, not to stand aloof from it and relinquish leadership of the revolution to the bourgeoisie but, on the contrary, to participate energetically in it and wage a resolute struggle for the most consistent democracy and the carrying through of the revolution to its conclusion. The working class is vitally interested in the most thorough elimination of all survivals of feudalism, the establishment of a democratic republic, the maximum extension of democracy. This form of state alone creates the most favourable conditions for the struggle to establish the power of the working class.

The question of the proletariat's allies in the revolution is directly linked to the theory of continuous revolution. The fundamental solution of this problem in the *Manifesto of the Communist Party* was confirmed and further developed on the basis of the experience of the 1848-49 revolution and the Paris Commune. In the revolutionary struggle the working class expresses the interests of all working people exploited by capital including, above all, the peasantry. "Hence the peasants find their natural ally and leader in the *urban proletariat*, whose task is the overthrow of the bourgeois order," Marx wrote in *The Eighteenth Brumaire of Louis Bonaparte* (Marx and Engels, *Selected Works*, Vol. 1, Moscow, 1976, p. 482). In the first edition of this work Marx further pointed out that when the peasantry becomes the ally of the proletariat, "*the proletarian revolution will obtain that chorus without which its solo song becomes a swan song in all peasant countries*" (ibid., p. 484). "...The whole thing in Germany," he wrote to Engels in 1856, "will depend on the possibility of backing the proletarian revolution by some second edition of the Peasant War. Then the affair will be splendid" (see p. 113 of this book). In these propositions Marx made a key political conclusion on the need for a revolutionary alliance between the working class and the peasantry and the leading role of the working class in this union.

Marx and Engels resolutely opposed Lassalle's thesis that, in relation to the proletariat, all the other classes represent "a single

23

reactionary mass". This thesis doomed the proletariat to isolation from the petty-bourgeois sections of the population in town and country, from the non-proletarian sections of the working people in its struggle for power. Engels' works occupy an important place in the elaboration of the problem of the proletariat's allies. In *The Peasant Question in France and Germany* Engels criticised the opportunist views which were being disseminated among socialists and set out theoretical principles for the agrarian programme of the socialist revolution, putting forward a number of profound propositions concerning the means and forms of socialist reconstruction of agriculture.

The conclusions of Marx and Engels were fully confirmed by history. Twentieth-century revolutions have shown that the most important preconditions for the development of the democratic revolution into the socialist revolution is an active participation by the working class in the democratic revolution, its alliance with the peasantry and other non-proletarian sections of the working people and its hegemony in the revolution.

An important constituent part of the revolutionary process is the movement of oppressed peoples for national liberation and independence. The teaching of Marx and Engels helps the working class reach a profound understanding of the very close interconnection and interdependence between the national liberation struggle and the struggle of the proletariat for social emancipation.

The position taken by Marx and Engels on the Irish question provides a notable example of how the proletariat of an oppressor nation should regard the national liberation movement. In the *Confidential Communication*—Marx regards the liberation of Ireland as a necessary condition for proletarian revolution in Britain, a country in which the material preconditions for revolution were more mature than in any other country. "Any nation that oppresses another forges its own chains," Marx wrote (see p. 124 of this book). Antagonism between nations is artificially inflamed and maintained by the bourgeoisie. "It knows that this scission is *the true secret of maintaining its power*" (see p. 124 of this book). The working class is the most active and consistent opponent of national oppression. Marxism teaches that socialist revolution alone leads to the complete elimination of national oppression. "In proportion as the exploitation of one individual by another is put an end to, the exploitation of one nation by another will also be put an end to. In proportion as the antagonism between classes within the nation vanishes, the hostility of one nation to another will come to an end," states the *Manifesto of the Communist Party* (see p. 73 of this book).

Marx and Engels invariably connected the success of the revolutionary struggle within national boundaries with the general course of the world revolutionary movement. The revolution of the proletariat has universal significance and all peoples will inevitably become involved in it. "...The emancipation of labour is neither a local nor a national, but a social problem, embracing all countries in which modern society exists...." (see p. 121 of this book).

In approximately the 1870s Marx and Engels conceived the scientifically-grounded idea of two streams in the world revolutionary process—the proletarian movement in the West and the peasant revolution in Russia—and their interaction. Marx and Engels closely followed the course of the revolutionary movement in Russia and emphasised that popular revolution in Russia could serve as a signal for the launching of proletarian revolution in the West "so that both complement each other" (see p. 292 of this book). In the Afterword to his work "On Social Relations in Russia", Engels wrote in 1894 that "the Russian revolution will ... give a fresh impulse to the labour movement in the West, creating for it new and better conditions for struggle and thereby advancing the victory of the modern industrial proletariat" (see p. 292 of this book).

Study of social movements in the countries of the East made possible the formulation of an important principle concerning the historical destinies of peoples which are backward in their development. Only in union with the proletarian revolution can they shorten the process of their development towards socialism. For this they must rely on the assistance and support of the victorious proletariat. "Only when the capitalist economy has been overcome at home and in the countries of its prime, only when the retarded countries have seen from their example 'how it's done', how the productive forces of modern industry are made to work as social property for society as a whole—only then will the retarded countries be able to start on this abbreviated process of development," Engels wrote. "But then their success will be assured" (see p. 291 of this book). This, he noted, relates "to all countries at the pre-capitalist stage of development" (see p. 291).

The works included in this book will acquaint the reader with the basic principles of the strategy and tactics of the proletariat's revolutionary struggle as worked out by Marx and Engels, their views on individual aspects of the theory of revolution—on armed uprising, the connection between war and revolution, etc.—and with their struggle against revolutionary phrase-mongering and opportunism and against the anarchists and other "alchemists of revolution", who sought "to make the revolution extempore", forcing the tactic of armed uprising upon the proletariat without taking into account the real situation or attempting to by-pass the necessary stages without consideration for objective social and economic conditions. Apart from adventurism and voluntarism, anarchism is distinguished by a lust for destruction and a rejection of the creative goals and tasks of the proletarian revolution which are connected with the building of a new society. In failing to understand the material basis of the revolutionary process, the anarchists divert the masses from actual revolutionary struggle. In Spain in 1873 they demonstrated in practice ' how not to make the revolution", and thereby doomed it to inevitable defeat.

The theory of socialist revolution created by Marx and Engels is not a dogma but a guide to action. For this reason its creators always demanded the most practical approach to the complex problems of the class struggle, condemning a dogmatic attitude towards theory. Choosing the means to win power, utilisation of peaceful and non-peaceful forms of revolutionary struggle, the change from one form to another, the combination of parliamentary and extra-parliamentary methods of struggle, etc. are all determined by concrete historical conditions and require of the proletarian party a sober and comprehensive assessment of the actual political situation and the balance of class forces within the country and on the international stage, combined with regard for the distinctive social and political features and national traditions and the level of development achieved by the labour movement.

Addressing the members of the International who had met for their London conference in 1871, soon after the defeat of the Paris Commune, Marx said: "We must declare to the governments: we know that you are the armed force which is directed against the proletarians; we shall proceed against you in a peaceful way where this is possible for us and with weapons should this prove necessary."

Marx and Engels elaborated the theory of socialist revolution in the era of pre-monopoly capitalism, when the objective conditions necessary for the victory of the working class were taking shape. The revolution of 1848-49 and the Paris Commune, Engels noted in 1895, showed that economic development in Europe was still not sufficiently mature to eliminate the capitalist mode of production.

26

In the 19th century the proletariat—the revolutionary class—, too, had yet to acquire great strength. Only with the beginning of the era of imperialism did the necessary conditions for a victorious socialist revolution come to maturity, as Lenin demonstrated.

In the new historical conditions of the 20th century the theoretical heritage of Marx and Engels was made use of by the advanced section of the working people and the oppressed majority of mankind in their struggle against exploitation, national enslavement, violence, wars and other social disasters engendered and spread by capitalism. The complete victory of Marxism and the steady growth of its influence on the development of mankind are bound up with the activity and ideas of Vladimir Lenin—with Leninism, which is a direct continuation and further development of Marxism in the historical conditions of the 20th century, a new, higher stage of Marxism.

Lenin comprehensively developed and enriched the theory of revolution created by Marx and Engels with new discoveries and new conclusions, raising it to a new, higher level. Lenin created the theory of imperialism on the basis of a profound generalisation of the latest trends in the development of capitalism. His analysis of the contradictions and laws of imperialism is a brilliant continuation and development of Marx's *Capital*. Lenin showed that imperialism is the last stage of capitalism, when the necessary conditions for its elimination have matured. Imperialism is the eve of socialist revolution, an era of unprecedented social upheavals and economic and political crises in bourgeois society. Discovery of the law that the capitalist economy and policy develop in an uneven, spasmodic way at the imperialist stage enabled Lenin to substantiate new and highly important propositions that different countries would attain socialism at different times, that this process need not begin in the most developed country and that the victory of socialism was possible initially in one country. These conclusions changed former conceptions of the course and conditions for victory of the socialist revolution and opened up new prospects for the revolutionary labour movement.

Lenin was the leader of the first victorious socialist revolution in the world, accomplished in Russia in October 1917. The Great October Socialist Revolution began a new age in world history—the age of mankind's transition from a capitalist to a communist socio-economic formation. The victory of socialist revolutions in a number of European, Asian and Latin American countries has turned socialism into a world system and made it the decisive factor in world development. With profound insight into the course and prospects for historical development after socialism's first victories, Lenin pointed to the inevitability of struggle on a world scale between the two social systems and revealed the importance of a socialist foreign policy, of consistent implementation of the principles of peaceful coexistence among states with different social systems. Acting in full conformity with the teaching of the creators of Marxist-Leninist theory, the Soviet Union and the other socialist countries are waging a tireless struggle in contemporary conditions for peace on earth, the prevention of wars, peaceful coexistence, implementation of detente and the reinforcement of political by military detente, the extension of detente to all parts of the world, giving it an irreversible, stable character, and for the consistent implementation of the principles contained in the Final Act of the Conference on Security and Co-operation in Europe, which was held in Helsinki in the summer of 1975.

The 20th century is the age of socialist revolution. The steadily growing economic, political and moral potential of the world socialist community—the principal revolutionary force of today, the struggle of the working class in the citadels of capitalism, the successes achieved by the national liberation movement, in fact, the entire course of mankind's development since October 1917, provide convincing evidence of the irrefutable correctness of the conclusions of Marxism-Leninism.

Life itself, the realities of today, have nullified the hopes of the apologists of capital that the class struggle will die down or can be eliminated in the world of capitalism. The latest pronouncements of the opponents of Marxism—different versions of the theory of modernisation and transformation of capitalism—have proved untenable as their numerous predecessors. Far from making socialist revolution, the inevitability of which was demonstrated by Marx and Engels, "superfluous", the contemporary scientific and technological revolution has made it increasingly necessary.

A profound and all-embracing crisis has struck the entire system of state-monopoly capitalism, involving every aspect of bourgeois society—the economy, politics, culture and ideology. The current slump in production, which is a traditional periodic phenomenon under capitalism and can now only be compared in strength and acuteness with the great depression of the 1930s, the highest level of unemployment in the entire post-war period, inflation, soaring prices and financial upheavals, combined with the energy and ecological crises and the crises of bourgeois democracy and culture

28

have given rise to a new wave of 'class battles between the proletariat and other sections of the working people on the one hand and the omnipotent monopolies on the other. The intensification and deepening of every kind of social conflict in most of the developed capitalist countries have dispelled the myths of the ideologists of the bourgeoisie concerning "harmony of class interests", "social partnership" and "class co-operation". "...This is an epoch of radical social change," said Leonid Brezhnev, General Secretary of the C.P.S.U. Central Committee, in his Report to the 25th Congress of the C.P.S.U. "Socialism's positions are expanding and growing stronger. The victories of the national liberation movement are opening up new horizons for countries that have won independence. The class struggle of the working people against monopoly oppression, against the exploiting order, is gaining in intensity. The scale of the revolutionary-democratic, anti-imperialist movement is steadily growing. Taken as a whole, this signifies development of the world revolutionary process.

"Such is the onward march of history. New generations and social strata, new parties and organisations are joining the revolutionary process" (*XXVth Congress of the C.P.S.U. Documents and Resolutions*, Moscow, 1976, pp. 32-33).

The transition from capitalism to a communist socio-economic formation constitutes the principal trend in the contemporary historical process.

KARL MARX

From
CONTRIBUTION
TO THE CRITIQUE
OF HEGEL'S PHILOSOPHY
OF LAW. INTRODUCTION

It is asked: can Germany attain a practice *à la hauteur des principes*, i.e., a *revolution* which will raise it not only to the *official level* of the modern nations but to the *height of humanity* which will be the near future of those nations?

The weapon of criticism cannot, of course, replace criticism by weapons, material force must be overthrown by material force; but theory also becomes a material force as soon as it has gripped the masses. Theory is capable of gripping the masses as soon as it demonstrates *ad hominem*, and it demonstrates *ad hominem* as soon as it becomes radical. To be radical is to grasp the root of the matter. But for man the root is man himself. The evident proof of the radicalism of German theory, and hence of its practical energy, is that it proceeds from a resolute *positive* abolition of religion. The criticism of religion ends with the teaching that *man is the highest being for man*, hence with the *categorical imperative to overthrow all relations* in which man is a debased, enslaved, forsaken, despicable being, relations which cannot be better described than by the exclamation of a Frenchman when it was planned to introduce a tax on dogs: Poor dogs! They want to treat you like human beings!

It is not the *radical* revolution, not the *general human* emancipation which is a utopian dream for Germany, but rather the partial, the *merely* political revolution, the revolution which leaves the pillars of the house standing. On what is a partial, a merely political revolution based? On the fact that *part of civil society* emancipates itself and attains *general* domination; on the fact that a definite class, proceeding from its *particular situation*, undertakes the general emancipation of society. This class emancipates the whole of society but only provided the whole of society is in the same situation as this class, e.g., possesses money and education or can acquire them at will.

No class of civil society can play this role without arousing a moment of enthusiasm in itself and in the masses, a moment in which it fraternises and merges with society in general, becomes confused with it and is perceived and acknowledged as its *general representative;* a moment in which its demands and rights are truly the rights and demands of society itself; a moment in which it is truly the social head and the social heart. Only in the name of the general rights of society can a particular class lay claim to general domination. For the storming of this emancipatory position, and hence for the political exploitation of all spheres of society in the interests of its own sphere, revolutionary energy and intellectual self-confidence alone are not sufficient. For the *revolution of a nation* and the *emancipation of a particular class* of civil society to coincide, for *one* estate to be acknowledged as the estate of the whole society, all the defects of society must conversely be concentrated in another class, a particular estate must be the general stumbling-block, the incorporation of the general limitation, a particular social sphere must be looked upon as the *notorious crime* of the whole of society, so that liberation from that sphere appears as general self-liberation. For *one* estate to be *par excellence* the estate of liberation, another estate must conversely be the obvious estate of oppression. The negative general significance of the French nobility and the French clergy determined the positive general significance of the immediately adjacent and opposed class of the *bourgeoisie.*

But no particular class in Germany has the consistency, the severity, the courage or the ruthlessness that could mark it out as the negative representative of society. No more has any estate the breadth of soul that identifies itself, even for a moment, with the soul of the nation, the genius that inspires material might to political violence, or that revolutionary audacity which flings at the adversary the defiant words: *I am nothing and I should be everything.* The main stem of German morals and honesty, of the classes as well as of individuals, is rather that *modest egoism* which asserts its limitedness and allows it to be asserted against itself. The relation of the various sections of German society is therefore

31

not dramatic but epic. Each of them begins to be aware of itself and to settle down beside the others with all its particular claims not as soon as it is oppressed, but as soon as the circumstances of the time, without the section's own participation, create a social substratum on which it can in turn exert pressure. Even the *moral self-confidence of the German middle class* rests only on the consciousness that it is the general representative of the philistine mediocrity of all the other classes. It is therefore not only the German kings who accede to the throne *mal à propos*; every section of civil society goes through a defeat before it has celebrated victory, develops its own limitations before it has overcome the limitations facing it and asserts its narrow-hearted essence before it has been able to assert its magnanimous essence. Thus the very opportunity of a great role has on every occasion passed away before it is to hand, thus every class, once it begins the struggle against the class above it, is involved in the struggle against the class below it. Hence the princes are struggling against the monarchy, the bureaucrats against the nobility, and the bourgeois against them all, while the proletariat is already beginning to struggle against the bourgeoisie. No sooner does the middle class dare to think of emancipation from its own standpoint than the development of the social conditions and the progress of political theory pronounce that standpoint antiquated or at least problematic.

In France it is enough for somebody to be something for him to want to be everything; in Germany one has to be nothing if one is not to forego everything. In France partial emancipation is the basis of universal emancipation; in Germany universal emancipation is the *conditio sine qua non* of any partial emancipation. In France it is the reality of gradual liberation, in Germany the impossibility of gradual liberation, that must give birth to complete freedom. In France every class is *politically idealistic* and becomes aware of itself at first not as a particular class but as the representative of social requirements generally. The role of *emancipator* therefore passes in dramatic motion to the various classes of the French nation one after the other until it finally comes to the class which implements social freedom no longer on the basis of certain conditions lying outside man and yet created by human society, but rather organises all conditions of human existence on the presupposition of social freedom. In Germany, on the contrary, where practical life is as spiritless as spiritual life is unpractical, no class in civil society has any need or capacity for

32

general emancipation until it is forced by its *immediate* condition, by *material* necessity, by its *very chains*.

Where, then, is the *positive* possibility of a German emancipation?

Answer: In the formation of a class with *radical chains*, a class of civil society which is not a class of civil society, an estate which is the dissolution of all estates, a sphere which has a universal character by its universal suffering and claims no *particular right* because no *particular wrong* but *wrong generally* is perpetrated against it; which can no longer invoke a *historical* but only a *human* title; which does not stand in any one-sided antithesis to the consequences but in an all-round antithesis to the premises of the German state; a sphere, finally, which cannot emancipate itself without emancipating itself from all other spheres of society and thereby emancipating all other spheres of society, which, in a word, is the *complete loss* of man and hence can win itself only through the *complete rewinning of man*. This dissolution of society as a particular estate is the *proletariat*.

The proletariat is coming into being in Germany only as a result of the rising *industrial* development. For it is not the *naturally arising* poor but the *artificially impoverished*, not the human masses mechanically oppressed by the gravity of society but the masses resulting from the *drastic dissolution* of society, mainly of the middle estate, that form the proletariat, although it is obvious that gradually the naturally arising poor and the Christian-Germanic serfs also join its ranks.

By proclaiming the *dissolution of the hitherto existing world order* the proletariat merely states the *secret of its own existence*, for it *is in fact* the dissolution of that world order. By demanding the *negation of private property*, the proletariat merely raises to the rank of a *principle of society* what society has made the principle of the *proletariat*, what, without its own co-operation, is already incorporated in *it* as the negative result of society. In regard to the world which is coming into being the proletarian then finds himself possessing the same right as the *German king* in regard to the world which has come into being when he calls the people *his* people as he calls the horse *his* horse. By declaring the people his private property the king simply states that the property-owner is king.

As philosophy finds its *material* weapons in the proletariat, so the proletariat finds its *spiritual* weapons in philosophy. And once the lightning of thought has squarely struck this ingenuous soil of the people the emancipation of the *Germans* into *human beings* will take place.

Let us sum up the result:

The only *practically* possible liberation of Germany is liberation that proceeds from the standpoint of *the* theory which proclaims man to be the highest being for man. In Germany emancipation from the *Middle Ages* is possible only as emancipation from the *partial* victories over the Middle Ages as well. In Germany *no* kind of bondage can be broken without breaking *every* kind of bondage. The *thorough* Germany cannot make a revolution without making a *thoroughgoing* revolution. The *emancipation of the German* is the *emancipation of the human being.* The *head* of this emancipation is *philosophy*, its *heart* is the *proletariat.* Philosophy cannot be made a reality without the abolition of the proletariat, the proletariat cannot be abolished without philosophy being made a reality.

When all inner requisites are fulfilled the *day of German resurrection* will be proclaimed by the *ringing call of the Gallic cock.*

Written at the end
of 1843-January 1844

Marx and Engels,
Collected Works, Vol. 3,
pp. 182, 184-87

KARL MARX

From

CRITICAL MARGINAL NOTES ON THE ARTICLE "THE KING OF PRUSSIA AND SOCIAL REFORM. BY A PRUSSIAN"

The "Prussian" prophesies the smothering of uprisings which break out in *"disastrous isolation of people from the community,* and in the *separation of their thoughts from social principles"*.

We have shown that the Silesian[1] uprising occurred by no means in circumstances of the separation of thoughts from social principles. It only remains for us to deal with the *"disastrous isolation of people from the community"*. By community here is meant the *political community*, the *state*. This is the old story about *unpolitical* Germany.

But do not *all* uprisings, without exception, break out in a *disastrous isolation of man from the community*? Does not *every* uprising necessarily presuppose isolation? Would the 1789 revolution have taken place without the disastrous isolation of French citizens from the community? It was intended precisely to abolish this isolation.

But the *community* from which the worker is *isolated* is a community the real character and scope of which is quite different from that of the *political* community. The community from which the worker is isolated by *his own labour* is *life* itself, physical and mental life, human morality, human activity, human enjoyment, *human* nature. *Human nature* is the *true community* of men. The disastrous isolation from this essential nature is incomparably more universal, more intolerable, more dreadful, and more contradictory, than isolation from the political community. Hence, too, the *abolition* of this isolation—and even a partial reaction to it, an *uprising* against it—is just as much more infinite as *man* is more infinite than the *citizen*, and human *life* more infinite than political life. Therefore, however *partial* the uprising of the *in-*

dustrial workers may be, it contains within itself a *universal* soul; however universal a *political* uprising may be, it conceals even in its *most grandiose* form a *narrow-minded* spirit.

The "Prussian" worthily concludes his article with the following sentence:

"*A social revolution without a political soul* (i.e., without an organising idea from the point of view of the whole) is impossible."

We have already seen that a *social* revolution is found to have the point of view of the *whole* because—even if it were to occur in only *one* factory district—it represents man's protest against a dehumanised life, because it starts out from the *point of view of a separate real individual*, because the *community*, against the separation of which from himself the individual reacts, is man's *true* community, *human* nature. The *political soul* of revolution, on the other hand, consists in the *tendency* of classes having no political influence to abolish their *isolation* from *statehood* and *rule*. Its point of view is that of the state, of an *abstract* whole, which exists *only* through separation from real life, and which is *inconceivable* without the *organised* contradiction between the universal idea of man and the individual existence of man. Hence, too, a revolution with a *political soul*, in accordance with the *limited* and *dichotomous* nature of this soul, organises a ruling stratum in society at the expense of society itself.

We want to divulge to the "Prussian" what a "*social revolution* with a *political* soul" actually is; we shall thereby at the same time confide the secret to him that he himself is unable, even in *words*, to rise above the narrow-minded political point of view.

A "*social*" revolution with a *political* soul is either a non-sensical concoction, if by "social" revolution the "Prussian" means a "social" as *opposed* to a political revolution, and nevertheless endows the social revolution with a political soul instead of a social one; or else a "*social revolution with a political soul*" is only a *paraphrase* for what was usually called a "*political revolution*", or "*simply a revolution*". Every revolution dissolves the *old society* and to that extent it is *social*. Every revolution overthrows the *old power* and to that extent it is *political*.

Let the "Prussian" choose between the *paraphrase* and the *nonsense*! But whereas a *social revolution* with a *political soul* is a paraphrase or nonsense, a *political revolution* with a *social* soul has a rational meaning. *Revolution* in general—the *overthrow* of the existing power and *dissolution* of the old relationship—is a

36

political act. But *socialism* cannot be realised without *revolution*. It needs this *political* act insofar as it needs *destruction* and *dissolution*. But where its *organising activity* begins, where its *proper object*, its *soul*, comes to the fore—there socialism throws off the *political* cloak.

Dated July 31, 1844

Marx and Engels,
Collected Works, Vol. 3,
pp. 204-06

KARL MARX
FREDERICK ENGELS
From
THE HOLY FAMILY,
OR CRITIQUE
OF CRITICAL
CRITICISM

**AGAINST BRUNO BAUER
AND COMPANY**

Proletariat and wealth are opposites; as such they form a single whole. They are both creations of the world of private property. The question is exactly what place each occupies in the antithesis. It is not sufficient to declare them two sides of a single whole.

Private property as private property, as wealth, is compelled to maintain *itself*, and thereby its opposite, the proletariat, in *existence*. That is the *positive* side of the antithesis, self-satisfied private property.

The proletariat, on the contrary, is compelled as proletariat to abolish itself and thereby its opposite, private property, which determines its existence, and which makes it proletariat. It is the *negative* side of the antithesis, its restlessness within its very self, dissolved and self-dissolving private property.

The propertied class and the class of the proletariat present the same human self-estrangement. But the former class feels at ease and strengthened in this self-estrangement, it recognises estrangement as *its own power* and has in it the *semblance* of a human existence. The latter feels annihilated in this estrangement; it sees in it its own powerlessness and the reality of an inhuman existence. It is, to use an expression of Hegel, in its abasement the *indignation* at that abasement, an indignation to which it is necessarily driven by the contradiction between its human *nature* and its condition of life, which is the outright, resolute and comprehensive negation of that nature.

Within this antithesis the private property-owner is therefore the *conservative* side, the proletarian the *destructive* side. From the former arises the action of preserving the antithesis, from the latter the action of annihilating it.

Indeed private property drives itself in its economic movement towards its own dissolution, but only through a development which does not depend on it, which is unconscious and which takes place against the will of private property by the very nature of things, only inasmuch as it produces the proletariat *as* proletariat, poverty which is conscious of its spiritual and physical poverty, dehumanisation which is conscious of its dehumanisation, and therefore self-abolishing. The proletariat executes the sentence that private property pronounces on itself by producing the proletariat, just as it executes the sentence that wage-labour pronounces on itself by producing wealth for others and poverty for itself. When the proletariat is victorious, it by no means becomes the absolute side of society, for it is victorious only by abolishing itself and its opposite. Then the proletariat disappears as well as the opposite which determines it, private property.

When socialist writers ascribe this world-historic role to the proletariat, it is not at all, as Critical Criticism pretends to believe, because they regard the proletarians as *gods*. Rather the contrary. Since in the fully-formed proletariat the abstraction of all humanity, even of the *semblance* of humanity, is practically complete; since the conditions of life of the proletariat sum up all the conditions of life of society today in their most inhuman form; since man has lost himself in the proletariat, yet at the same time has not only gained theoretical consciousness of that loss, but through urgent, no longer removable, no longer disguisable, absolutely imperative *need*—the practical expression of *necessity*—is driven directly to revolt against this inhumanity, it follows that the proletariat can and must emancipate itself. But it cannot emancipate itself without abolishing the conditions of its own life. It cannot abolish the conditions of its life without abolishing *all* the inhuman conditions of life of society today which are summed up in its own situation. Not in vain does it go through the stern but steeling school of *labour*. It is not a question of what this or that proletarian, or even the whole proletariat, at the moment *regards* as its aim. It is a question of *what the proletariat is*, and what, in accordance with this *being*, it will historically be compelled to do. Its aim and historical action is visibly and irrevocably foreshadowed in its own life situation as well as in the whole organisation of bourgeois society today. There is no need to explain here that a large part of the English and French proletariat is already *conscious* of its historic task and is constantly working to develop that consciousness into complete clarity.

Written in September-
November 1844

Marx and Engels,
Collected Works, Vol. 4,
pp. 35-37

FREDERICK ENGELS

SPEECHES IN ELBERFELD[2]

From
Speech of February 15, 1845

The unavoidable result of our existing social relations, under all circumstances, and in all cases, will be a *social revolution*. With the same certainty with which we can develop from given mathematical principles a new mathematical proposition, with the same certainty we can deduce from the existing economic relations and the principles of political economy the imminence of social revolution. Let us, however, look at this upheaval a little closer; what form will it take, what will be its results, in what ways will it differ from the previous violent upheavals? A social revolution, gentlemen, is something quite different from the political revolutions which have taken place so far. It is not directed, as these have been, against the property of monopoly, but against the monopoly of property; a social revolution, gentlemen, is *the open war of the poor against the rich*. And such a struggle, in which all the mainsprings and causes, which in previous historical conflicts lay dark and hidden at the bottom, operate openly and without concealment, such a struggle, to be sure, threatens to be far fiercer and bloodier than all those that preceded it. The result of this struggle can be twofold. Either the rebellious party only attacks the appearance, not the essence, only the form, not the thing itself, or it goes for the thing itself, grasps the evil itself by the root. In the first case private property will be allowed to continue and will only be distributed differently, so that the causes which have led to the present situation remain in operation and must sooner or later bring about a similar situation and another revolution. But, gentlemen, is this possible? Has there been a revolution which did not really carry out what it was out for? The English revolution realised both the religious and the political principles whose suppression by Charles I caused it to break out;

the French bourgeoisie in its fight against the aristocracy and the old monarchy achieved everything that it aimed for, made an end to all the abuses which drove it to insurrection.[3] And should the insurrection of the poor cease before poverty and its causes have been eliminated? It is not possible, gentlemen; it would be flying in the face all historical experience to suppose such a thing. Furthermore, the level of education of the workers, especially in England and France, forbids us to consider this possible. There only remains, then, the other alternative, namely, that the future social revolution will deal with the real causes of want and poverty, of ignorance and crime, that it will therefore carry through a real social reform. And this can only happen by the proclamation of the principles of communism. Just consider, gentlemen, the ideas which actuate the worker in those countries where the worker too thinks. Look at France, at the different sections of the labour movement, whether they are not *all* communistic; go to England and listen to the kind of proposals being made to the workers for the improvement of their position—are they not *all* based on the principle of common property; study the different systems of social reform and how many will you find that are not communistic? Of all the systems which are still of any importance today, the only one which is not communistic is that of Fourier, who devoted more attention to the social organisation of human activity than to the distribution of its products. All these facts justify the conclusion that a future social revolution will end with the implementation of the principles of communism and hardly permit any other possibility.

If, gentlemen, these conclusions are correct, if the social revolution and practical communism are the necessary result of our existing conditions—then we will have to concern ourselves above all with the measures by which we can avoid a violent and bloody overthrow of the social conditions. And there is only *one* means, namely, the peaceful introduction or at least preparation of communism. If we do not want the *bloody* solution of the social problem, if we do not want to permit the daily growing contradiction between the education and the condition of our proletarians to come to a head, which, according to all our experience of human nature, will mean that this contradiction will be solved by brute force, desperation and thirst for revenge, then, gentlemen, we must apply ourselves seriously and without prejudice to the social problem; then we must make it our business to contribute our share towards humanising the condition of the

41

modern helots. And if it should perhaps appear to some of you that the raising of the hitherto abased classes will not be possible without an abasement of your own condition, then you ought to bear in mind that what is involved is to create for *all people* such a condition that everyone can freely develop his human nature and live in a human relationship with his neighbours, and has no need to fear any violent shattering of his condition; it must be borne in mind that what some individuals have to sacrifice is not their real human enjoyment of life, but only the semblance of this enjoyment produced by our bad conditions, something which conflicts with the reason and the heart of those who now enjoy these apparent advantages. Far from wishing to destroy real human life with all its requirements and needs, we wish on the contrary really to bring it into being. And if, even apart from this, you will only seriously consider for a moment what the consequences of our present situation are bound to be, into what labyrinths of contradictions and disorders it is leading us—then, gentlemen, you will certainly find it worth the trouble to study the social question seriously and thoroughly. And if I can induce you to do this, I shall have achieved the purpose of my talk.

Marx and Engels,
Collected Works, Vol. 4,
pp. 262-64

KARL MARX
FREDERICK ENGELS

From
CHAPTER I
OF THE GERMAN IDEOLOGY

[6. CONCLUSIONS FROM
THE MATERIALIST CONCEPTION
OF HISTORY: HISTORY AS
A CONTINUOUS PROCESS,
HISTORY AS BECOMING WORLD
HISTORY, THE NECESSITY
OF COMMUNIST REVOLUTION]

...Finally, from the conception of history set forth by us we obtain these further conclusions: 1) In the development of productive forces there comes a stage when productive forces and means of intercourse are brought into being which, under the existing relations, only cause mischief, and are no longer productive but destructive forces (machinery and money); and connected with this a class is called forth which has to bear all the burdens of society without enjoying its advantages, which is ousted from society and forced into the sharpest contradiction to all other classes; a class which forms the majority of all members of society, and from which emanates the consciousness of the necessity of a fundamental revolution, the communist consciousness, which may, of course, arise among the other classes too through the contemplation of the situation of this class. 2) The conditions under which definite productive forces can be applied are the conditions of the rule of a definite class of society, whose social power, deriving from its property, has its *practical*-idealistic expression in each case in the form of the state and, therefore, every revolutionary struggle is directed against a class which till then has been in power. 3) In all previous revolutions the mode of activity always remained unchanged and it was only a question of a different distribution of this activity, a new distribution of labour to other persons, whilst the communist revolution is directed against the hitherto existing *mode* of activity, does away with *labour*,[4] and abolishes the rule of all classes with the classes themselves, because it is carried through by the class which no longer counts as a class in society, which is not recognised as a class, and is in itself the expression of the dissolution of all classes, nationalities, etc., within present society, and 4) both for the production on a mass scale of this communist consciousness, and for the success of the cause itself, the alteration of men on a mass scale is necessary, an alteration which can only take place in a practical movement, a *revolution*; the revolution is necessary, therefore, not only because the *ruling* class cannot be overthrown in any other way, but also because the class *overthrowing* it can only in a revolution succeed in ridding itself of all the muck of ages and become fitted to found society anew.

Written in 1845-1846

Marx and Engels, *Collected Works*, Vol. 5, pp. 52-53

FREDERICK ENGELS

From
LETTER
TO THE COMMUNIST
CORRESPONDENCE
COMMITTEE
IN BRUSSELS[5]

Paris, October 23, 1846

I therefore defined the objects of the Communists in this way:
1) to safeguard the interests of the proletariat as against those of
the bourgeoisie; 2) to do this through the abolition of private
property and its replacement by community of goods; 3) to
recognise no means of carrying out these objects other than a
democratic revolution by force.

Marx and Engels,
Selected Correspondence,
Moscow, 1975, p. 27

From

THE POVERTY OF PHILOSOPHY

ANSWER TO THE *PHILOSOPHY OF POVERTY* BY M. PROUDHON

An oppressed class is the vital condition for every society founded on the antagonism of classes. The emancipation of the oppressed class thus implies necessarily the creation of a new society. For the oppressed class to be able to emancipate itself it is necessary that the productive powers already acquired and the existing social relations should no longer be capable of existing side by side. Of all the instruments of production, the greatest productive power is the revolutionary class itself. The organisation of revolutionary elements as a class supposes the existence of all the productive forces which could be engendered in the bosom of the old society.

Does this mean that after the fall of the old society there will be a new class domination culminating in a new political power? No.

The condition for the emancipation of the working class is the abolition of all classes, just as the condition for the emancipation of the third estate, of the bourgeois order, was the abolition of all estates* and all orders.

The working class, in the course of its development, will substitute for the old civil society an association which will exclude classes and their antagonism, and there will be no more political power properly socalled, since political power is precisely the official expression of antagonism in civil society.

---

*Estates here in the historical sense of the estates of feudalism, estates with definite and limited privileges. The revolution of the bourgeoisie abolished the estates and their privileges. Bourgeois society knows only *classes.* It was, therefore, absolutely in contradiction with history to describe the proletariat as the "fourth estate". F. E. [*Note to the German edition, 1885.*]

Meanwhile the antagonism between the proletariat and the bourgeoisie is a struggle of class against class, a struggle which carried to its highest expression is a total revolution. Indeed, is it at all surprising that a society founded on the *opposition* of classes should culminate in brutal *contradiction*, the shock of body against body, as its final denouement.

Do not say that social movement excludes political movement. There is never a political movement which is not at the same time social.

It is only in an order of things in which there are no more classes and class antagonisms that *social evolutions* will cease to be *political revolutions*. Till then, on the eve of every general reshuffling of society, the last word of social science will always be:

"Le combat ou la mort; la lutte sanguinaire ou le néant. C'est ainsi que la question est invinciblement posée."[a]

George Sand[6]

Written in the
first half of 1847

Marx and Engels,
Collected Works, Vol. 6,
pp. 211-12

---

[a] "Combat or death, bloody struggle or extinction. Thus the question is inexorably put."— *Ed.*

FREDERICK ENGELS

From

PRINCIPLES
OF COMMUNISM

Question 14: What kind of new social order will this have to be?

Answer: Above all, it will have to take the running of industry and all branches of production in general out of the hands of separate individuals competing with each other and instead will have to ensure that all these branches of production are run by society as a whole, i.e., for the social good, according to a social plan and with the participation of all members of society. It will therefore do away with competition and replace it by association. Since the running of industry by individuals has private ownership as its necessary consequence and since competition is nothing but the manner in which industry is run by individual private owners, private ownership cannot be separated from the individual running of industry and competition. Hence, private ownership will also have to be abolished, and in its stead there will be common use of all the instruments of production and the distribution of all products by common agreement, or the so-called community of property. The abolition of private ownership is indeed the most succinct and characteristic summary of the transformation of the entire social system necessarily following from the development of industry, and it is therefore rightly put forward by the Communists as their main demand.

Question 15: The abolition of private property was therefore not possible earlier?

Answer: No. Every change in the social order, every revolution in property relations, has been the necessary result of the creation of new productive forces which would no longer conform to the old property relations. Private property itself arose in this way. For private property has not always existed, but when towards the end

F Engels

of the Middle Ages a new mode of production appeared in the form of manufacture which could not be subordinated to the then existing feudal and guild property, manufacture, having outgrown the old property relations, created a new form of ownership—private ownership. For manufacture and the first stage of development of large-scale industry, no other form of ownership was possible than private ownership and no other order of society than that founded upon private ownership. So long as it is not possible to produce so much that not only is there enough for all, but also a surplus for the increase of social capital and for the further development of the productive forces, so long must there always be a ruling class disposing of the productive forces of society, and a poor, oppressed class. How these classes are composed will depend upon the stage of development of production. In the Middle Ages, which were dependent upon agriculture, we find the lord and the serf; the towns of the later Middle Ages show us the master guildsman and the journeyman and day labourer; the seventeenth century has the manufacturer and the manufactory worker; the nineteenth century the big factory-owner and the proletarian. It is obvious that hitherto the productive forces had not yet been so far developed that enough could be produced for all or to make private property a fetter, a barrier, to these productive forces. Now, however, when the development of large-scale industry has, *firstly*, created capital and productive forces on a scale hitherto unheard of and the means are available to increase these productive forces in a short time to an infinite extent; when, *secondly*, these productive forces are concentrated in the hands of a few bourgeois whilst the great mass of the people are more and more becoming proletarians, and their condition more wretched and unendurable in the same measure in which the riches of the bourgeois increase; when, *thirdly*, these powerful productive forces that can easily be increased have so enormously outgrown private property and the bourgeois that at every moment they provoke the most violent disturbances in the social order—only now has the abolition of private property become not only possible but even absolutely necessary.

Question 16: Will it be possible to bring about the abolition of private property by peaceful methods?

Answer: It is to be desired that this could happen, and Communists certainly would be the last to resist it. The Communists know only too well that all conspiracies are not only futile but even harmful. They know only too well that revolutions are not made deliberately and arbitrarily, but that everywhere and at all times they have been the necessary outcome of circumstances entirely independent of the will and the leadership of particular parties and entire classes. But they also see that the development of the proletariat is in nearly every civilised country forcibly suppressed, and that thus the opponents of the Communists are working with all their might towards a revolution. Should the oppressed proletariat in the end be goaded into a revolution, we Communists will then defend the cause of the proletarians by deed just as well as we do now by word.

Question 17: Will it be possible to abolish private property at one stroke?

Answer: No, such a thing would be just as impossible as at *one* stroke to increase the existing productive forces to the degree necessary for instituting community of property. Hence, the proletarian revolution, which in all probability is impending, will transform existing society only gradually, and be able to abolish private property only when the necessary quantity of the means of production has been created.

Question 18: What will be the course of this revolution?

Answer: In the first place it will inaugurate a *democratic constitution* and thereby, directly or indirectly, the political rule of the proletariat. Directly in England, where the proletariat already constitutes the majority of the people. Indirectly in France and in Germany, where the majority of the people consists not only of proletarians but also of small peasants and urban petty bourgeois, who are only now being proletarianised and in all their political interests are becoming more and more dependent on the proletariat and therefore soon will have to conform to the demands of the proletariat. This will perhaps involve a second fight, but one that can end only in the victory of the proletariat.

Democracy would be quite useless to the proletariat if it were not immediately used as a means of carrying through further measures directly attacking private ownership and securing the means of subsistence of the proletariat. Chief among these measures, already made necessary by the existing conditions, are the following:

1. Limitation of private ownership by means of progressive taxation, high inheritance taxes, abolition of inheritance by collateral lines (brothers, nephews, etc.), compulsory loans and so forth.

2. Gradual expropriation of landed proprietors, factory-owners, railway and shipping magnates, partly through competition on the

part of state industry and partly directly through compensation in assignations.

3. Confiscation of the property of all emigrants and rebels against the majority of the people.

4. Organisation of the labour or employment of the proletarians on national estates, in national factories and workshops, thereby putting an end to competition among the workers themselves and compelling the factory-owners, as long as they still exist, to pay the same increased wages as the State.

5. Equal liability to work for all members of society until complete abolition of private ownership. Formation of industrial armies, especially for agriculture.

6. Centralisation of the credit and banking systems in the hands of the State by means of a national bank with state capital and the suppression of all private banks and bankers.

7. Increase of national factories, workshops, railways, and ships, cultivation of all uncultivated land and improvement of land already cultivated in the same proportion in which the capital and workers at the disposal of the nation increase.

8. Education of all children, as soon as they are old enough to do without the first maternal care, in national institutions and at the expense of the nation. Education combined with production.

9. The erection of large palaces on national estates as common dwellings for communities of citizens engaged in industry as well as agriculture, and combining the advantages of both urban and rural life without the one-sidedness and disadvantages of either.

10. The demolition of all insanitary and badly built dwellings and town districts.

11. Equal right of inheritance to be enjoyed by illegitimate and legitimate children.

12. Concentration of all means of transport in the hands of the nation.

Of course, all these measures cannot be carried out at once. But one will always lead on to the other. Once the first radical onslaught upon private ownership has been made, the proletariat will see itself compelled to go always further, to concentrate all capital, all agriculture, all industry, all transport, and all exchange more and more in the hands of the State. All these measures work towards such results; and they will become realisable and will develop their centralising consequences in the same proportion in which the productive forces of the country will be multiplied by the labour of the proletariat. Finally, when all capital, all production, and all exchange are concentrated in the hands of the nation, private ownership will automatically have ceased to exist, money will have become superfluous, and production will have so increased and men will be so much changed that the last forms of the old social relations will also be able to fall away.

Question 19: Will it be possible for this revolution to take place in one country alone?

Answer: No. Large-scale industry, already by creating the world market, has so linked up all the peoples of the earth, and especially the civilised peoples, that each people is dependent on what happens to another. Further, in all civilised countries large-scale industry has so levelled social development that in all these countries the bourgeoisie and the proletariat have become the two decisive classes of society and the struggle between them the main struggle of the day. The communist revolution will therefore be no merely national one; it will be a revolution taking place simultaneously in all civilised countries, that is, at least in England, America, France and Germany. In each of these countries it will develop more quickly or more slowly according to whether the country has a more developed industry, more wealth, and a more considerable mass of productive forces. It will therefore be slowest and most difficult to carry out in Germany, quickest and easiest in England. It will also have an important effect upon the other countries of the world, and will completely change and greatly accelerate their previous manner of development. It is a world-wide revolution and will therefore be world-wide in scope.[8]

Question 20: What will be the consequences of the final abolition of private ownership?

Answer: Above all, through society's taking out of the hands of the private capitalists the use of all the productive forces and means of communication as well as the exchange and distribution of products and managing them according to a plan corresponding to the means available and the needs of the whole of society, all the evil consequences of the present running of large-scale industry will be done away with. There will be an end of crises; the extended production, which under the present system of society means over-production and is such a great cause of misery, will then not even be adequate and will have to be expanded much further. Instead of creating misery, over-production beyond the immediate needs of society will mean the satisfaction of the needs of all, create new needs and at the same time the means to satisfy them. It will be the condition and the cause of new advances, and it will achieve these advances without thereby, as always hitherto, bringing the order of society into confusion. Once liberated from the pressure of private ownership, large-scale industry will develop on a scale that will make its present level of development seem as paltry as seems the manufacturing system compared with the large-scale industry of our time. This development of industry will provide society with a sufficient quantity of products to satisfy the needs of all. Similarly agriculture, which is also hindered by the pressure of private ownership and the parcelling of land from introducing the improvements already available and scientific advancements, will be given a quite new impulse, and place at society's disposal an ample quantity of products. Thus society will produce enough products to be able so to arrange distribution that the needs of all its members will be satisfied. The division of society into various antagonistic classes will thereby become superfluous. Not only will it become superfluous, it is even incompatible with the new social order. Classes came into existence through the division of labour and the division of labour in its hitherto existing form will entirely disappear. For in order to bring industrial and agricultural production to the level described, mechanical and chemical aids alone are not enough; the abilities of the people who set these aids in motion must also be developed to a corresponding degree. Just as in the last century the peasants and the manufactory workers changed their entire way of life, and themselves became quite different people when they were drawn into large-scale industry, so also will the common management of production by the whole of society and the resulting new development of production require and also produce quite different people. The common management of production cannot be effected by people as they are today, each one being assigned to a single branch of production, shackled to it, exploited by it, each having developed only *one* of his abilities at the cost of all the others and knowing only *one* branch, or only a branch of a branch of the total production. Even present-day industry finds less and less use for such people. Industry carried on in common and according to plan by the whole of society presupposes moreover people of all-round development, capable of surveying the entire system of production. Thus the division of labour making one man a peasant, another a shoemaker, a third a factory worker, a fourth a stockjobber, which has already been undermined by machines, will completely disappear. Education will enable young people quickly to go through the whole system of production, it will enable them to pass

53

from one branch of industry to another according to the needs of society or their own inclinations. It will therefore free them from that one-sidedness which the present division of labour stamps on each one of them. Thus the communist organisation of society will give its members the chance of an all-round exercise of abilities that have received all-round development. With this, the various classes will necessarily disappear. Thus the communist organisation of society is, on the one hand, incompatible with the existence of classes and, on the other, the very establishment of this society furnishes the means to do away with these class differences.

It follows from this that the antagonism between town and country will likewise disappear. The carrying on of agriculture and industrial production by the same people, instead of by two different classes, is already for purely material reasons an essential condition of communist association. The scattering of the agricultural population over the countryside, along with the crowding of the industrial population into the big towns, is a state which corresponds only to an undeveloped stage of agriculture and industry, an obstacle to all further development which is already now making itself very keenly felt.

The general association of all members of society for the common and planned exploitation of the productive forces, the expansion of production to a degree where it will satisfy the needs of all, the termination of the condition where the needs of some are satisfied at the expense of others, the complete annihilation of classes and their antagonisms, the all-round development of the abilities of all the members of society through doing away with the hitherto existing division of labour, through industrial education, through change of activity, through the participation of all in the enjoyments provided by all, through the merging of town and country—such are the main results of the abolition of private property.

Written at the end of
October 1847

Marx and Engels,
Collected Works, Vol. 6,
pp. 348-54

KARL MARX

FREDERICK ENGELS

From

MANIFESTO
OF THE
COMMUNIST PARTY[9]

A spectre is haunting Europe—the spectre of Communism. All the Powers of old Europe have entered into a holy alliance to exorcise this spectre: Pope and Czar, Metternich and Guizot, French Radicals and German police-spies.

Where is the party in opposition that has not been decried as Communistic by its opponents in power? Where the Opposition that has not hurled back the branding reproach of Communism, against the more advanced opposition parties, as well as against its reactionary adversaries?

Two things result from this fact:

I. Communism is already acknowledged by all European Powers to be itself a Power.

II. It is high time that Communists should openly, in the face of the whole world, publish their views, their aims, their tendencies, and meet this nursery tale of the Spectre of Communism with a Manifesto of the party itself.

To this end, Communists of various nationalities have assembled in London, and sketched the following Manifesto, to be published in the English, French, German, Italian, Flemish and Danish languages.

BOURGEOIS AND PROLETARIANS *

The history of all hitherto existing society** is the history of class struggles.

Freeman and slave, patrician and plebeian, lord and serf, guild-master*** and journeyman, in a word, oppressor and oppressed,

---

*By bourgeoisie is meant the class of modern Capitalists, owners of the means of social production and employers of wage-labour. By proletariat, the class of modern wage-labourers who, having no means of production of their own, are reduced to selling their labour-power in order to live. [*Note by Engels to the English edition of 1888.*]

**That is, all *written* history. In 1847, the pre-history of society, the social organisation existing previous to recorded history, was all but unknown. Since then, Haxthausen discovered common ownership of land in Russia, Maurer proved it to be the social foundation from which all Teutonic races started in history, and by and by village communities were found to be, or to have been the primitive form of society everywhere from India to Ireland. The inner organisation of this primitive Communistic society was laid bare, in its typical form, by Morgan's crowning discovery of the true nature of the *gens* and its relation to the *tribe*. With the dissolution of these primeval communities society begins to be differentiated into separate and finally antagonistic classes. I have attempted to retrace this process of dissolution in *Der Ursprung der Familie, des Privateigenthums und des Staats,* 2nd edition, Stuttgart, 1886. [*Note by Engels to the English edition of 1888, and— less the last sentence—to the German edition of 1890.*]

***Guild-master, that is, a full member of a guild, a master within, not a head of a guild. [*Note by Engels to the English edition of 1888.*]

stood in constant opposition to one another, carried on an uninterrupted, now hidden, now open fight, a fight that each time ended, either in a revolutionary re-constitution of society at large, or in the common ruin of the contending classes.

In the earlier epochs of history, we find almost everywhere a complicated arrangement of society into various orders, a manifold gradation of social rank. In ancient Rome we have patricians, knights, plebeians, slaves; in the Middle Ages, feudal lords, vassals, guild-masters, journeymen, apprentices, serfs; in almost all of these classes, again, subordinate gradations.

The modern bourgeois society that has sprouted from the ruins of feudal society has not done away with class antagonisms. It has but established new classes, new conditions of oppression, new forms of struggle in place of the old ones.

Our epoch, the epoch of the bourgeoisie, possesses, however, this distinctive feature: it has simplified the class antagonisms. Society as a whole is more and more splitting up into two great hostile camps, into two great classes directly facing each other: Bourgeoisie and Proletariat.

From the serfs of the Middle Ages sprang the chartered burghers of the earliest towns. From these burgesses the first elements of the bourgeoisie were developed.

The discovery of America, the rounding of the Cape, opened up fresh ground for the rising bourgeoisie. The East-Indian and Chinese markets, the colonisation of America, trade with the colonies, the increase in the means of exchange and in commodities generally, gave to commerce, to navigation, to industry, an impulse never before known, and thereby, to the revolutionary element in the tottering feudal society, a rapid development.

The feudal system of industry, under which industrial production was monopolised by closed guilds, now no longer sufficed for the growing wants of the new markets. The manufacturing system took its place. The guild-masters were pushed on one side by the manufacturing middle class; division of labour between the different corporate guilds vanished in the face of division of labour in each single workshop.

Meantime the markets kept ever growing, the demand ever rising. Even manufacture no longer sufficed. Thereupon, steam and machinery revolutionised industrial production. The place of manufacture was taken by the giant, Modern Industry, the place of the industrial middle class, by industrial millionaires, the leaders of whole industrial armies, the modern bourgeois.

57

Modern industry has established the world market, for which the discovery of America paved the way. This market has given an immense development to commerce, to navigation, to communication by land. This development has, in its turn, reacted on the extension of industry; and in proportion as industry, commerce, navigation, railways extended, in the same proportion the bourgeoisie developed, increased its capital, and pushed into the background every class handed down from the Middle Ages.

We see, therefore, how the modern bourgeoisie is itself the product of a long course of development, of a series of revolutions in the modes of production and of exchange.

Each step in the development of the bourgeoisie was accompanied by a corresponding political advance of that class. An oppressed class under the sway of the feudal nobility, an armed and self-governing association in the medieval commune*; here independent urban republic (as in Italy and Germany), there taxable "third estate" of the monarchy (as in France), afterwards, in the period of manufacture proper, serving either the semi-feudal or the absolute monarchy as a counterpoise against the nobility, and, in fact, cornerstone of the great monarchies in general, the bourgeoisie has at last, since the establishment of Modern Industry and of the world market, conquered for itself, in the modern representative State, exclusive political sway. The executive of the modern State is but a committee for managing the common affairs of the whole bourgeoisie.

The bourgeoisie, historically, has played a most revolutionary part.

The bourgeoisie, wherever it has got the upper hand, has put an end to all feudal, patriarchal, idyllic relations. It has pitilessly torn asunder the motley feudal ties that bound man to his "natural

---

* "Commune" was the name taken, in France, by the nascent towns even before they had conquered from their feudal lords and masters local self-government and political rights as the "Third Estate". Generally speaking, for the economical development of the bourgeoisie, England is here taken as the typical country; for its political development, France. [*Note by Engels to the English edition of 1888.*]

This was the name given their urban communities by the townsmen of Italy and France, after they had purchased or wrested their initial rights of self-government from their feudal lords. [*Note by Engels to the German edition of 1890.*]

superiors", and has left remaining no other nexus between man and man than naked self-interest, than callous "cash payment". It has drowned the most heavenly ecstasies of religious fervour, of chivalrous enthusiasm, of philistine sentimentalism, in the icy water of egotistical calculation. It has resolved personal worth into exchange value, and in place of the numberless indefeasible chartered freedoms, has set up that single, unconscionable freedom—Free Trade. In one word, for exploitation, veiled by religious and political illusions, it has substituted naked, shameless, direct, brutal exploitation.

The bourgeoisie has stripped of its halo every occupation hitherto honoured and looked up to with reverent awe. It has converted the physician, the lawyer, the priest, the poet, the man of science, into its paid wage-labourers.

The bourgeoisie has torn away from the family its sentimental veil, and has reduced the family relation to a mere money relation.

The bourgeoisie has disclosed how it came to pass that the brutal display of vigour in the Middle Ages, which Reactionists so much admire, found its fitting complement in the most slothful indolence. It has been the first to show what man's activity can bring about. It has accomplished wonders far surpassing Egyptian pyramids, Roman aqueducts, and Gothic cathedrals; it has conducted expeditions that put in the shade all former Exoduses of nations and crusades.

The bourgeoisie cannot exist without constantly revolutionising the instruments of production, and thereby the relations of production, and with them the whole relations of society. Conservation of the old modes of production in unaltered form, was, on the contrary, the first condition of existence for all earlier industrial classes. Constant revolutionising of production, uninterrupted disturbance of all social conditions, everlasting uncertainty and agitation distinguish the bourgeois epoch from all earlier ones. All fixed, fast-frozen relations, with their train of ancient and venerable prejudices and opinions, are swept away, all new-formed ones become antiquated before they can ossify. All that is solid melts into air, all that is holy is profaned, and man is at last compelled to face with sober senses, his real conditions of life, and his relations with his kind.

The need of a constantly expanding market for its products chases the bourgeoisie over the whole surface of the globe. It must nestle everywhere, settle everywhere, establish connexions everywhere.

The bourgeoisie has through its exploitation of the world market given a cosmopolitan character to production and consumption in every country. To the great chagrin of Reactionists, it has drawn from under the feet of industry the national ground on which it stood. All old-established national industries have been destroyed or are daily being destroyed. They are dislodged by new industries, whose introduction becomes a life and death question for all civilised nations, by industries that no longer work up indigenous raw material, but raw material drawn from the remotest zones; industries whose products are consumed, not only at home, but in every quarter of the globe. In place of the old wants, satisfied by the productions of the country, we find new wants, requiring for their satisfaction the products of distant lands and climes. In place of the old local and national seclusion and self-sufficiency, we have intercourse in every direction, universal interdependence of nations. And as in material, so also in intellectual production. The intellectual creations of individual nations become common property. National one-sidedness and narrow-mindedness become more and more impossible, and from the numerous national and local literatures, there arises a world literature.

The bourgeoisie, by the rapid improvement of all instruments of production, by the immensely facilitated means of communication, draws all, even the most barbarian, nations into civilisation. The cheap prices of its commodities are the heavy artillery with which it batters down all Chinese walls, with which it forces the barbarians' intensely obstinate hatred of foreigners to capitulate. It compels all nations, on pain of extinction, to adopt the bourgeois mode of production; it compels them to introduce what it calls civilisation into their midst, i.e., to become bourgeois themselves. In one word, it creates a world after its own image.

The bourgeoisie has subjected the country to the rule of the towns. It has created enormous cities, has greatly increased the urban population as compared with the rural, and has thus rescued a considerable part of the population from the idiocy of rural life. Just as it has made the country dependent on the towns, so it has made barbarian and semi-barbarian countries dependent on the civilised ones, nations of peasants on nations of bourgeois, the East on the West.

The bourgeoisie keeps more and more doing away with the scattered state of the population, of the means of production, and of property. It has agglomerated population, centralised means of production, and has concentrated property in a few hands. The necessary consequence of this was political centralisation. Independent, or but loosely connected provinces with separate interests, laws, governments and systems of taxation, became lumped together into one nation, with one government, one code of laws, one national class-interest, one frontier and one customs-tariff.

The bourgeoisie, during its rule of scarce one hundred years, has created more massive and more colossal productive forces than have all preceding generations together. Subjection of Nature's forces to man, machinery, application of chemistry to industry and agriculture, steam-navigation, railways, electric telegraphs, clearing of whole continents for cultivation, canalisation of rivers, whole populations conjured out of the ground—what earlier century had even a presentiment that such productive forces slumbered in the lap of social labour?

We see then: the means of production and of exchange, on whose foundation the bourgeoisie built itself up, were generated in feudal society. At a certain stage in the development of these means of production and of exchange, the conditions under which feudal society produced and exchanged, the feudal organisation of agriculture and manufacturing industry, in one word, the feudal relations of property became no longer compatible with the already developed productive forces; they became so many fetters. They had to be burst asunder; they were burst asunder.

Into their place stepped free competition, accompanied by a social and political constitution adapted to it, and by the economical and political sway of the bourgeois class.

A similar movement is going on before our own eyes. Modern bourgeois society with its relations of production, of exchange and of property, a society that has conjured up such gigantic means of production and of exchange, is like the sorcerer, who is no longer able to control the powers of the nether world whom he has called up by his spells. For many a decade past the history of industry and commerce is but the history of the revolt of modern productive forces against modern conditions of production, against the property relations that are the conditions for the existence of the bourgeoisie and of its rule. It is enough to mention the commercial crises that by their periodical return put on its trial, each time more threateningly, the existence of the entire bourgeois society. In these crises a great part not only of the existing products, but also of the previously created productive forces, are periodically destroyed. In these crises there breaks out an epidemic that, in all earlier epochs, would have seemed an absurdity—the epidemic of over-production. Society suddenly finds itself put back into a state of momentary barbarism; it appears as if a famine, a universal war of devastation had cut off the supply of every means of subsistence; industry and commerce seem to be destroyed; and why? Because there is too much civilisation, too much means of subsistence, too much industry, too much commerce. The productive forces at the disposal of society no longer tend to further the development of the conditions of bourgeois property; on the contrary, they have become too powerful for these conditions, by which they are fettered, and so soon as they overcome these fetters, they bring disorder into the whole of bourgeois society, endanger the existence of bourgeois property. The conditions of bourgeois society are too narrow to comprise the wealth created by them. And how does the bourgeoisie get over these crises? On the one hand by enforced destruction of a mass of productive forces; on the other, by the conquest of new markets, and by the more thorough exploitation of the old ones. That is to say, by paving the way for more extensive and more destructive crises, and by diminishing the means whereby crises are prevented.

The weapons with which the bourgeoisie felled feudalism to the ground are now turned against the bourgeoisie itself.

But not only has the bourgeoisie forged the weapons that bring death to itself; it has also called into existence the men who are to wield those weapons—the modern working class—the proletarians.

In proportion as the bourgeoisie, i.e., capital, is developed, in the same proportion is the proletariat, the modern working class, developed—a class of labourers who live only so long as they find work, and who find work only so long as their labour increases capital. These labourers, who must sell themselves piecemeal, are a commodity, like every other article of commerce, and are consequently exposed to all the vicissitudes of competition, to all the fluctuations of the market.

Owing to the extensive use of machinery and to division of labour, the work of the proletarians has lost all individual character, and, consequently, all charm for the workman. He becomes an appendage of the machine, and it is only the most simple, most monotonous, and most easily acquired knack, that is required of him. Hence, the cost of production of a workman is restricted, almost entirely, to the means of subsistence that he requires for his maintenance, and for the propagation of his race. But the price of a commodity, and therefore also of labour,[10] is equal to its cost of production. In proportion, therefore, as the repulsiveness of the work increases, the wage decreases. Nay more, in proportion as the use of machinery and division of labour increases, in the same proportion the burden of toil also increases, whether by prolongation of the working hours, by increase of the work exacted in a given time or by increased speed of the machinery, etc.

Modern industry has converted the little workshop of the patriarchal master into the great factory of the industrial capitalist. Masses of labourers, crowded into the factory, are organised like soldiers. As privates of the industrial army they are placed under the command of a perfect hierarchy of officers and sergeants. Not only are they slaves of the bourgeois class, and of the bourgeois State; they are daily and hourly enslaved by the machine, by the overlooker, and, above all, by the individual bourgeois manufacturer himself. The more openly this despotism proclaims gain to be its end and aim, the more petty, the more hateful and the more embittering it is.

The less the skill and exertion of strength implied in manual labour, in other words, the more modern industry becomes developed, the more is the labour of men superseded by that of women. Differences of age and sex have no longer any distinctive social validity for the working class. All are instruments of labour, more or less expensive to use, according to their age and sex.

No sooner is the exploitation of the labourer by the manufacturer, so far, at an end, and he receives his wages in cash, than he is set upon by the other portions of the bourgeoisie, the landlord, the shopkeeper, the pawnbroker, etc.

The lower strata of the middle class—the small tradespeople, shopkeepers, and retired tradesmen generally, the handicraftsmen and peasants—all these sink gradually into the proletariat, partly because their diminutive capital does not suffice for the scale on which Modern Industry is carried on, and is swamped in the competition with the large capitalists, partly because their specialised skill is rendered worthless by new methods of production. Thus the proletariat is recruited from all classes of the population.

The proletariat goes through various stages of development. With its birth begins its struggle with the bourgeoisie. At first the contest is carried on by individual labourers, then by the workpeople of a factory, then by the operatives of one trade, in one locality, against the individual bourgeois who directly exploits them. They direct their attacks not against the bourgeois conditions of production, but against the instruments of production themselves; they destroy imported wares that compete with their labour, they smash to pieces machinery, they set factories ablaze, they seek to restore by force the vanished status of the workman of the Middle Ages.

At this stage the labourers still form an incoherent mass scattered over the whole country, and broken up by their mutual competition. If anywhere they unite to form more compact bodies, this is not yet the consequence of their own active union, but of the union of the bourgeoisie, which class, in order to attain its own political ends, is compelled to set the whole proletariat in motion, and is moreover yet, for a time, able to do so. At this stage, therefore, the proletarians do not fight their enemies, but the enemies of their enemies, the remnants of absolute monarchy, the landowners, the non-industrial bourgeois, the petty bourgeoisie. Thus the whole historical movement is concentrated in the hands of the bourgeoisie; every victory so obtained is a victory for the bourgeoisie.

But with the development of industry the proletariat not only increases in number; it becomes concentrated in greater masses, its strength grows, and it feels that strength more. The various interests and conditions of life within the ranks of the proletariat are more and more equalised, in proportion as machinery obliterates all distinctions of labour, and nearly everywhere reduces wages to the same low level. The growing competition among the bourgeois, and the resulting commercial crises, make the wages of the workers ever more fluctuating. The unceasing improvement of machinery, ever more rapidly developing, makes their livelihood more and more precarious; the collisions between individual workmen and individual bourgeois take more and more the character of collisions between two classes. Thereupon the workers begin to form combinations (Trades' Unions) against the bourgeois; they club together in order to keep up the rate of wages; they found permanent associations in order to make provision beforehand for these occasional revolts. Here and there the contest breaks out into riots.

Now and then the workers are victorious, but only for a time. The real fruit of their battles lies, not in the immediate result, but in the ever-expanding union of the workers. This union is helped on by the improved means of communication that are created by modern industry and that place the workers of different localities in contact with one another. It was just this contact that was needed to centralise the numerous local struggles, all of the same character, into one national struggle between classes. But every class struggle is a political struggle. And that union, to attain which the burghers of the Middle Ages, with their miserable highways, required centuries, the modern proletarians, thanks to railways, achieve in a few years.

This organisation of the proletarians into a class, and consequently into a political party, is continually being upset again by the competition between the workers themselves. But it ever rises up again, stronger, firmer, mightier. It compels legislative recognition of particular interests of the workers, by taking advantage of the divisions among the bourgeoisie itself. Thus the ten-hours' bill in England was carried.[11]

Altogether collisions between the classes of the old society further, in many ways, the course of development of the proletariat. The bourgeoisie finds itself involved in a constant battle. At first with the aristocracy; later on, with those portions of the bourgeoisie itself, whose interests have become antagonistic to the progress of industry; at all times, with the bourgeoisie of foreign countries. In all these battles it sees itself compelled to appeal to the proletariat, to ask for its help, and thus, to drag it into the political arena. The bourgeoisie itself, therefore, supplies the proletariat with its own elements of political and general education, in other words, it furnishes the proletariat with weapons for fighting the bourgeoisie.

Further, as we have already seen, entire sections of the ruling classes are, by the advance of industry, precipitated into the proletariat, or are at least threatened in their conditions of existence. These also supply the proletariat with fresh elements of enlightenment and progress.

Finally, in times when the class struggle nears the decisive hour, the process of dissolution going on within the ruling class, in fact within the whole range of old society, assumes such a violent, glaring character, that a small section of the ruling class cuts itself adrift, and joins the revolutionary class, the class that holds the future in its hands. Just as, therefore, at an earlier period, a section of the nobility went over to the bourgeoisie, so now a portion of the bourgeoisie goes over to the proletariat, and in particular, a portion of the bourgeois ideologists, who have raised themselves to the level of comprehending theoretically the historical movement as a whole.

Of all the classes that stand face to face with the bourgeoisie today, the proletariat alone is a really revolutionary class. The other classes decay and finally disappear in the face of Modern Industry; the proletariat is its special and essential product.

The lower middle class, the small manufacturer, the shopkeeper, the artisan, the peasant, all these fight against the bourgeoisie, to save from extinction their existence as fractions of the middle class. They are therefore not revolutionary, but conservative. Nay more, they are reactionary, for they try to roll back the wheel of history. If by chance they are revolutionary, they are so only in view of their impending transfer into the proletariat, they thus defend not their present, but their future interests, they desert their own standpoint to place themselves at that of the proletariat.

The "dangerous class", the social scum, that passively rotting mass thrown off by the lowest layers of old society may, here and there, be swept into the movement by a proletarian revolution; its conditions of life, however, prepare it far more for the part of a bribed tool of reactionary intrigue.

In the conditions of the proletariat, those of old society at large are already virtually swamped. The proletarian is without property; his relation to his wife and children has no longer anything in common with the bourgeois family relations; modern industrial labour, modern subjection to capital, the same in England as in France, in America as in Germany, has stripped him of every trace of national character. Law, morality, religion, are to him so many bourgeois prejudices, behind which lurk in ambush just as many bourgeois interests.

All the preceding classes that got the upper hand, sought to fortify their already acquired status by subjecting society at large to their conditions of appropriation. The proletarians cannot become masters of the productive forces of society, except by abolishing their own previous mode of appropriation, and thereby also every other previous mode of appropriation. They have nothing of their own to secure and to fortify; their mission is to destroy all previous securities for, and insurances of, individual property.

All previous historical movements were movements of minorities, or in the interest of minorities. The proletarian movement is the self-conscious, independent movement of the immense majority, in the interest of the immense majority. The proletariat, the lowest stratum of our present society, cannot stir, cannot raise itself up, without the whole superincumbent strata of official society being sprung into the air.

Though not in substance, yet in form, the struggle of the proletariat with the bourgeoisie is at first a national struggle. The proletariat of each country must, of course, first of all settle matters with its own bourgeoisie.

In depicting the most general phases of the development of the proletariat, we traced the more or less veiled civil war, raging within existing society, up to the point where that war breaks out into open revolution, and where the violent overthrow of the bourgeoisie lays the foundation for the sway of the proletariat.

Hitherto, every form of society has been based, as we have already seen, on the antagonism of oppressing and oppressed classes. But in order to oppress a class, certain conditions must be assured to it under which it can, at least, continue its slavish existence. The serf, in the period of serfdom, raised himself to membership in the commune, just as the petty bourgeois, under the yoke of feudal absolutism, managed to develop into a bourgeois. The modern labourer, on the contrary, instead of rising with the progress of industry, sinks deeper and deeper below the conditions of existence of his own class. He becomes a pauper, and pauperism develops more rapidly than population and wealth. And here it becomes evident, that the bourgeoisie is unfit any longer to be the ruling class in society, and to impose its conditions of existence upon society as an over-riding law. It is unfit to rule because it is incompetent to assure an existence to its slave within his slavery, because it cannot help letting him sink into such a state, that it has to feed him, instead of being fed by him. Society can no longer live under this bourgeoisie, in other words, its existence is no longer compatible with society.

The essential condition for the existence, and for the sway of the bourgeois class, is the formation and augmentation of capital; the condition for capital is wage-labour. Wage-labour rests exclusively on competition between the labourers. The advance of industry, whose involuntary promoter is the bourgeoisie, replaces the isolation of the labourers, due to competition, by their revolutionary combination, due to association. The development of Modern Industry, therefore, cuts from under its feet the very foundation on which the bourgeoisie produces and appropriates products. What the bourgeoisie, therefore, produces, above all, is its own grave-diggers. Its fall and the victory of the proletariat are equally inevitable.

II

PROLETARIANS AND COMMUNISTS

In what relation do the Communists stand to the proletarians as a whole?

The Communists do not form a separate party opposed to other working-class parties.

They have no interests separate and apart from those of the proletariat as a whole.

They do not set up any sectarian principles of their own, by which to shape and mould the proletarian movement.

The Communists are distinguished from the other working-class parties by this only: 1. In the national struggles of the proletarians of the different countries, they point out and bring to the front the common interests of the entire proletariat, independently of all nationality. 2. In the various stages of development which the struggle of the working class against the bourgeoisie has to pass through, they always and everywhere represent the interests of the movement as a whole.

The Communists, therefore, are on the one hand, practically, the most advanced and resolute section of the working-class parties of every country, that section which pushes forward all others; on the other hand, theoretically, they have over the great mass of the proletariat the advantage of clearly understanding the line of march, the conditions, and the ultimate general results of the proletarian movement.

The immediate aim of the Communists is the same as that of all the other proletarian parties: formation of the proletariat into a class, overthrow of the bourgeois supremacy, conquest of political power by the proletariat.

The theoretical conclusions of the Communists are in no way based on ideas or principles that have been invented, or discovered by this or that would-be universal reformer.

They merely express, in general terms, actual relations springing from an existing class struggle, from a historical movement going on under our very eyes. The abolition of existing property relations is not at all a distinctive feature of Communism.

All property relations in the past have continually been subject to historical change consequent upon the change in historical conditions.

The French Revolution, for example, abolished feudal property in favour of bourgeois property.

The distinguishing feature of Communism is not the abolition of property generally, but the abolition of bourgeois property. But modern bourgeois private property is the final and most complete expression of the system of producing and appropriating products, that is based on class antagonisms, on the exploitation of the many by the few.

In this sense, the theory of the Communists may be summed up in the single sentence: Abolition of private property.

We Communists have been reproached with the desire of abolishing the right of personally acquiring property as the fruit of a man's own labour, which property is alleged to be the groundwork of all personal freedom, activity and independence.

Hard-won, self-acquired, self-earned property! Do you mean the property of the petty artisan and of the small peasant, a form of property that preceded the bourgeois form? There is no need to abolish that; the development of industry has to a great extent already destroyed it, and is still destroying it daily.

Or do you mean modern bourgeois private property?

But does wage-labour create any property for the labourer? Not a bit. It creates capital, i.e., that kind of property which exploits wage-labour, and which cannot increase except upon condition of begetting a new supply of wage-labour for fresh exploitation. Property, in its present form, is based on the antagonism of capital and wage-labour. Let us examine both sides of this antagonism.

To be a capitalist is to have not only a purely personal, but a social *status* in production. Capital is a collective product, and only by the united action of many members, nay, in the last resort, only by the united action of all members of society, can it be set in motion.

Capital is, therefore, not a personal, it is a social power.

When, therefore, capital is converted into common property, into the property of all members of society, personal property is not thereby transformed into social property. It is only the social character of the property that is changed. It loses its class character.

Let us now take wage-labour.

The average price of wage-labour is the minimum wage, *i.e.*, that quantum of the means of subsistence, which is absolutely requisite to keep the labourer in bare existence as a labourer. What, therefore, the wage-labourer appropriates by means of his labour, merely suffices to prolong and reproduce a bare existence. We by no means intend to abolish this personal appropriation of the products of labour, an appropriation that is made for the maintenance and reproduction of human life, and that leaves no surplus wherewith to command the labour of others. All that we want to do away with is the miserable character of this appropriation, under which the labourer lives merely to increase capital, and is allowed to live only in so far as the interest of the ruling class requires it.

In bourgeois society, living labour is but a means to increase accumulated labour. In Communist society, accumulated labour is but a means to widen, to enrich, to promote the existence of the labourer.

In bourgeois society, therefore, the past dominates the present; in Communist society, the present dominates the past. In bourgeois society capital is independent and has individuality, while the living person is dependent and has no individuality.

And the abolition of this state of things is called by the bourgeois abolition of individuality and freedom! And rightly so. The abolition of bourgeois individuality, bourgeois independence, and bourgeois freedom is undoubtedly aimed at.

By freedom is meant, under the present bourgeois conditions of production, free trade, free selling and buying.

But if selling and buying disappears, free selling and buying disappears also. This talk about free selling and buying, and all the other "brave words" of our bourgeoisie about freedom in general, have a meaning, if any, only in contrast with restricted selling and buying, with the fettered traders of the Middle Ages, but have no meaning when opposed to the Communistic abolition of buying and selling, of the bourgeois conditions of production, and of the bourgeoisie itself.

You are horrified at our intending to do away with private property. But in your existing society, private property is already done away with for nine-tenths of the population; its existence for the few is solely due to its non-existence in the hands of those nine-tenths. You reproach us, therefore, with intending to do away with a form of property, the necessary condition for whose existence is the non-existence of any property for the immense majority of society.

In one word, you reproach us with intending to do away with your property. Precisely so; that is just what we intend.

From the moment when labour can no longer be converted into capital, money, or rent, into a social power capable of being monopolised, i.e., from the moment when individual property can no longer be transformed into bourgeois property, into capital, from that moment, you say, individuality vanishes.

You must, therefore, confess that by "individual" you mean no other person than the bourgeois, than the middle-class owner of property. This person must, indeed, be swept out of the way, and made impossible.

Communism deprives no man of the power to appropriate the products of society; all that it does is to deprive him of the power to subjugate the labour of others by means of such appropriation.

It has been objected that upon the abolition of private property all work will cease, and universal laziness will overtake us.

According to this, bourgeois society ought long ago to have gone to the dogs through sheer idleness; for those of its members who work, acquire nothing, and those who acquire anything, do not work. The whole of this objection is but another expression of the tautology: that there can no longer be any wage-labour when there is no longer any capital.

All objections urged against the Communistic mode of producing and appropriating material products, have, in the same way, been urged against the Communistic modes of producing and appropriating intellectual products. Just as, to the bourgeois, the disappearance of class property is the disappearance of production itself, so the disappearance of class culture is to him identical with the disappearance of all culture.

That culture, the loss of which he laments, is, for the enormous majority, a mere training to act as a machine.

But don't wrangle with us so long as you apply, to our intended abolition of bourgeois property, the standard of your bourgeois notions of freedom, culture, law, &c. Your very ideas are but the outgrowth of the conditions of your bourgeois production and bourgeois property, just as your jurisprudence is but the will of

71

your class made into a law for all, a will, whose essential character and direction are determined by the economical conditions of existence of your class.

The selfish misconception that induces you to transform into eternal laws of nature and of reason, the social forms springing from your present mode of production and form of property—historical relations that rise and disappear in the progress of production—this misconception you share with every ruling class that has preceded you. What you see clearly in the case of ancient property, what you admit in the case of feudal property, you are of course forbidden to admit in the case of your own bourgeois form of property.

Abolition of the family! Even the most radical flare up at this infamous proposal of the Communists.

On what foundation is the present family, the bourgeois family, based? On capital, on private gain. In its completely developed form this family exists only among the bourgeoisie. But this state of things finds its complement in the practical absence of the family among the proletarians, and in public prostitution.

The bourgeois family will vanish as a matter of course when its complement vanishes, and both will vanish with the vanishing of capital.

Do you charge us with wanting to stop the exploitation of children by their parents? To this crime we plead guilty.

But, you will say, we destroy the most hallowed of relations, when we replace home education by social.

And your education! Is not that also social, and determined by the social conditions under which you educate, by the intervention, direct or indirect, of society, by means of schools, &c? The Communists have not invented the intervention of society in education; they do but seek to alter the character of that intervention, and to rescue education from the influence of the ruling class.

The bourgeois clap-trap about the family and education, about the hallowed co-relation of parent and child, becomes all the more disgusting, the more, by the action of Modern Industry, all family ties among the proletarians are torn asunder, and their children transformed into simple articles of commerce and instruments of labour.

But you Communists would introduce community of women, screams the whole bourgeoisie in chorus.

The bourgeois sees in his wife a mere instrument of production. He hears that the instruments of production are to be exploited in common, and, naturally, can come to no other conclusion than the lot of being common to all will likewise fall to the women.

He has not even a suspicion that the real point aimed at is to do away with the status of women as mere instruments of production.

For the rest, nothing is more ridiculous than the virtuous indignation of our bourgeois at the community of women which, they pretend, is to be openly and officially established by the Communists. The Communists have no need to introduce community of women; it has existed almost from time immemorial.

Our bourgeois, not content with having the wives and daughters of their proletarians at their disposal, not to speak of common prostitutes, take the greatest pleasure in seducing each other's wives.

Bourgeois marriage is in reality a system of wives in common and thus, at the most, what the Communists might possibly be reproached with, is that they desire to introduce, in substitution for a hypocritically concealed, an openly legalised community of women. For the rest, it is self-evident that the abolition of the present system of production must bring with it the abolition of the community of women springing from that system, *i.e.*, of prostitution both public and private.

The Communists are further reproached with desiring to abolish countries and nationality.

The working men have no country. We cannot take from them what they have not got. Since the proletariat must first of all acquire political supremacy, must rise to be the leading class of the nation, must constitute itself *the* nation, it is so far, itself national, though not in the bourgeois sense of the word.

National differences and antagonisms between peoples are daily more and more vanishing, owing to the development of the bourgeoisie, to freedom of commerce, to the world market, to uniformity in the mode of production and in the conditions of life corresponding thereto.

The supremacy of the proletariat will cause them to vanish still faster. United action, of the leading civilised countries at least, is one of the first conditions for the emancipation of the proletariat.

In proportion as the exploitation of one individual by another is put an end to, the exploitation of one nation by another will also be put an end to. In proportion as the antagonism between classes within the nation vanishes, the hostility of one nation to another will come to an end.

The charges against Communism made from a religious, a

philosophical, and, generally, from an ideological standpoint, are not deserving of serious examination.

Does it require deep intuition to comprehend that man's ideas, views and conceptions, in one word, man's consciousness changes with every change in the conditions of his material existence, in his social relations and in his social life?

What else does the history of ideas prove, than that intellectual production changes its character in proportion as material production is changed? The ruling ideas of each age have ever been the ideas of its ruling class.

When people speak of ideas that revolutionise society, they do but express the fact, that within the old society, the elements of a new one have been created, and that the dissolution of the old ideas keeps even pace with the dissolution of the old conditions of existence.

When the ancient world was in its last throes, the ancient religions were overcome by Christianity. When Christian ideas succumbed in the 18th century to rationalist ideas, feudal society fought its death battle with the then revolutionary bourgeoisie. The ideas of religious liberty and freedom of conscience merely gave expression to the sway of free competition within the domain of knowledge.

"Undoubtedly," it will be said, "religious, moral, philosophical and juridical ideas have been modified in the course of historical development. But religion, morality, philosophy, political science, and law, constantly survived this change.

"There are, besides, eternal truths, such as Freedom, Justice, etc., that are common to all states of society. But Communism abolishes eternal truths, it abolishes all religion and all morality, instead of constituting them on a new basis; it therefore acts in contradiction to all past historical experience."

What does this accusation reduce itself to? The history of all past society has consisted in the development of class antagonisms, antagonisms that assumed different forms at different epochs.

But whatever form they may have taken, one fact is common to all past ages, *viz.*, the exploitation of one part of society by the other. No wonder, then, that the social consciousness of past ages, despite all the multiplicity and variety it displays, moves within certain common forms, or general ideas, which cannot completely vanish except with the total disappearance of class antagonisms.

The Communist revolution is the most radical rupture with traditional property relations; no wonder that its development involves the most radical rupture with traditional ideas.

But let us have done with the bourgeois objections to Communism.

We have seen above, that the first step in the revolution by the working class is to raise the proletariat to the position of ruling class, to win the battle of democracy.

The proletariat will use its political supremacy to wrest, by degrees, all capital from the bourgeoisie, to centralise all instruments of production in the hands of the State, *i.e.*, of the proletariat organised as the ruling class; and to increase the total of productive forces as rapidly as possible.

Of course, in the beginning, this cannot be effected except by means of despotic inroads on the rights of property, and on the conditions of bourgeois production; by means of measures, therefore, which appear economically insufficient and untenable, but which, in the course of the movement, outstrip themselves, necessitate further inroads upon the old social order, and are unavoidable as a means of entirely revolutionising the mode of production.

These measures will of course be different in different countries.

Nevertheless in the most advanced countries, the following will be pretty generally applicable:

1. Abolition of property in land and application of all rents of land to public purposes.

2. A heavy progressive or graduated income tax.

3. Abolition of all right of inheritance.

4. Confiscation of the property of all emigrants and rebels.

5. Centralisation of credit in the hands of the State, by means of a national bank with State capital and an exclusive monopoly.

6. Centralisation of the means of communication and transport in the hands of the State.

7. Extension of factories and instruments of production owned by the State; the bringing into cultivation of waste-lands, and the improvement of the soil generally in accordance with a common plan.

8. Equal liability of all to labour. Establishment of industrial armies, especially for agriculture.

9. Combination of agriculture with manufacturing industries; gradual abolition of the distinction between town and country, by a more equable distribution of the population over the country.

10. Free education for all children in public schools. Abolition of children's factory labour in its present form. Combination of education with industrial production, &c., &c.

75

When, in the course of development, class distinctions have disappeared, and all production has been concentrated in the hands of a vast association of the whole nation, the public power will lose its political character. Political power, properly so called, is merely the organised power of one class for oppressing another. If the proletariat during its contest with the bourgeoisie is compelled, by the force of circumstances, to organise itself as a class, if, by means of a revolution, it makes itself the ruling class, and, as such, sweeps away by force the old conditions of production, then it will, along with these conditions, have swept away the conditions for the existence of class antagonisms and of classes generally, and will thereby have abolished its own supremacy as a class.

In place of the old bourgeois society, with its classes and class antagonisms, we shall have an association, in which the free development of each is the condition for the free development of all.

Written in December
1847-January 1848

Marx and Engels,
Collected Works, Vol. 6,
pp. 481-506

KARL MARX
FREDERICK ENGELS

ADDRESS
OF THE
CENTRAL COMMITTEE
TO THE
COMMUNIST LEAGUE[12]

MARCH 1850

The Central Committee
to the League

Brothers! In the two revolutionary years 1848-49 the League proved itself in double fashion: first, in that its members energetically took part in the movement in all places, that in the press, on the barricades and on the battle-fields, they stood in the front ranks of the only decidedly revolutionary class, the proletariat. The League further proved itself in that its conception of the movement as laid down in the circulars of the congresses and of the Central Committee of 1847 as well as in the *Communist Manifesto* turned out to be the only correct one, that the expectations expressed in those documents were completely fulfilled and the conception of present-day social conditions, previously propagated only in secret by the League, is now on everyone's lips and is openly preached in the market places. At the same time the former firm organisation of the League was considerably slackened. A large part of the members who directly participated in the revolutionary movement believed the time for secret societies to have gone by and public activities alone sufficient. The individual circles and communities allowed their connections with the Central Committee to become loose and gradually dormant. Consequently, while the democratic party, the party of the petty bourgeoisie, organised itself more and more in Germany, the workers' party lost its only firm foothold, remained organised at the most in separate localities for local purposes and in the general movement thus came completely under the domination and leadership of the petty-bourgeois democrats. An end must be put to this state of affairs, the independence of the workers must be restored. The Central Committee realised this necessity and therefore already in the winter of 1848-49 it sent an emissary, Josef Moll, to Germany for the reorganisation of the League. Moll's mission, however, was without lasting effect, partly because the German workers at that time had not acquired sufficient experience and partly because it was interrupted by the insurrection of the previous May. Moll himself took up the musket, entered the Baden-Palatinate army and fell on July 19[a] in the encounter at the Murg. The League lost in him one of its oldest, most active and most trustworthy members, one who had been active in all the congresses and Central Committees and even prior to this had carried out a series of missions with great success. After the defeat of the revolutionary parties of Germany and France in July 1849, almost all the members of the Central Committee came together again in London, replenished their numbers with new revolutionary forces and set about the reorganisation of the League with renewed zeal.

Reorganisation can only be carried out by an emissary, and the Central Committee considers it extremely important that the emissary should leave precisely at this moment when a new revolution is impending, when the workers' party, therefore, must act in the most organised, most unanimous and most independent fashion possible if it is not to be exploited and taken in tow again by the bourgeoisie as in 1848.

Brothers! We told you as early as 1848 that the German liberal bourgeois would soon come to power and would immediately turn their newly acquired power against the workers. You have seen how this has been fulfilled. In fact it was the bourgeois who, immediately after the March movement of 1848,[13] took possession of the state power and used this power to force back at once the workers, their allies in the struggle, into their former oppressed position. Though the bourgeoisie was not able to accomplish this without uniting with the feudal party, which had been disposed of in March, without finally even surrendering power once again to this feudal absolutist party, still it has secured conditions for itself which, in the long run, owing to the financial embarrassment of the government, would place power in its hands and would safeguard all its interests, if it were possible for the revolutionary movement to assume already now a so-called peaceful development. The bourgeoisie, in order to safeguard its rule, would not even need to make itself obnoxious by violent measures against the people, since all such violent steps have already been taken by the feudal counter-revolution. Developments, however, will not take

---

[a] A mistake: should read "June 29".—Ed.

this peaceful course. On the contrary, the revolution, which will accelerate this development, is near at hand, whether it will be called forth by an independent uprising of the French proletariat or by an invasion of the Holy Alliance against the revolutionary Babylon.

And the role, this so treacherous role which the German liberal bourgeois played in 1848 against the people, will in the impending revolution be taken over by the democratic petty bourgeois, who at present occupy the same position in the opposition as the liberal bourgeois before 1848. This party, the democratic party, which is far more dangerous to the workers than the previous liberal one, consists of three elements:

I. Of the most advanced sections of the big bourgeoisie, which pursue the aim of the immediate complete overthrow of feudalism and absolutism. This faction is represented by the one-time Berlin compromisers, by the tax resisters.

II. Of the democratic-constitutional petty bourgeois, whose main aim during the previous movement was the establishment of a more or less democratic federal state as striven for by their representatives, the Lefts in the Frankfort Assembly, and later by the Stuttgart parliament,[14] and by themselves in the campaign for the Reich Constitution.

III. Of the republican petty bourgeois, whose ideal is a German federative republic after the manner of Switzerland, and who now call themselves Red and Social-Democratic because they cherish the pious wish of abolishing the pressure of big capital on small capital, of the big bourgeois on the small bourgeois. The representatives of this faction were the members of the democratic congresses and committees, the leaders of the democratic associations, the editors of the democratic newspapers.

Now, after their defeat, all these factions call themselves Republicans or Reds, just as the republican petty bourgeois in France now call themselves Socialists. Where, as in Württemberg, Bavaria, etc., they still find opportunity to pursue their aims constitutionally, they seize the occasion to retain their old phrases and to prove by deeds that they have not changed in the least. It is evident, moreover, that the altered name of this party does not make the slightest difference in its attitude to the workers, but merely proves that they are now obliged to turn against the bourgeoisie, which is united with absolutism, and to seek support in the proletariat.

The petty-bourgeois democratic party in Germany is very

powerful; it comprises not only the great majority of the bourgeois inhabitants of the towns, the small people in industry and trade and the guild-masters; it numbers among its followers also the peasants and the rural proletariat, in so far as the latter has not yet found a support in the independent urban proletariat.

The relation of the revolutionary workers' party to the petty-bourgeois democrats is this: it marches together with them against the faction which it aims at overthrowing, it opposes them in everything whereby they seek to consolidate their position in their own interests.

Far from desiring to revolutionise all society for the revolutionary proletarians, the democratic petty bourgeois strive for a change in social conditions by means of which existing society will be made as tolerable and comfortable as possible for them. Hence they demand above all diminution of state expenditure by a curtailment of the bureaucracy and shifting the chief taxes on to the big landowners and bourgeois. Further, they demand the abolition of the pressure of big capital on small, through public credit institutions and laws against usury, by which means it will be possible for them and the peasants to obtain advances, on favourable conditions, from the state instead of from the capitalists; they also demand the establishment of bourgeois property relations in the countryside by the complete abolition of feudalism. To accomplish all this they need a democratic state structure, either constitutional or republican, that will give them and their allies, the peasants, a majority; also a democratic communal structure that will give them direct control over communal property and over a series of functions now performed by the bureaucrats.

The domination and speedy increase of capital is further to be counteracted partly by restricting the right of inheritance and partly by transferring as many jobs of work as possible to the state. As far as the workers are concerned, it remains certain above all that they are to remain wage-workers as before; the democratic petty bourgeois only desire better wages and a more secure existence for the workers and hope to achieve this through partial employment by the state and through charity measures; in short, they hope to bribe the workers by more or less concealed alms and to break their revolutionary potency by making their position tolerable for the moment. The demands of the petty-bourgeois democracy here summarised are not put forward by all of its factions at the same time and only a very few members of them consider that these demands constitute definite aims in their entirety. The further separate individuals or factions among them go, the more of these demands will they make their own, and those few who see their own programme in what has been outlined above might believe that thereby they have put forward the utmost that can be demanded from the revolution. But these demands can in no wise suffice for the party of the proletariat. While the democratic petty bourgeois wish to bring the revolution to a conclusion as quickly as possible, and with the achievement, at most, of the above demands, it is our interest and our task to make the revolution permanent, until all more or less possessing classes have been forced out of their position of dominance, until the proletariat has conquered state power, and the association of proletarians, not only in one country but in all the dominant countries of the world, has advanced so far that competition among the proletarians of these countries has ceased and that at least the decisive productive forces are concentrated in the hands of the proletarians. For us the issue cannot be the alteration of private property but only its annihilation, not the smoothing over of class antagonisms but the abolition of classes, not the improvement of existing society but the foundation of a new one. That, during the further development of the revolution, the petty-bourgeois democracy will for a moment obtain predominating influence in Germany is not open to doubt. The question, therefore, arises as to what the attitude of the proletariat and in particular of the League will be in relation to it:

1. During the continuance of the present conditions where the petty-bourgeois democrats are likewise oppressed;

2. In the next revolutionary struggle, which will give them the upper hand;

3. After this struggle, during the period of preponderance over the overthrown classes and the proletariat.

1. At the present moment, when the democratic petty bourgeois are everywhere oppressed, they preach in general unity and reconciliation to the proletariat, they offer it their hand and strive for the establishment of a large opposition party which will embrace all shades of opinion in the democratic party, that is, they strive to entangle the workers in a party organisation in which general social-democratic phrases predominate, behind which their special interests are concealed and in which the particular demands of the proletariat may not be brought forward for the sake of beloved peace. Such a union would turn out solely to their

advantage and altogether to the disadvantage of the proletariat. The proletariat would lose its whole independent, laboriously achieved position and once more sink down to being an appendage of official bourgeois democracy. This union must, therefore, be most decisively rejected. Instead of once again stooping to serve as the applauding chorus of the bourgeois democrats, the workers, and above all the League, must exert themselves to establish an independent, secret and public organisation of the workers' party alongside of the official democrats and make each section the central point and nucleus of workers' societies in which the attitude and interests of the proletariat will be discussed independently of bourgeois influences. How far the bourgeois democrats are from seriously considering an alliance in which the proletarians would stand side by side with them with equal power and equal rights is shown, for example, by the Breslau democrats who, in their organ, the *Neue Oder-Zeitung*, most furiously attack the independently organised workers, whom they style Socialists. In the case of a struggle against a common adversary no special union is required. As soon as such an adversary has to be fought directly, the interests of both parties, for the moment, coincide, and, as previously, so also in the future, this connection, calculated to last only for the moment, will arise of itself. It is self-evident that in the impending bloody conflicts, as in all earlier ones, it is the workers who, in the main, will have to win the victory by their courage, determination and self-sacrifice. As previously, so also in this struggle, the mass of the petty bourgeois will as long as possible remain hesitant, undecided and inactive, and then, as soon as the issue has been decided, will seize the victory for themselves, will call upon the workers to maintain tranquillity and return to their work, will guard against so-called excesses and bar the proletariat from the fruits of victory. It is not in the power of the workers to prevent the petty-bourgeois democrats from doing this, but it is in their power to make it difficult for them to gain the upper hand as against the armed proletariat, and to dictate such conditions to them that the rule of the bourgeois democrats will from the outset bear within it the seeds of their downfall, and that their subsequent extrusion by the rule of the proletariat will be considerably facilitated. Above all things, the workers must counteract, as much as is at all possible, during the conflict and immediately after the struggle, the bourgeois endeavours to allay the storm, and must compel the democrats to carry out their present terrorist phrases. Their actions must be so aimed as to prevent the direct revolutionary excitement from being suppressed again immediately after the victory. On the contrary, they must keep it alive as long as possible. Far from opposing so-called excesses, instances of popular revenge against hated individuals or public buildings that are associated only with hateful recollections, such instances must not only be tolerated but the leadership of them taken in hand. During the struggle and after the struggle, the workers must, at every opportunity, put forward their own demands alongside of the demands of the bourgeois democrats. They must demand guarantees for the workers as soon as the democratic bourgeois set about taking over the government. If necessary they must obtain these guarantees by force and in general they must see to it that the new rulers pledge themselves to all possible concessions and promises—the surest way to compromise them. In general, they must in every way restrain as far as possible the intoxication of victory and the enthusiasm for the new state of things, which make their appearance after every victorious street battle, by a calm and dispassionate estimate of the situation and by unconcealed mistrust in the new government. Alongside of the new official governments they must establish simultaneously their own revolutionary workers' governments, whether in the form of municipal committees and municipal councils or in the form of workers' clubs or workers' committees, so that the bourgeois-democratic governments not only immediately lose the support of the workers but from the outset see themselves supervised and threatened by authorities which are backed by the whole mass of the workers. In a word, from the first moment of victory, mistrust must be directed no longer against the conquered reactionary party, but against the workers' previous allies, against the party that wishes to exploit the common victory for itself alone.

2. But in order to be able energetically and threateningly to oppose this party, whose treachery to the workers will begin from the first hour of victory, the workers must be armed and organised. The arming of the whole proletariat with rifles, muskets, cannon and munitions must be put through at once, the revival of the old Citizens' Guard directed against the workers must be resisted. However, where the latter is not feasible the workers must attempt to organise themselves independently as a proletarian guard with commanders elected by themselves and with a general staff of their own choosing, and to put themselves at the command not of the state authority but of the revolutionary community councils which the workers will have managed to get adopted. Where workers are

employed at the expense of the state they must see that they are armed and organised in separate corps with commanders of their own choosing or as part of the proletarian guard. Arms and ammunition must not be surrendered on any pretext; any attempt at disarming must be frustrated, if necessary by force. Destruction of the influence of the bourgeois democrats upon the workers, immediate independent and armed organisation of the workers and the enforcement of conditions as difficult and compromising as possible upon the inevitable momentary rule of the bourgeois democracy—these are the main points which the proletariat and hence the League must keep in view during and after the impending insurrection.

3. As soon as the new governments have consolidated their positions to some extent, their struggle against the workers will begin. Here, in order to be able to offer energetic opposition to the democratic petty bourgeois, it is above all necessary that the workers shall be independently organised and centralised in clubs. After the overthrow of the existing governments, the Central Committee will, as soon as it is at all possible, betake itself to Germany, immediately convene a congress and put before the latter the necessary proposals for the centralisation of the workers' clubs under a leadership established in the chief seat of the movement. The speedy organisation of at least a provincial interlinking of the workers' clubs is one of the most important points for the strengthening and development of the workers' party; the immediate consequence of the overthrow of the existing governments will be the election of a national representative assembly. Here the proletariat must see to it:

I. That no groups of workers are barred on any pretext or by any kind of trickery on the part of local authorities or government commissioners.

II. That everywhere workers' candidates are put up alongside of the bourgeois-democratic candidates, that they should consist as far as possible of members of the League, and that their election is promoted by all possible means. Even where there is no prospect whatsoever of their being elected, the workers must put up their own candidates in order to preserve their independence, to count their forces and to bring before the public their revolutionary attitude and party standpoint. In this connection they must not allow themselves to be seduced by such arguments of the democrats as, for example, that by so doing they are splitting the democratic party and making it possible for the reactionaries to win. The ultimate intention of all such phrases is to dupe the proletariat. The advance which the proletarian party is bound to make by such independent action is infinitely more important than the disadvantage that might be incurred by the presence of a few reactionaries on the representative body. If the democracy from the outset comes out resolutely and terroristically against the reaction, the influence of the latter in the elections will be destroyed in advance.

The first point on which the bourgeois democrats will come into conflict with the workers will be the abolition of feudalism. As in the first French Revolution, the petty bourgeois will give the feudal lands to the peasants as free property, that is to say, try to leave the rural proletariat in existence and form a petty-bourgeois peasant class which will go through the same cycle of impoverishment and indebtedness which the French peasant is now still going through.

The workers must oppose this plan in the interest of the rural proletariat and in their own interest. They must demand that the confiscated feudal property remain state property and be converted into workers' colonies cultivated by the associated rural proletariat with all the advantages of large-scale agriculture, through which the principle of common property immediately obtains a firm basis in the midst of the tottering bourgeois property relations. Just as the democrats combine with the peasants so much the workers combine with the rural proletariat. Further, the democrats will work either directly for a federative republic or, if they cannot avoid a single and indivisible republic, they will at least attempt to cripple the central government by the utmost possible autonomy and independence for the communities and provinces. The workers, in opposition to this plan, must not only strive for a single and indivisible German republic, but also within this republic for the most determined centralisation of power in the hands of the state authority. They must not allow themselves to be misguided by the democratic talk of freedom for the communities, of self-government, etc. In a country like Germany where there are still so many relics of the Middle Ages to be abolished, where there is so much local and provincial obstinacy to be broken, it must under no circumstances be permitted that every village, every town and every province should put a new obstacle in the path of revolutionary activity, which can proceed with full force only from the centre. It is not to be tolerated that the present state of affairs should be renewed, that Germans must fight separately in every town and in every province for one and the same advance. Least of all is it to be tolerated that a form of property, namely, communal property, which still lags behind modern private property and which everywhere is necessarily passing into the latter, together with the quarrels resulting from it between poor and rich communities, as well as communal civil law, with its trickery against the workers, that exists alongside of state civil law, should be perpetuated by a so-called free communal constitution. As in France in 1793 so today in Germany it is the task of the really revolutionary party to carry through the strictest centralisation.*

We have seen how the democrats will come to power with the next movement, how they will be compelled to propose more or less socialistic measures. It will be asked what measures the workers ought to propose in reply. At the beginning of the movement, of course, the workers cannot yet propose any directly communistic measures. But they can:

1. Compel the democrats to interfere in as many spheres as possible of the hitherto existing social order, to disturb its regular course and to compromise themselves as well as to concentrate the utmost possible productive forces, means of transport, factories, railways, etc., in the hands of the state;

2. They must drive the proposals of the democrats, who in any case will not act in a revolutionary but in a merely reformist manner, to the extreme and transform them into direct attacks upon private property; thus, for example, if the petty bourgeois

---

* It must be recalled today that this passage is based on a misunderstanding. At that time—thanks to the Bonapartist and liberal falsifiers of history—it was considered as established that the French centralised machine of administration had been introduced by the Great Revolution and in particular that it had been operated by the Convention as an indispensable and decisive weapon for defeating the royalist and federalist reaction and the external enemy. It is now, however, a well-known fact that throughout the whole revolution up the eighteenth Brumaire the whole administration of the departments, arrondissements and communes consisted of authorities elected by the respective constituents themselves, and that these authorities acted with complete freedom within the general state laws; that precisely this provincial and local self-government, similar to the American, became the most powerful lever of the revolution and indeed to such an extent that Napoleon, immediately after his *coup d'état* of the eighteenth Brumaire, hastened to replace it by an administration by prefects, which still exists and which, therefore, was a pure instrument of reaction from the beginning. But just as little as local and provincial self-government is in contradiction to political, national centralisation, so is it to an equally small extent necessarily bound up with that narrow-minded, cantonal or communal self-seeking which strikes us as so repulsive in Switzerland, and which all the South German federal republicans wanted to make the rule in Germany in 1849. [*Note by Engels to the 1885 edition.*]

86

propose purchase of the railways and factories, the workers must demand that these railways and factories shall be simply confiscated by the state without compensation as being the property of reactionaries. If the democrats propose proportional taxes, the workers must demand progressive taxes; if the democrats themselves put forward a moderately progressive tax, the workers must insist on a tax with rates that rise so steeply that big capital will be ruined by it; if the democrats demand the regulation of state debts, the workers must demand state bankruptcy. Thus, the demands of the workers must everywhere be governed by the concessions and measures of the democrats.

If the German workers are not able to attain power and achieve their own class interests without completely going through a lengthy revolutionary development, they at least know for a certainty this time that the first act of this approaching revolutionary drama will coincide with the direct victory of their own class in France and will be very much accelerated by it.

But they themselves must do the utmost for their final victory by clarifying their minds as to what their class interests are, by taking up their position as an independent party as soon as possible and by not allowing themselves to be seduced for a single moment by the hypocritical phrases of the democratic petty bourgeois into refraining from the independent organisation of the party of the proletariat. Their battle cry must be: The Revolution in Permanence.

London, March 1850

Marx and Engels,
Selected Works in 3 vols.,
Vol. 1, Moscow, 1976,
pp. 175-85

KARL MARX

[a]TO THE EDITOR
OF THE
"NEUE ,DEUTSCHE ZEITUNG"

In an article which appeared in your newspaper on June 22 of this year you rebuke me for advocating the *domination and dictatorship of the working class,* while you, on the contrary, urge the *general abolition of class differences.* I do not understand this amendment.

You knew very well that the *Manifesto of the Communist Party* (published before the February revolution of 1848), p. 16 reads: "If the proletariat during its contest with the bourgeoisie is compelled, by the force of circumstances, to organise itself as a class, if, by means of a revolution, it makes itself the ruling class and, as such, sweeps away by force the old conditions of production, then it will, along with these conditions, have swept away the conditions for the existence of class antagonisms and of classes generally, and will thereby have abolished its own supremacy as a class".

You know that, in opposing Proudhon, I advocated this very same view in the *Misère de la philosophie* prior to February 1848.

Finally, the article which you criticise (p. 32, No. 3 of the *Neue Rheinische Zeitung*) itself states: "This socialism (i.e. communism) is the declaration of the permanence of the revolution, the class dictatorship of the proletariat as the necessary transit point to the abolition of class distinctions generally, to the abolition of all the relations of production on which they rest, to the abolition of all the social relations that correspond to these relations of production, to the revolutionising of all the ideas that result from these social relations".[15]

K. Marx

Written in June 1850

Marx/Engels, *Werke,* Bd. 7, S. 323

FREDERICK ENGELS

From
REVOLUTION
AND
COUNTER-REVOLUTION
IN GERMANY

In revolution, as in war, it is always necessary to show a strong front, and he who attacks is in the advantage; ... in revolution, as in war, it is of the highest necessity to stake everything on the decisive moment, whatever the odds may be. There is not a single successful revolution in history that does not prove the truth of these axioms.

Insurrection is an art quite as much as war or any other, and subject to certain rules of proceeding, which, when neglected, will produce the ruin of the party neglecting them. Those rules, logical deductions from the nature of the parties and the circumstances one has to deal with in such a case, are so plain and simple that the short experience of 1848 had made the Germans pretty well acquainted with them. Firstly, never play with insurrection unless you are fully prepared to face the consequences of your play. Insurrection is a calculus with very indefinite magnitudes, the value of which may change every day; the forces opposed to you have all the advantage of organisation, discipline and habitual authority; unless you bring strong odds against them, you are defeated and ruined. Secondly, the insurrectionary career once entered upon, act with the greatest determination, and on the offensive. The defensive is the death of every armed rising; it is lost before it measures itself with its enemies. Surprise your antagonists while their forces are scattering, prepare new successes, however small but daily; keep up the moral ascendant which the first successful rising has given to you; rally thus those vacillating elements to your side which always follow the strongest impulse, and which always look out for the safer side; force your enemies to a retreat before they can collect their strength against you; in the words of Danton, the greatest master of revolutionary policy yet known: *de l'audace, de l'audace, encore de l'audace*!

Written in August 1851-
September 1852

Marx and Engels,
Selected Works in 3 vols.,
Vol. 1, Moscow, 1976,
pp. 361, 377

KARL MARX

From
THE EIGHTEENTH
BRUMAIRE
OF LOUIS BONAPARTE

Hegel remarks somewhere that all facts and personages of great importance in world history occur, as it were, twice. He forgot to add: the first time as tragedy, the second as farce. Caussidière for Danton, Louis Blanc for Robespierre, the *Montagne* of 1848 to 1851 for the *Montagne* of 1793 to 1795, the Nephew for the Uncle. And the same caricature occurs in the circumstances attending the second edition of the eighteenth Brumaire![16]

Men make their own history, but they do not make it just as they please; they do not make it under circumstances chosen by themselves, but under circumstances directly encountered, given and transmitted from the past. The tradition of all the dead generations weighs like a nightmare on the brain of the living. And just when they seem engaged in revolutionising themselves and things, in creating something that has never yet existed, precisely in such periods of revolutionary crisis they anxiously conjure up the spirits of the past to their service and borrow from them names, battle cries and costumes in order to present the new scene of world history in this time-honoured disguise and this borrowed language. Thus Luther donned the mask of the Apostle Paul, the Revolution of 1789 to 1814 draped itself alternately as the Roman republic and the Roman empire, and the Revolution of 1848 knew nothing better to do than to parody, now 1789, now the revolutionary tradition of 1793 to 1795. In like manner a beginner who has learnt a new language always translates it back into his mother tongue, but he has assimilated the spirit of the new language and can freely express himself in it only when he finds his way in it without recalling the old and forgets his native tongue in the use of the new.

Consideration of this conjuring up of the dead of world history reveals at once a salient difference. Camille Desmoulins, Danton, Robespierre, Saint-Just, Napoleon, the heroes as well as the parties and the masses of the old French Revolution, performed the task of their time in Roman costume and with Roman phrases, the task of unchaining and setting up modern *bourgeois* society. The first ones knocked the feudal basis to pieces and mowed off the feudal heads which had grown on it. The other created inside France the conditions under which alone free competition could be developed, parcelled landed property exploited and the unchained industrial productive power of the nation employed; and beyond the French borders he everywhere swept the feudal institutions away, so far as was necessary to furnish bourgeois society in France with a suitable up-to-date environment on the European Continent. The new social formation once established, the antediluvian Colossi disappeared and with them resurrected Romanity—the Brutuses, Gracchi, Publicolas, the tribunes, the senators, and Caesar himself. Bourgeois society in its sober reality had begotten its true interpreters and mouthpieces in the Says, Cousins, Royer-Collards, Benjamin Constants and Guizots; its real military leaders sat behind the office desks, and the hogheaded Louis XVIII was its political chief. Wholly absorbed in the production of wealth and in peaceful competitive struggle, it no longer comprehended that ghosts from the days of Rome had watched over its cradle. But unheroic as bourgeois society is, it nevertheless took heroism, sacrifice, terror, civil war and battles of peoples to bring it into being. And in the classically austere traditions of the Roman republic its gladiators found the ideals and the art forms, the self-deceptions that they needed in order to conceal from themselves the bourgeois limitations of the content of their struggles and to keep their enthusiasm on the high plane of the great historical tragedy. Similarly, at another stage of development, a century earlier, Cromwell and the English people had borrowed speech, passions and illusions from the Old Testament for their bourgeois revolution. When the real aim had been achieved, when the bourgeois transformation of English society had been accomplished, Locke supplanted Habakkuk.

Thus the awakening of the dead in those revolutions served the purpose of glorifying the new struggles, not of parodying the old; of magnifying the given task in imagination, not of fleeing from its solution in reality; of finding once more the spirit of revolution, not of making its ghost walk about again.

From 1848 to 1851 only the ghost of the old revolution walked about, from Marrast, the *républicain en gants jaunes*,[a] who disguised himself as the old Bailly, down to the adventurer, who hides his commonplace repulsive features under the iron death mask of Napoleon. An entire people, which had imagined that by means of a revolution it had imparted to itself an accelerated power of motion, suddenly finds itself set back into a defunct epoch and, in order that no doubt as to the relapse may be possible, the old dates arise again, the old chronology, the old names, the old edicts, which had long become a subject of antiquarian erudition, and the old minions of the law, who had seemed long decayed. The nation feels like that mad Englishman in Bedlam who fancies that he lives in the times of the ancient Pharaohs and daily bemoans the hard labour that he must perform in the Ethiopian mines as a gold digger, immured in this subterranean prison, a dimly burning lamp fastened to his head, the overseer of the slaves behind him with a long whip, and at the exits a confused welter of barbarian mercenaries, who understand neither the forced labourers in the mines nor one another, since they speak no common language. "And all this is expected of me," sighs the mad Englishman, "of me, a freeborn Briton, in order to make gold for the old Pharaohs." "In order to pay the debts of the Bonaparte family," sighs the French nation. The Englishman, so long as he was in his right mind could not get rid of the fixed idea of making gold. The French, so long as they were engaged in revolution, could not get rid of the memory of Napoleon, as the election of December 10[17] proved. They hankered to return from the perils of revolution to the flesh-pots of Egypt, and December 2, 1851 was the answer. They have not only a caricature of the old Napoleon, they have the old Napoleon himself, caricatured as he must appear in the middle of the nineteenth century.

The social revolution of the nineteenth century cannot draw its poetry from the past, but only from the future. It cannot begin with itself before it has stripped off all superstition in regard to the past. Earlier revolutions required recollections of past world history in order to drug themselves concerning their own content. In order to arrive at its own content, the revolution of the nineteenth century must let the dead bury their dead. There the phrase went beyond the content; here the content goes beyond the phrase.

The February Revolution was a surprise attack, a *taking* of the old society *unawares*, and the people proclaimed this unexpected

[a] Republican in yellow gloves.—*Ed.*

stroke as a deed of world importance, ushering in a new epoch. On December 2 the February Revolution is conjured away by a card-sharper's trick, and what seems overthrown is no longer the monarchy but the liberal concessions that were wrung from it by centuries of struggle. Instead of *society* having conquered a new content for itself, it seems that the *state* only returned to its oldest form, to the shamelessly simple domination of the sabre and the cowl. This is the answer to the *coup de main* of February 1848, given by the *coup de tête* of December 1851. Easy come, easy go. Meanwhile the interval of time has not passed by unused. During the years 1848 to 1851 French society has made up, and that by an abbreviated because revolutionary method, for the studies and experiences which, in a regular, so to speak, textbook course of development, would have had to precede the February Revolution, if it was to be more than a ruffling of the surface. Society now seems to have fallen back behind its point of departure; it has in truth first to create for itself the revolutionary point of departure, the situation, the relations, the conditions under which alone modern revolution becomes serious.

Bourgeois revolutions, like those of the eighteenth century, storm swiftly from success to success; their dramatic effects outdo each other; men and things seem set in sparkling brilliants; ecstasy is the everyday spirit; but they are short-lived; soon they have attained their zenith, and a long crapulent depression lays hold of society before it learns soberly to assimilate the results of its storm-and-stress period. On the other hand, proletarian revolutions, like those of the nineteenth century, criticise themselves constantly, interrupt themselves continually in their own course, come back to the apparently accomplished in order to begin it afresh, deride with unmerciful thoroughness the inadequacies, weaknesses and paltrinesses of their first attempts, seem to throw down their adversary only in order that he may draw new strength from the earth and rise again, more gigantic, before them, recoil ever and anon from the indefinite prodigiousness of their own aims, until a situation has been created which makes all turning back impossible, and the conditions themselves cry out:

> Hic Rhodus, hic salta!
> Here is the rose, here dance! [18]

For the rest, every fairly competent observer, even if he had not followed the course of French development step by step, must have had a presentiment that an unheard-of fiasco was in store for the revolution. It was enough to hear the self-complacent howl of victory with which Messieurs the Democrats congratulated each other on the expected gracious consequences of the second Sunday in May 1852.[19] In their minds the second Sunday in May 1852 had become a fixed idea, a dogma, like the day on which Christ should reappear and the millennium begin, in the minds of the Chiliasts. As ever, weakness had taken refuge in a belief in miracles, fancied the enemy overcome when he was only conjured away in imagination, and it lost all understanding of the present in a passive glorification of the future that was in store for it and of the deeds it had *in petto* but which it merely did not want to carry out as yet. Those heroes who seek to disprove their demonstrated incapacity by mutually offering each other their sympathy and getting together in a crowd had tied up their bundles, collected their laurel wreaths in advance and were just then engaged in discounting on the exchange market the republics *in partibus*[a] for which they had already providently organised the government personnel with all the calm of their unassuming disposition. December 2 struck them like a thunderbolt from a clear sky, and the peoples that in periods of pusillanimous depression gladly let their inward apprehension be drowned out by the loudest bawlers will perchance have convinced themselves that the times are past when the cackle of geese could save the Capitol.

The Constitution, the National Assembly, the dynastic parties, the blue and the red republicans, the heroes of Africa, the thunder from the platform, the sheet lightning of the daily press, the entire literature, the political names and the intellectual reputations, the civil law and the penal code, the *liberté, égalité, fraternité* and the second Sunday in May 1852—all has vanished like a phantasmagoria before the spell of a man whom even his enemies do not make out to be a magician. Universal suffrage seems to have survived only for a moment, in order that with its own hand it may make its last will and testament before the eyes of all the world and declare in the name of the people itself: All that exists deserves to perish.[20]

It is not enough to say, as the French do, that their nation was taken unawares. A nation and a woman are not forgiven the unguarded hour in which the first adventurer that came along

---

[a] *In partibus infidelium* (literally, in the country of the infidels)—an addition to the title of Catholic bishops appointed to a purely nominal dioceses in non-Christian countries. This expression is frequently used in Marx's and Engels' writings to describe émigré governments formed abroad ignoring the real situation in a country.—*Ed.*

could violate them. The riddle is not solved by such turns of speech, but merely formulated differently. It remains to be explained how a nation of thirty-six millions can be surprised and delivered unresisting into captivity by three swindlers.

Let us recapitulate in general outline the phases that the French Revolution went through from February 24, 1848, to December 1851.

Three main periods are unmistakable: *the February period*; May 4, 1848, to May 28, 1849: *the period of the constitution of the republic*, or *of the Constituent National Assembly*; May 28, 1849, to December 2, 1851: *the period of the constitutional republic* or *of the Legislative National Assembly*.

The *first period*, from February 24, or the overthrow of Louis Philippe, to May 4, 1848, the meeting of the Constituent Assembly, the *February period* proper, may be described as the *prologue* to the revolution. Its character was officially expressed in the fact that the government improvised by it itself declared that it was *provisional* and, like the government, everything that was mooted, attempted or enunciated during this period proclaimed itself to be only *provisional*. Nothing and nobody ventured to lay claim to the right of existence and of real action. All the elements that had prepared or determined the revolution, the dynastic opposition, the republican bourgeoisie, the democratic-republican petty bourgeoisie and the social-democratic workers, provisionally found their place in the February *government*.

It could not be otherwise. The February days originally intended an electoral reform, by which the circle of the politically privileged among the possessing class itself was to be widened and the exclusive domination of the aristocracy of finance overthrown. When it came to the actual conflict, however, when the people mounted the barricades, the National Guard maintained a passive attitude, the army offered no serious resistance and the monarchy ran away, the republic appeared to be a matter of course. Every party construed it in its own way. Having secured it arms in hand, the proletariat impressed its stamp upon it and proclaimed it to be a *social republic*. There was thus indicated the general content of the modern revolution, a content which was in most singular contradiction to everything that, with the material available, with the degree of education attained by the masses, under the given circumstances and relations, could be immediately realised in practice. On the other hand, the claims of all the remaining elements that had collaborated in the February Revolution were recognised by the lion's share that they obtained in the government. In no period do we, therefore, find a more confused mixture of high-flown phrases and actual uncertainty and clumsiness, of more enthusiastic striving for innovation and more deeply-rooted domination of the old routine, of more apparent harmony of the whole of society and more profound estrangement of its elements. While the Paris proletariat still revelled in the vision of the wide prospects that had opened before it and indulged in seriously-meant discussions on social problems, the old powers of society had grouped themselves, assembled, reflected and found unexpected support in the mass of the nation, the peasants and petty-bourgeois, who all at once stormed on to the political stage, after the barriers of the July monarchy had fallen.

The *second period*, from May 4, 1848, to the end of May 1849, is the period of the *constitution*, the *foundation, of the bourgeois republic*. Directly after the February days not only had the dynastic opposition been surprised by the republicans and the republicans by the Socialists, but all France by Paris. The National Assembly, which met on May 4, 1848, had emerged from the national elections and represented the nation. It was a living protest against the pretensions of the February days and was to reduce the results of the revolution to the bourgeois scale. In vain the Paris proletariat, which immediately grasped the character of this National Assembly, attempted on May 15, a few days after it met, forcibly to negate its existence, to dissolve it, to disintegrate again into its constituent parts the organic form in which the proletariat was threatened by the reacting spirit of the nation. As is known, May 15 had no other result save that of removing Blanqui and his comrades, that is, the real leaders of the proletarian party, from the public stage for the entire duration of the cycle we are considering.[21]

The *bourgeois monarchy* of Louis Philippe can be followed only by a *bourgeois republic*, that is to say, whereas a limited section of the bourgeoisie ruled in the name of the king, the whole of the bourgeoisie will now rule on behalf of the people. The demands of the Paris proletariat are utopian nonsense, to which an end must be put. To this declaration of the Constituent National Assembly the Paris proletariat replied with the *June Insurrection*,[22] the most colossal event in the history of European civil wars. The bourgeois republic triumphed. On its side stood the aristocracy of finance, the industrial bourgeoisie, the middle class, the petty bourgeois, the army, the *lumpenproletariat* organised as the Mobile Guard, the intellectual lights, the clergy and the rural population. On the side of the Paris proletariat stood none but itself. More than three thousand insurgents were butchered after the victory, and fifteen thousand were transported without trial. With this defeat the proletariat passes into the *background* of the revolutionary stage. It attempts to press forward again on every occasion, as soon as the movement appears to make a fresh start, but with ever decreased expenditure of strength and always slighter results. As soon as one of the social strata situated above it gets into revolutionary ferment, the proletariat enters into an alliance with it and so shares all the defeats that the different parties suffer, one after another. But these subsequent blows become the weaker, the greater the surface of society over which they are distributed. The more important leaders of the proletariat in the Assembly and in the press successively fall victims to the courts, and ever more equivocal figures come to head it. In part it throws itself into *doctrinaire experiments, exchange banks and workers' associations, hence into a movement in which it renounces the revolutionising of the old world by means of the latter's own great, combined resources, and seeks, rather, to achieve its salvation behind society's back, in private fashion, within its limited conditions of existence, and hence necessarily suffers shipwreck*. It seems to be unable either to rediscover revolutionary greatness in itself or to win new energy from the connections newly entered into, until *all classes* with which it contended in June themselves lie prostrate beside it. But at least it succumbs with the honours of the great, world-historic struggle; not only France, but all Europe trembles at the June earthquake, while the ensuing defeats of the upper classes are so cheaply bought that they require barefaced exaggeration by the victorious party to be able to pass for events at all, and become the more ignominious the further the defeated party is removed from the proletarian party.

The defeat of the June insurgents, to be sure, had now prepared, had levelled the ground on which the bourgeois republic could be founded and built up, but it had shown at the same time that in Europe the questions at issue are other than that of "republic or monarchy". It had revealed that here *bourgeois republic* signifies the unlimited despotism of one class over other classes. It had proved that in countries with an old civilisation, with a developed formation of classes, with modern conditions of production and with an intellectual consciousness in which all traditional ideas have been dissolved by the work of centuries, *the republic* signifies

in general only the political form of revolution of bourgeois society
and not its *conservative form of life*, as, for example, in the United
States of North America, where, though classes already exist, they
have not yet become fixed, but continually change and interchange
their elements in constant flux, where the modern means of
production, instead of coinciding with a stagnant surplus
population, rather compensate for the relative deficiency of heads
and hands, and where, finally, the feverish, youthful movement
of material production, which has to make a new world its own,
has left neither time nor opportunity for abolishing the old spirit
world.

During the June days all classes and parties had united in the
Party of Order against the proletarian class as the *party of
Anarchy*, of socialism, of communism. They had "saved" society
from *"the enemies of society"*. They had given out the watchwords
of the old society, *"property, family, religion, order"*, to their army
as passwords and had proclaimed to the counter-revolutionary
crusaders: "By this sign thou shalt conquer!" From that
moment, as soon as one of the numerous parties which had
gathered under this sign against the June insurgents seeks to hold
the revolutionary battlefield in its own class interest, it goes down
before the cry: "Property, family, religion, order". Society is saved
just as often as the circle of its rulers contracts, as a more exclusive
interest is maintained against a wider one. Every demand of the
simplest bourgeois financial reform, of the most ordinary
liberalism, of the most formal republicanism, of the most shallow
democracy, is simultaneously castigated as an "attempt on society"
and stigmatised as "socialism". And, finally, the high priests of
"the religion of order" themselves are driven with kicks from their
Pythian tripods, hauled out of their beds in the darkness of night,
put in prison-vans, thrown into dungeons or sent into exile; their
temple is razed to the ground, their mouths are sealed, their pens
broken, their law torn to pieces in the name of religion, of property,
of the family, of order. Bourgeois fanatics for order are shot down
on their balconies by mobs of drunken soldiers, their domestic
sanctuaries profaned, their houses bombarded for amusement—
in the name of property, of the family, of religion and of order.
Finally, the scum of bourgeois society forms the *holy phalanx of
order* and the hero Crapulinski[23] installs himself in the Tuileries
as the *"saviour of society"*....

On the threshold of the February Revolution, the *social republic*
appeared as a phrase, as a prophecy. In the June days of 1848, it

was drowned in the blood of the *Paris proletariat*, but it haunts the subsequent acts of the drama like a ghost. The *democratic republic* announces its arrival. On June 13, 1849, it is dissipated together with its *petty bourgeois*,[24] who have taken to their heels, but in its flight it blows its own trumpet with redoubled boastfulness. The *parliamentary republic*, together with the bourgeoisie, takes possession of the entire stage; it enjoys its existence to the full, but December 2, 1851 buries it to the accompaniment of the anguished cry of the royalists in coalition: "Long live the Republic!"

The French bourgeoisie balked at the domination of the working proletariat; it has brought the *lumpenproletariat* to domination, with the chief of the Society of December 10[25] at the head. The bourgeoisie kept France in breathless fear of the future terrors of red anarchy; Bonaparte discounted this future for it when, on December 4, he had the eminent bourgeois of the Boulevard Montmartre and the Boulevard des Italiens shot down at their windows by the liquor-inspired army of order. It apotheosised the sword; the sword rules it. It destroyed the revolutionary press; its own press has been destroyed. It placed popular meetings under police supervision; its salons are under the supervision of the police. It disbanded the democratic National Guards; its own National Guard is disbanded. It imposed a state of siege; a state of siege is imposed upon it. It supplanted the juries by military commissions; its juries are supplanted by military commissions. It subjected public education to the sway of the priests; the priests subject it to their own education. It transported people without trial; it is being transported without trial. It repressed every stirring in society by means of the state power; every stirring in its society is suppressed by means of the state power. Out of enthusiasm for its purse, it rebelled against its own politicians and men of letters; its politicians and men of letters are swept aside, but its purse is being plundered now that its mouth has been gagged and its pen broken. The bourgeoisie never wearied of crying out to the revolution what Saint Arsenius cried out to the Christians: *"Fuge, tace, quiesce!* Flee, be silent, keep still!"* Bonaparte cries to the bourgeoisie: *"Fuge, tace, quiesce!* Flee, be silent, keep still!"

The French bourgeoisie had long ago found the solution to Napoleon's dilemma: *"Dans cinquante ans l'Europe sera républicaine ou cosaque."*[a] It had found the solution to it in the *"république cosaque"*. No Circe, by means of black magic, has

---

[a] "In fifty years Europe will be republican or Cossack."—*Ed.*

distorted that work of art, the bourgeois republic, into a monstrous shape. That republic has lost nothing but the semblance of respectability. Present-day[a] France was contained in a finished state within the parliamentary republic. It only required a bayonet thrust for the bubble to burst and the monster to spring forth before our eyes.

Why did the Paris proletariat not rise in revolt after December 2?

The overthrow of the bourgeoisie had as yet been only decreed: the decree had not been carried out. Any serious insurrection of the proletariat would at once have put fresh life into the bourgeoisie, would have reconciled it with the army and ensured a second June defeat for the workers.

On December 4 the proletariat was incited by bourgeois and *épicier* to fight. On the evening of that day several legions of the National Guard promised to appear, armed and uniformed, on the scene of battle. For the bourgeois and the *épicier* had got wind of the fact that in one of his decrees of December 2 Bonaparte abolished the secret ballot and enjoined them to record their "yes" or "no" in the official registers after their names. The resistance of December 4 intimidated Bonaparte. During the night he caused placards to be posted on all the street corners of Paris, announcing the restoration of the secret ballot. The bourgeois and the *épicier* believed that they had gained their end. Those who failed to appear next morning were the bourgeois and the *épicier*.

By a *coup de main* during the night of December 1 to 2, Bonaparte had robbed the Paris proletariat of its leaders, the barricade commanders. An army without officers, averse to fighting under the banner of the *Montagnards* because of the memories of June 1848 and 1849 and May 1850, it left to its vanguard, the secret societies, the task of saving the insurrectionary honour of Paris, which the bourgeoisie had so unresistingly surrendered to the soldiery that, later on, Bonaparte could sneeringly give as his motive for disarming the National Guard—his fear that its arms would be turned against it itself by the anarchists!

"*C'est le triomphe complet et définitif du Socialisme!*"[b] Thus Guizot characterised December 2. But if the overthrow of the parliamentary republic contains within itself the germ of the

---

[a] I.e., after the *coup d'état* of 1851.—*Ed.*
[b] "This is the complete and final triumph of socialism!"—*Ed.*

triumph of the proletarian revolution, its immediate and palpable result was *the victory of Bonaparte over parliament, of the executive power over the legislative power, of force without phrases over the force of phrases.* In parliament the nation made its general will the law, that is, it made the law of the ruling class its general will. Before the executive power it renounces all will of its own and submits to the superior command of an alien will, to authority. The executive power, in contrast to the legislative power, expresses the heteronomy of a nation, in contrast to its autonomy. France, therefore, seems to have escaped the despotism of a class only to fall back beneath the despotism of an individual, and, what is more, beneath the authority of an individual without authority. The struggle seems to be settled in such a way that all classes, equally impotent and equally mute, fall on their knees before the rifle butt.

But the revolution is thoroughgoing. It is still journeying through purgatory. It does its work methodically. By December 2, 1851, it had completed one half of its preparatory work; it is now completing the other half. First it perfected the parliamentary power, in order to be able to overthrow it. Now that it has attained this, it perfects the *executive power*, reduces it to its purest expression, isolates it, sets it up against itself as the sole target, in order to concentrate all its forces of destruction against it. And when it has done this second half of its preliminary work, Europe will leap from its seat and exultantly exclaim: Well grubbed, old mole!

This executive power with its enormous bureaucratic and military organisation, with its ingenious state machinery, embracing wide strata, with a host of officials numbering half a million, besides an army of another half million, this appalling parasitic body, which enmeshes the body of French society like a net and chokes all its pores, sprang up in the days of the absolute monarchy, with the decay of the feudal system, which it helped to hasten. The seignorial privileges of the landowners and towns became transformed into so many attributes of the state power, the feudal dignitaries into paid officials and the motley pattern of conflicting mediaeval plenary powers into the regulated plan of a state authority whose work is divided and centralised as in a factory. The first French Revolution, with its task of breaking all separate local, territorial, urban and provincial powers in order to create the civil unity of the nation, was bound to develop what the absolute monarchy had begun: centralisation, but at the same time the extent, the attributes and the agents of governmental power. Napoleon perfected this state machinery. The Legitimist monarchy and the July monarchy added nothing but a greater division of labour, growing in the same measure as the division of labour within bourgeois society created new groups of interests, and, therefore, new material for state administration. Every *common* interest was straightway severed from society, counterposed to it as a higher, *general* interest, snatched from the activity of society's members themselves and made an object of government activity, from a bridge, a schoolhouse and the communal property of a village community to the railways, the national wealth and the national university of France. Finally, in its struggle against the revolution, the parliamentary republic found itself compelled to strengthen, along with the repressive measures, the resources and centralisation of governmental power. All revolutions perfected this machine instead of smashing it. The parties that contended in turn for domination regarded the possession of this huge state edifice as the principal spoils of the victor.

Written in December 1851-
March 1852

Marx and Engels
Selected Works in 3 vols.,
Vol. 1, Moscow, 1976,
pp. 398-406, 474-77

KARL MARX

From
LETTER
TO JOSEPH WEYDEMEYER
IN NEW YORK

London, March 5, 1852

As to myself, no credit is due to me for discovering either the existence of classes in modern society or the struggle between them. Long before me bourgeois historians had described the historical development of this class struggle and bourgeois economists the economic anatomy of the classes. What I did that was new was to demonstrate: 1) that the *existence of classes* is merely linked to *particular historical phases in the development of production*, 2) that class struggle necessarily leads to the *dictatorship of the proletariat*, 3) that this dictatorship itself only constitutes the transition to the *abolition of all classes* and to a *classless society*. Ignorant louts like Heinzen, who deny not merely the class struggle but even the existence of classes, only prove that, despite all their blood-curdling yelps and the humanitarian airs they give themselves, they regard the social conditions under which the bourgeoisie rules as the final product, the *non plus ultra*[a] of history, and that they are only the servants of the bourgeoisie. And the less these louts realise the magnitude and the transitory necessity of the bourgeois regime the more disgusting is their servitude.

Marx and Engels,
Selected Correspondence,
Moscow, 1975, p. 64

---

[a] Highest point attainable.—*Ed.*

KARL MARX

From the pamphlet
[a]REVELATIONS CONCERNING THE COMMUNIST TRIAL IN COLOGNE

We accordingly quote a few short passages from the latest minutes of the London Central authority for September 15, 1850.

In justifying his proposal for a separation Marx said inter alia: "The minority replaces the critical view with a dogmatic one and the materialist view with an idealistic one. Instead of the real conditions *naked will* is made the motive force of the revolution. While we say to the workers: You have 15, 20 or 50 years of civil wars and international conflicts to go through, not just in order to change prevailing conditions but also to change yourselves and to qualify for political control, you say, on the contrary: 'We must immediately come to power, or we can go to sleep.' While we specifically point out to the German workers the undeveloped form of the German proletariat, you lavish compliments in the grossest fashion on national feeling and the class prejudices of the German artisans, which is certainly a more popular approach. Like the democrats make a sacred thing of the word *people*, so do you of the word *proletariat*. In the same way as the democrats you substitute the catchword of revolution for revolutionary development" etc.

Written at the end
of October-beginning
of December 1852

Marx/Engels, *Werke*,
Bd. 8, S. 412-13

KARL MARX

From

THE FUTURE RESULTS OF THE BRITISH RULE IN INDIA

All the English bourgeoisie may be forced to do will neither emancipate nor materially mend the social condition of the mass of the people, depending not only on the development of the productive powers, but on their appropriation by the people. But what they will not fail to do is to lay down the material premises for both. Has the bourgeoisie ever done more? Has it ever effected a progress without dragging individuals and peoples through blood and dirt, through misery and degradation?

The Indians will not reap the fruits of the new elements of society scattered among them by the British bourgeoisie, till in Great Britain itself the now ruling classes shall have been supplanted by the industrial proletariat, or till the Hindoos themselves shall have grown strong enough to throw off the English yoke altogether. At all events, we may safely expect to see, at a more or less remote period, the regeneration of that great and interesting country, whose gentle natives are, to use the expression of Prince Saltykov, even in the most inferior classes, *"sont plus fins et plus adroits que les Italiens"*,[a] whose submission even is counterbalanced by a certain calm nobility, who, notwithstanding their natural languor, have astonished the British officers by their bravery, whose country has been the source of our languages, our religions, and who

---

[a] are more refined and more skilful than the Italians.—*Ed.*

represent the type of the ancient German in the *Jat* and the type of the ancient Greek in the Brahmin.

I cannot part with the subject of India without some concluding remarks.

The profound hypocrisy and inherent barbarism of bourgeois civilisation lies unveiled before our eyes, turning from its home, where it assumes respectable forms, to the colonies, where it goes naked. They are the defenders of property, but did any revolutionary party ever originate agrarian revolutions like those in Bengal, in Madras, and in Bombay? Did they not, in India, to borrow an expression of that great robber, Lord Clive himself, resort to atrocious extortion, when simple corruption could not keep pace with their rapacity? While they prated in Europe about the inviolable sanctity of the national debt, did they not confiscate in India the dividends of the *rayahs*, who had invested their private savings in the Company's own funds? While they combated the French Revolution under the pretext of defending "our holy religion", did they not forbid, at the same time, Christianity to be propagated in India, and did they not, in order to make money out of the pilgrims streaming to the temples of Orissa and Bengal, take up the trade in the murder and prostitution perpetrated in the temple of Juggernaut? These are the men of "Property, Order, Family, and Religion".

The devastating effects of English industry, when contemplated with regard to India, a country as vast as Europe, and containing 150 millions of acres, are palpable and confounding. But we must not forget that they are only the organic results of the whole system of production as it is now constituted. That production rests on the supreme rule of capital. The centralisation of capital is essential to the existence of capital as an independent power. The destructive influence of that centralisation upon the markets of the world does but reveal, in the most gigantic dimensions, the inherent organic laws of political economy now at work in every civilised town. The bourgeois period of history has to create the material basis of the new world — on the one hand the universal intercourse founded upon the mutual dependency of mankind, and the means of that intercourse; on the other hand the development of the productive powers of man and the transformation of material production into a scientific domination of natural agencies. Bourgeois industry and commerce create these material conditions of a new world in the same way as geological revolutions have created the surface of the earth. When a great social revolution shall have mastered the results of the bourgeois epoch, the market of the world and the modern powers of production, and subjected them to the common control of the most advanced peoples, then only will human progress cease to resemble that hideous pagan idol, who would not drink the nectar but from the skulls of the slain.

Written on
July 22, 1853

Marx and Engels,
Articles on Britain,
Moscow, 1975,
pp. 201-03

KARL MARX

From
LETTER
TO THE
LABOUR PARLIAMENT[26]

London, 9 March, 1854
28, Dean Street, Soho

I regret deeply to be unable, for the moment at least, to leave London, and thus to be prevented from expressing verbally my feelings of pride and gratitude on receiving the invitation to sit as Honorary Delegate at the Labour Parliament. The mere assembling of such a Parliament marks a new epoch in the history of the world. The news of this great fact will arouse the hopes of the working classes throughout Europe and America.

Great Britain, of all other countries, has seen developed on the greatest scale, the despotism of Capital and the slavery of Labour. In no other country have the intermediate stations between the millionaire commanding whole industrial armies and the wages-slave living only from hand to mouth so gradually been swept away from the soil. There exist here no longer, as in continental countries, large classes of peasants and artisans almost equally dependent on their own property and their own labour. A complete divorce of property from labour has been effected in Great Britain. In no other country, therefore, the war between the two classes that constitute modern society has assumed so colossal dimensions and features so distinct and palpable.

But it is precisely from these facts that the working classes of Great Britain, before all others, are competent and called for to act as leaders in the great movement that must finally result in the absolute emancipation of Labour. Such they are from the conscious clearness of their position, the vast superiority of their numbers, the disastrous struggles of their past, and the moral strength of their present.

It is the working millions of Great Britain who first have laid down the real basis of a new society—modern industry, which transformed the destructive agencies of nature into the productive power of man. The English working classes, with invincible energies, by the sweat of their brows and brains, have called into life the material means of ennobling labour itself, and of multiplying its fruits to such a degree as to make general abundance possible.

By creating the inexhaustible productive powers of modern industry they have fulfilled the first condition of the emancipation of labour. They have now to realise its other condition. They have to free those wealth-producing powers from the infamous shackles of monopoly, and subject them to the joint control of the producers, who, till now, allowed the very products of their hands to turn against them and be transformed into as many instruments of their own subjugation.

The labouring classes have conquered nature: they have now to conquer man. To succeed in this attempt they do not want strength, but the organisation of their common strength, organisation of the labouring classes on a national scale—such, I suppose, is the great and glorious end aimed at by the Labour Parliament.

If the Labour Parliament proves true to the idea that called it to life, some future historian will have to record that there existed in the year 1854 two Parliaments in England, a Parliament at London, and a Parliament at Manchester—a Parliament of the rich, and a Parliament of the poor—but that men sat only in the Parliament of the men and not in the Parliament of the masters.

Yours truly,

Karl Marx

Written on March 9, 1854
Published in
The People's Paper
No. 98, March 18, 1854

Marx and Engels,
Articles on Britain,
Moscow, 1975,
pp. 216-17

KARL MARX

From

SPEECH
AT THE ANNIVERSARY
OF "THE PEOPLE'S PAPER"[27]

DELIVERED IN LONDON,
APRIL 14, 1856

The so-called Revolutions of 1848 were but poor
incidents—small fractures and fissures in the dry crust of
European society. However, they denounced the abyss. Beneath the
apparently solid surface, they betrayed oceans of liquid matter,
only needing expansion to rend into fragments continents of hard
rock. Noisily and confusedly they proclaimed the emancipation of
the Proletarian, i.e., the secret of the nineteenth century, and of the
revolution of that century.

That social revolution, it is true, was no novelty invented in 1848.
Steam, electricity, and the self-acting mule were revolutionists of a
rather more dangerous character than even citizens Barbès,
Raspail and Blanqui. But, although the atmosphere in which we
live, weighs upon everyone with a 20,000 lb. force, do you feel it?
No more than European society before 1848 felt the revolutionary
atmosphere enveloping and pressing it from all sides.

There is one great fact, characteristic of this our nineteenth
century, a fact which no party dares deny. On the one hand, there
have started into life industrial and scientific forces, which no
epoch of the former human history had ever suspected. On the
other hand, there exist symptoms of decay, far surpassing the
horrors recorded of the latter times of the Roman Empire.

In our days everything seems pregnant with its contrary.
Machinery, gifted with the wonderful power of shortening and
fructifying human labour, we behold starving and overworking it.
The new-fangled sources of wealth, by some strange weird spell, are
turned into sources of want. The victories of art seem to be bought
by the loss of character. At the same pace that mankind masters

nature, man seems to become enslaved to other men or to his own infamy. Even the pure light of science seems unable to shine but on the dark background of ignorance. All our invention and progress seem to result in endowing material forces with intellectual life, and in stultifying human life into a material force. This antagonism between modern industry and science on the one hand, modern misery and dissolution on the other hand; this antagonism between the productive powers and the social relations of our epoch is a fact, palpable, overwhelming, and not to be controverted. Some parties may wail over it; others may wish to get rid of modern arts, in order to get rid of modern conflicts. Or they may imagine that so signal a progress in industry wants to be completed by as signal a regress in politics. On our part, we do not mistake the shape of the shrewd spirit that continues to mark all these contradictions. We know that to work well the new-fangled forces of society, they only want to be mastered by new-fangled men—and such are the working men. They are as much the invention of modern time as machinery itself. In the signs that bewilder the middle class, the aristocracy and the poor prophets of regression, we do recognise our brave friend, Robin Goodfellow, the old mole that can work in the earth so fast, that worthy pioneer—the Revolution. The English working men are the first-born sons of modern industry. They will then, certainly, not be the last in aiding the social revolution produced by that industry, a revolution, which means the emancipation of their own class all over the world, which is as universal as capital-rule and wages-slavery. I know the heroic struggles the English working class have gone through since the middle of the last century—struggles less glorious, because they are shrouded in obscurity, and burked by the middle-class historian. To revenge the misdeeds of the ruling class, there existed in the Middle Ages, in Germany, a secret tribunal, called the "*Vehmgericht*". If a red cross was seen marked on a house, people knew that its owner was doomed by the "*Vehm*". All the houses of Europe are now marked with the mysterious red cross. History is the judge—its executioner, the proletarian.

Published in
The People's Paper
No. 207, April 19, 1856

Marx and Engels,
Articles on Britain,
Moscow, 1975,
pp. 262-64

KARL MARX

From
LETTER
TO ENGELS
IN MANCHESTER

London, [April 16,] 1856

The whole thing in Germany will depend on the possibility of backing the proletarian revolution by some second edition of the Peasant War. Then the affair will be splendid.

Marx and Engels,
Selected Correspondence,
Moscow, 1975, p. 86

FREDERICK ENGELS

From
LETTER
TO MARX
IN LONDON

Manchester, October 7, 1858

The business with Jones is very nasty. He has held a meeting here and spoken entirely along the lines of the new alliance.[28] After this affair one is really almost driven to believe that the English proletarian movement in its old traditional Chartist form must perish completely before it can develop in a new, viable form. And yet one cannot foresee what this new form will look like. It seems to me moreover that Jones' new move, together with the former more or less successful attempts at such an alliance, are indeed connected with the fact that the English proletariat is actually becoming more and more bourgeois, so that this most bourgeois of all nations is apparently aiming ultimately at the possession of a bourgeois aristocracy and a bourgeois proletariat *alongside* the bourgeoisie. For nation which exploits the whole world this is of course to a certain extent justifiable. The only thing that would help here would be a few thoroughly bad years, but since the gold discoveries these no longer seem so easy to come by.

Marx and Engels,
Selected Correspondence,
Moscow, 1975, pp. 102-03

KARL MARX

From
LETTER
TO ENGELS
IN MANCHESTER

London, Friday [October 8], 1858

We cannot deny that bourgeois society has experienced its sixteenth century a second time—a sixteenth century which will, I hope, sound the death-knell of bourgeois society just as the first one thrust it into existence. The specific task of bourgeois society is the establishment of a world market, at least in outline, and of production based upon this world market. As the world is round, this seems to have been completed by the colonisation of California and Australia and the opening up of China and Japan. The difficult question for us is this: on the Continent the revolution is imminent and will moreover immediately assume a socialist character. Is it not bound to be crushed in this little corner, considering that in a far greater territory the movement of bourgeois society is still in the ascendant?

Marx and Engels,
Selected Correspondence,
Moscow, 1975, pp. 103-04

From

PREFACE
TO "A CONTRIBUTION
TO THE CRITIQUE
OF POLITICAL ECONOMY"

My investigation led to the result that legal relations as well as forms of state are to be grasped neither from themselves nor from the so-called general development of the human mind, but rather have their roots in the material conditions of life, the sum total of which Hegel, following the example of the Englishmen and Frenchmen of the eighteenth century, combines under the name of "civil society", that, however, the anatomy of civil society is to be sought in political economy. The investigation of the latter, which I began in Paris, I continued in Brussels, whither I had emigrated in consequence of an expulsion order of M. Guizot. The general result at which I arrived and which, once won, served as a guiding thread for my studies, can be briefly formulated as follows: In the social production of their life, men enter into definite relations that are indispensable and independent of their will, relations of production which correspond to a definite stage of development of their material productive forces. The sum total of these relations of production constitutes the economic structure of society, the real foundation, on which rises a legal and political superstructure and to which correspond definite forms of social consciousness. The mode of production of material life conditions the social, political and intellectual life process in general. It is not the consciousness of men that determines their being, but, on the contrary, their social being that determines their consciousness. At a certain stage of their development, the material productive forces of society come in conflict with the existing relations of production, or—what is but a legal expression for the same thing—with the property relations within which they have been at work hitherto. From forms

116

of development of the productive forces these relations turn into their fetters. Then begins an epoch of social revolution. With the change of the economic foundation the entire immense superstructure is more or less rapidly transformed. In considering such transformations a distinction should always be made between the material transformation of the economic conditions of production, which can be determined with the precision of natural science, and the legal, political, religious, aesthetic or philosophic—in short, ideological forms in which men become conscious of this conflict and fight it out. Just as our opinion of an individual is not based on what he thinks of himself, so can we not judge of such a period of transformation by its own consciousness; on the contrary, this consciousness must be explained rather from the contradictions of material life, from the existing conflict between the social productive forces and the relations of production. No social order ever perishes before all the productive forces for which there is room in it have developed; and new, higher relations of production never appear before the material conditions of their existence have matured in the womb of the old society itself. Therefore mankind always sets itself only such tasks as it can solve; since, looking at the matter more closely, it will always be found that the task itself arises only when the material conditions for its solution already exist or are at least in the process of formation. In broad outlines Asiatic, ancient, feudal, and modern bourgeois modes of production can be designated as progressive epochs in the economic formation of society. The bourgeois relations of production are the last antagonistic form of the social process of production—antagonistic not in the sense of individual antagonism, but of one arising from the social conditions of life of the individuals; at the same time the productive forces developing in the womb of bourgeois society create the material conditions for the solution of that antagonism. This social formation brings, therefore, the prehistory of human society to a close.

London, January 1859

Marx and Engels, *Selected Works* in 3 vols., Vol. 1, Moscow, 1976, pp. 503-04

From

INAUGURAL ADDRESS
OF THE WORKING MEN'S
INTERNATIONAL
ASSOCIATION

ESTABLISHED
SEPTEMBER 28, 1864,
AT A PUBLIC MEETING
HELD AT ST. MARTIN'S HALL,
LONG ACRE, LONDON[29]

But there was in store a still greater victory of the political economy of labour over the political economy of property. We speak of the co-operative movement, especially the co-operative factories raised by the unassisted efforts of a few bold "hands". The value of these great social experiments cannot be overrated. By deed, instead of by argument, they have shown that production on a large scale, and in accord with the behests of modern science, may be carried on without the existence of a class of masters employing a class of hands; that to bear fruit, the means of labour need not be monopolised as a means of dominion over, and of extortion against, the labouring man himself; and that, like slave labour, like serf labour, hired labour is but a transitory and inferior form, destined to disappear before associated labour plying its toil with a willing hand, a ready mind, and a joyous heart. In England, the seeds of the co-operative system were sown by Robert Owen; the working men's experiments, tried on the Continent, were, in fact, the practical upshot of the theories, not invented, but loudly proclaimed, in 1848.

At the same time, the experience of the period from 1848 to 1864, has proved beyond doubt that, however excellent in principle, and however useful in practice, co-operative labour, if kept within the narrow circle of the casual efforts of private workmen, will never be able to arrest the growth in geometrical progression of monopoly, to free the masses, nor even to perceptibly lighten the burden of their miseries. It is perhaps for this very reason that plausible noblemen, philanthropic middle-class spouters, and even keen political economists, have all at once turned nauseously complimentary to the very co-operative labour system they had vainly tried to nip in the bud by deriding it as the Utopia of the dreamer, or stigmatising it as the sacrilege of the Socialist. To save the industrious masses, co-operative labour ought to be developed to national dimensions, and consequently, to be fostered by national means. Yet, the lords of land and the lords of capital will always use their political privileges for the defence and perpetuation of their economical monopolies. So far from promoting, they will continue to lay every possible impediment in the way of the emancipation of labour. Remember the sneer with which, last session, Lord Palmerston put down the advocates of the Irish Tenants' Right Bill. The House of Commons, cried he, is a house of landed proprietors.

To conquer political power has therefore become the great duty of the working classes. They seem to have comprehended this, for in England, Germany, Italy, and France there have taken place simultaneous revivals, and simultaneous efforts are being made at the political reorganisation of the working men's party.

One element of success they possess—numbers; but numbers weigh only in the balance, if united by combination and led by knowledge. Past experience has shown how disregard of that bond of brotherhood which ought to exist between the workmen of different countries, and incite them to stand firmly by each other in all their struggles for emancipation, will be chastised by the common discomfiture of their incoherent efforts. This thought prompted the working men of different countries assembled on September 28, 1864, in public meeting at St. Martin's Hall, to found the International Association.

Another conviction swayed that meeting.

If the emancipation of the working classes requires their fraternal concurrence, how are they to fulfil that great mission with a foreign policy in pursuit of criminal designs, playing upon national prejudices and squandering in piratical wars the people's blood and treasure? It was not the wisdom of the ruling classes, but the heroic resistance to their criminal folly by the working classes of England that saved the West of Europe from plunging headlong into an infamous crusade for the perpetuation and propagation of slavery on the other side of the Atlantic. The shameless approval, mock sympathy, or idiotic indifference, with which the upper classes of Europe have witnessed the mountain fortress of the Caucasus falling a prey to, and heroic Poland being assassinated by, Russia; the immense and unresisted encroachments of that barbarous power, whose head is at St. Petersburg, and whose hands are in every cabinet of Europe, have taught the working classes the duty to master themselves the mysteries of international politics; to watch the diplomatic acts of their respective Governments; to counteract them, if necessary, by all means in their power; when unable to prevent, to combine in simultaneous denunciations, and to vindicate the simple laws of morals and justice, which ought to govern the relations of private individuals, as the rules paramount of the intercourse of nations.

The fight for such a foreign policy forms part of the general struggle for the emancipation of the working classes.

Proletarians of all countries, Unite!

Written between
October 21 and 27,
1864

Marx and Engels,
Articles on Britain,
Moscow, 1975,
pp. 346-49

KARL MARX

From
GENERAL RULES OF THE INTERNATIONAL WORKING MEN'S ASSOCIATION

Considering,

That the emancipation of the working classes must be conquered by the working classes themselves; that the struggle for the emancipation of the working classes means not a struggle for class privileges and monopolies, but for equal rights and duties, and the abolition of all class rule;

That the economical subjection of the man of labour to the monopoliser of the means of labour, that is, the sources of life, lies at the bottom of servitude in all its forms, of all social misery, mental degradation, and political dependence;

That the economical emancipation of the working classes is therefore the great end to which every political movement ought to be subordinate as a means;

That all efforts aiming at that great end have hitherto failed from the want of solidarity between the manifold divisions of labour in each country, and from the absence of a fraternal bond of union between the working classes of different countries;

That the emancipation of labour is neither a local nor a national, but a social problem, embracing all countries in which modern society exists, and depending for its solution on the concurrence, practical and theoretical, of the most advanced countries;

That the present revival of the working classes in the most industrious countries of Europe, while it raises a new hope, gives solemn warning against a relapse into the old errors, and calls for the immediate combination of the still disconnected movements;

For These Reasons—

The International Working Men's Association has been founded.

It declares:

That all societies and individuals adhering to it will acknowledge truth, justice, and morality, as the basis of their conduct towards each other and towards all men, without regard to colour, creed, or nationality;

That it acknowledges *no rights without duties, no duties without rights*;

And in this spirit the following Rules have been drawn up.

1. This Association is established to afford a central medium of communication and co-operation between Working Men's Societies existing in different countries and aiming at the same end, *viz.*, the protection, advancement, and complete emancipation of the working classes.

Written between
October 21 and 27,
1864

Marx and Engels,
Selected Works in 3 vols.,
Vol. 2, Moscow, 1973,
pp. 19-20

KARL MARX

From
CONFIDENTIAL
COMMUNICATION[30]

5) *Question of the General Council Resolution on the Irish Amnesty.*[31]

If England is the bulwark of landlordism and European capitalism, the only point where one can hit official England really hard is *Ireland*.

In the first place, Ireland is the *bulwark* of English landlordism. If it fell in Ireland it would fall in England. In Ireland this is a hundred times easier since *the economic struggle there is concentrated exclusively on landed property*, since this struggle is at the same time national, and since the people there are more revolutionary and exasperated than in England. Landlordism in Ireland is maintained solely by the *English army*. The moment the forced union[32] between the two countries ends, a social revolution will immediately break out in Ireland, though in outmoded forms. English landlordism would not only lose a great source of wealth, but also its *greatest moral force*, i.e., that of *representing the domination of England over Ireland*. On the other hand, by maintaining the power of their landlords in Ireland, the English proletariat makes them invulnerable in England itself.

In the second place, the *English bourgeoisie* has not only exploited the Irish poverty to keep down the working class in England by *forced immigration* of poor Irishmen, but it has also divided the proletariat into two hostile camps. The revolutionary fire of the Celtic worker does not go well with the nature of the Anglo-Saxon worker, solid, but slow. On the contrary, in *all the big industrial centres in England* there is profound antagonism between the Irish proletariat and the English proletariat. The average English worker hates the Irish worker as a competitor who lowers wages and the *standard of life*. He feels national and religious antipathies for him. He regards him somewhat like the *poor whites* of the Southern States of North America regard their black slaves. This antagonism among the proletarians of England is artificially nourished and supported by the bourgeoisie. It knows that this scission is the *true secret of maintaining its power*.

This antagonism is reproduced on the other side of the Atlantic. The Irish, chased from their native soil by the bulls and the sheep, reassemble in North America where they constitute a huge, ever growing section of the population. Their only thought, their only passion, is hatred for England. The English and American governments (or the classes they represent) play on these feelings in order to perpetuate the covert *struggle between the United States and England.* They thereby prevent a sincere and lasting alliance between the workers on both sides of the Atlantic, and consequently, their emancipation.

Furthermore, Ireland is the only pretext the English Government has for retaining a *big standing army*, which, if need be, as has happened before, can be used against the English workers after having done its military training in Ireland.

Lastly, England today is seeing a repetition of what happened on a monstrous scale in ancient Rome. Any nation that oppresses another forges its own chains.

Thus, the attitude of the International Association to the Irish question is very clear. Its first need is to encourage the social revolution in England. To this end a great blow must be struck in Ireland.

The General Council's resolution on the Irish amnesty serves only as an introduction to other resolutions which will affirm that, quite apart from international justice, it is a *precondition to the emancipation of the English working class* to transform the present *forced union* (i.e., the enslavement of Ireland) into *equal and free confederation* if possible, into *complete separation* if need be.

Written about
March 28, 1870

Marx and Engels,
Selected Works in 3 vols.,
Vol. 2, Moscow, 1973,
pp. 175-77

KARL MARX

From
CAPITAL
VOLUME I

GENESIS OF THE
INDUSTRIAL CAPITALIST

The genesis of the industrial* capitalist did not proceed in such a
gradual way as that of the farmer. Doubtless many small guild-
masters, and yet more independent small artisans, or even wage-
labourers, transformed themselves into small capitalists, and (by
gradually extending exploitation of wage-labour and corresponding accumulation) into full-blown capitalists. In the infancy of
capitalist production, things often happened as in the infancy of
mediaeval towns, where the question, which of the escaped serfs
should be master and which servant, was in great part decided by
the earlier or later date of their flight. The snail's pace of this
method corresponded in no wise with the commercial requirements
of the new world-market that the great discoveries of the end of the
15th century created. But the middle ages had handed down two
distinct forms of capital, which mature in the most different
economic social formations, and which, before the era of the
capitalist mode of production, are considered as capital quand
même—usurer's capital and merchant's capital.

"At present, all the wealth of society goes first into the possession
of the capitalist ... he pays the landowner his rent, the labourer his

---

* Industrial here in contradistinction to agricultural. In the "categoric" sense
the farmer is an industrial capitalist as much as the manufacturer.

125

wages, the tax and tithe gatherer their claims, and keeps a large, indeed the largest, and a continually augmenting share, of the annual produce of labour for himself. The capitalist may now be said to be the first owner of all the wealth of the community, though no law has conferred on him the right to this property ... this change has been effected by the taking of interest on capital ... and it is not a little curious that all the law-givers of Europe endeavoured to prevent this by statutes, viz., statutes against usury.... The power of the capitalist over all the wealth of the country is a complete change in the right of property, and by what law, or series of laws, was it effected? "* The author should have remembered that revolutions are not made by laws.

The money capital formed by means of usury and commerce was prevented from turning into industrial capital, in the country by the feudal constitution, in the towns by the guild organisation.** These fetters vanished with the dissolution of feudal society, with the expropriation and partial eviction of the country population. The new manufactures were established at sea-ports, or at inland points beyond the control of the old municipalities and their guilds. Hence in England an embittered struggle of the corporate towns against these new industrial nurseries.

The discovery of gold and silver in America, the extirpation, enslavement and entombment in mines of the aboriginal population, the beginning of the conquest and looting of the East Indies, the turning of Africa into a warren for the commercial hunting of black-skins, signalised the rosy dawn of the era of capitalist production. These idyllic proceedings are the chief momenta of primitive accumulation. On their heels treads the commercial war of the European nations, with the globe for a theatre. It begins with the revolt of the Netherlands from Spain, assumes giant dimensions in England's Anti-Jacobin War, and is still going on in the opium wars against China, &c.

The different momenta of primitive accumulation distribute themselves now, more or less in chronological order, particularly

---

*"The Natural and Artificial Rights of Property Contrasted." Lond., 1832, pp. 98-99. Author of the anonymous work: "Th. Hodgskin."

** Even as late as 1794, the small cloth-makers of Leeds sent a deputation to Parliament, with a petition for a law to forbid any merchant from becoming a manufacturer.(Dr. Aikin, "Description of the Country from 30 to 40 miles round Manchester." Lond., 1795.)

over Spain, Portugal, Holland, France, and England. In England at the end of the 17th century, they arrive at a systematical combination, embracing the colonies, the national debt, the modern mode of taxation, and the protectionist system. These methods depend in part on brute force, *e.g.,* the colonial system. But they all employ the power of the State, the concentrated and organised force of society, to hasten, hot-house fashion, the process of transformation of the feudal mode of production into the capitalist mode, and to shorten the transition. Force is the midwife of every old society pregnant with a new one. It is itself an economic power.

Of the Christian colonial system, W. Howitt, a man who makes a speciality of Christianity, says: "The barbarities and desperate outrages of the so-called Christian race, throughout every region of the world, and upon every people they have been able to subdue, are not to be paralleled by those of any other race, however fierce, however untaught, and however reckless of mercy and of shame, in any age of the earth."[*] The history of the colonial administration of Holland—and Holland was the head capitalistic nation of the 17th century—"is one of the most extraordinary relations of treachery, bribery, massacre, and meanness".[**] Nothing is more characteristic than their system of stealing men, to get slaves for Java. The men stealers were trained for this purpose. The thief, the interpreter, and the seller, were the chief agents in this trade, native princes the chief sellers. The young people stolen, were thrown into the secret dungeons of Celebes, until they were ready for sending to the slave-ships. An official report says: "This one town of Macassar, e.g., is full of secret prisons, one more horrible than the other, crammed with unfortunates, victims of greed and tyranny fettered in chains, forcibly torn from their families." To secure Malacca, the Dutch corrupted the Portuguese governor. He let them into the town in 1641. They hurried at once to his house

---

[*] William Howitt: "Colonization and Christianity: A Popular History of the Treatment of the Natives by the Europeans in all their Colonies." London, 1838, p. 9. On the treatment of the slaves there is a good compilation in Charles Comte, "Traité de la Législation." 3me éd. Bruxelles, 1837. This subject one must study in detail, to see what the bourgeoisie makes of itself and of the labourer, wherever it can, without restraint, model the world after its own image.

[**] Thomas Stamford Raffles, late Lieut.-Gov. of that island: "The History of Java," Lond., 1817.

and assassinated him, to "abstain" from the payment of £21,875, the price of his treason. Wherever they set foot, devastation and depopulation followed. Banjuwangi, a province of Java, in 1750 numbered over 80,000 inhabitants, in 1811 only 8,000. Sweet commerce!

The English East India Company, as is well known, obtained, besides the political rule in India, the exclusive monopoly of the tea-trade, as well as of the Chinese trade in general, and of the transport of goods to and from Europe. But the coasting trade of India and between the islands, as well as the internal trade of India, were the monopoly of the higher employés of the company. The monopolies of salt, opium, betel and other commodities, were inexhaustible mines of wealth. The employés themselves fixed the price and plundered at will the unhappy Hindus. The Governor-General took part in this private traffic. His favourites received contracts under conditions whereby they, cleverer than the alchemists, made gold out of nothing. Great fortunes sprang up like mushrooms in a day; primitive accumulation went on without the advance of a shilling. The trial of Warren Hastings swarms with such cases. Here is an instance. A contract for opium was given to a certain Sullivan at the moment of his departure on an offical mission to a part of India far removed from the opium district. Sullivan sold his contract to one Binn for £40,000; Binn sold it the same day for £60,000, and the ultimate purchaser who carried out the contract declared that after all he realised an enormous gain. According to one of the lists laid before Parliament, the Company and its employés from 1757-1766 got £6,000,000 from the Indians as gifts. Between 1769 and 1770, the English manufactured a famine by buying up all the rice and refusing to sell it again, except at fabulous prices.*

The treatment of the aborigines was, naturally, most frightful in plantation-colonies destined for export trade only, such as the West Indies, and in rich and well-populated countries, such as Mexico and India, that were given over to plunder. But even in the colonies properly so called, the Christian character of primitive accumulation did not belie itself. Those sober virtuosi of Protestantism, the Puritans of New England, in 1703, by decrees of their assembly set a premium of £40 on every Indian scalp and

---

* In the year 1866 more than a million Hindus dies of hunger in the province of Orissa alone. Nevertheless, the attempt was made to enrich the Indian treasury by the price at which the necessaries of life were sold to the starving people.

every captured red-skin: in 1720 a premium of £100 on every scalp; in 1744, after Massachusetts-Bay had proclaimed a certain tribe as rebels, the following prices: for a male scalp of 12 years and upwards £100 (new currency), for a male prisoner £105, for women and children prisoners £55, for scalps of women and children £50. Some decades later, the colonial system took its revenge on the descendants of the pious pilgrim fathers, who had grown seditious in the meantime. At English instigation and for English pay they were tomahawked by red-skins. The British Parliament proclaimed blood-hounds and scalping as "means that God and Nature had given into its hand."

The colonial system ripened, like a hot-house, trade and navigation. The "societies Monopolia" of Luther were powerful levers for concentration of capital. The colonies secured a market for the budding manufactures, and, through the monopoly of the market, an increased accumulation. The treasures captured outside Europe by undisguised looting, enslavement, and murder, floated back to the mother-country and were there turned into capital. Holland, which first fully developed the colonial system, in 1648 stood already in the acme of its commercial greatness. It was "in almost exclusive possession of the East Indian trade and the commerce between the south-west and north-east of Europe. Its fisheries, marine, manufactures, surpassed those of any other country. The total capital of the Republic was probably more important than that of all the rest of Europe put together." Gülich forgets to add that by 1648, the people of Holland were more overworked, poorer and more brutally oppressed than those of all the rest of Europe put together.

To-day industrial supremacy implies commercial supremacy. In the period of manufacture properly so called, it is, on the other hand, the commercial supremacy that gives industrial predominance. Hence the preponderant rôle that the colonial system plays at that time. It was "the strange God" who perched himself on the altar cheek by jowl with the old Gods of Europe, and one fine day with a shove and a kick chucked them all of a heap. It proclaimed surplus-value making as the sole end and aim of humanity.

The system of public credit, *i.e.*, of national debts, whose origin we discover in Genoa and Venice as early as the middle ages, took possession of Europe generally during the manufacturing period. The colonial system with its maritime trade and commercial wars served as a forcing-house for it. Thus it first took root in Holland.

129

National debts, *i. e.,* the alienation of the state—whether despotic, constitutional or republican—marked with its stamp the capitalistic era. The only part of the so-called national wealth that actually enters into the collective possessions of modern peoples is—their national debt.* Hence, as a necessary consequence, the modern doctrine that a nation becomes the richer the more deeply it is in debt. Public credit becomes the *credo* of capital. And with the rise of national debt-making, want of faith in the national debt takes the place of the blasphemy against the Holy Ghost, which may not be forgiven.

The public debt becomes one of the most powerful levers of primitive accumulation. As with the stroke of an enchanter's wand, it endows barren money with the power of breeding and thus turns it into capital, without the necessity of its exposing itself to the troubles and risks inseparable from its employment in industry or even in usury. The state creditors actually give nothing away, for the sum lent is transformed into public bonds, easily negotiable, which go on functioning in their hands just as so much hard cash would. But further, apart from the class of lazy annuitants thus created, and from the improvised wealth of the financiers, middlemen between the government and the nation—as also apart from the tax-farmers, merchants, private manufacturers, to whom a good part of every national loan renders the service of a capital fallen from heaven—the national debt has given rise to joint-stock companies, to dealings in negotiable effects of all kinds, and to agiotage, in a word to stock-exchange gambling and the modern bankocracy.

At their birth the great banks, decorated with national titles, were only associations of private speculators, who placed themselves by the side of governments, and, thanks to the privileges they received, were in a position to advance money to the State. Hence the accumulation of the national debt has no more infallible measure than the successive rise in the stock of these banks, whose full development dates from the founding of the Bank of England in 1694. The Bank of England began with lending its money to the Government at 8%; at the same time it was empowered by Parliament to coin money out of the same capital, by lending it again to the public in the form of banknotes. It was allowed to use these notes for discounting bills, making advances on commodities,

---

* William Cobbett remarks that in England all public institutions are designated "royal"; as compensation for this, however, there is the "national" debt.

and for buying the precious metals. It was not long ere this credit-money, made by the bank itself, became the coin in which the Bank of England made its loans to the State, and paid, on account of the State, the interest on the public debt. It was not enough that the bank gave with one hand and took back more with the other; it remained, even whilst receiving, the eternal creditor of the nation down to the last shilling advanced. Gradually it became inevitably the receptacle of the metallic hoard of the country, and the centre of gravity of all commercial credit. What effect was produced on their contemporaries by the sudden uprising of this brood of bankocrats, financiers, rentiers, brokers, stock-jobbers, &c., is proved by the writings of that time, *e.g.*, by Bolingbroke's.[*]

With the national debt arose an international credit system, which often conceals one of the sources of primitive accumulation in this or that people. Thus the villainies of the Venetian thieving system formed one of the secret bases of the capital-wealth of Holland to whom Venice in her decadence lent large sums of money. So also was it with Holland and England. By the beginning of the 18th century the Dutch manufactures were far outstripped. Holland had ceased to be the nation preponderant in commerce and industry. One of its main lines of business, therefore, from 1701-1776, is the lending out of enormous amounts of capital, especially to its great rival England. The same thing is going on today between England and the United States. A great deal of capital, which appears today in the United States without any certificate of birth, was yesterday, in England, the capitalised blood of children.

As the national debt finds its support in the public revenue, which must cover the yearly payments for interest, &c., the modern system of taxation was the necessary complement of the system of national loans. The loans enable the government to meet extraordinary expenses, without the tax-payers feeling it immediately, but they necessitate, as a consequence, increased taxes. On the other hand, the raising of taxation caused by the accumulation of debts contracted one after another, compels the government always to have recourse to new loans for new extraordinary expenses. Modern fiscality, whose pivot is formed by taxes on the most necessary means of subsistence (thereby increasing their price), thus contains within itself the germ of

---

[*] "Si les Tartares inondaient l'Europe aujourd'hui, il faudrait bien des affaires pour leur faire entendre ce que c'est qu'un financier parmi nous." Montesquieu, "Esprit des lois," t. IV., p. 33, éd. Londres, 1769.

automatic progression. Over-taxation is not an incident, but rather a principle. In Holland, therefore, where this system was first inaugurated, the great patriot, De Witt, has in his "Maxims" extolled it as the best system for making the wage-labourer submissive, frugal, industrious, and overburdened with labour. The destructive influence that it exercises on the condition of the wage-labourer concerns us less however, here, than the forcible expropriation, resulting from it, of peasants, artisans, and in a word, all elements of the lower middle-class. On this there are not two opinions, even among the bourgeois economists. Its expropriating efficacy is still further heightened by the system of protection, which forms one of its integral parts.

The great part that the public debt, and the fiscal system corresponding with it, has played in the capitalisation of wealth and the expropriation of the masses, has led many writers, like Cobbett, Doubleday and others, to seek in this, incorrectly, the fundamental cause of the misery of the modern peoples.

The system of protection was an artificial means of manufacturing manufacturers, of expropriating independent labourers, of capitalising the national means of production and subsistence, of forcibly abbreviating the transition from the mediaeval to the modern mode of production. The European states tore one another to pieces about the patent of this invention, and, once entered into the service of the surplus-value makers, did not merely lay under contribution in the pursuit of this purpose their own people, indirectly through protective duties, directly through export premiums. They also forcibly rooted out, in their dependent countries, all industry, as, e.g., England did with the Irish woollen manufacture. On the continent of Europe, after Colbert's example, the process was much simplified. The primitive industrial capital, here, came in part directly out of the state treasury. "Why," cries Mirabeau, "why go so far to seek the cause of the manufacturing glory of Saxony before the war? 180,000,000 of debts contracted by the sovereigns!"*

Colonial system, public debts, heavy taxes, protection, commercial wars, &c., these children of the true manufacturing period, increase gigantically during the infancy of Modern Industry. The birth of the latter is heralded by a great slaughter of the innocents. Like the royal navy, the factories were recruited by means of the

---

*Mirabeau, "De la Monarchie Prussienne sous Frédéric le Grand," t. VI., p. 101.

press-gang. Blasé as Sir F. M. Eden is as to the horrors of the expropriation of the agricultural population from the soil, from the last third of the 15th century to his own time; with all the self-satisfaction with which he rejoices in this process, "essential" for establishing capitalistic agriculture and "the due proportion between arable and pasture land"—he does not show, however, the same economic insight in respect to the necessity of child-stealing and child-slavery for the transformation of manufacturing exploitation into factory exploitation, and the establishment of the "true relation" between capital and labour-power. He says: "It may, perhaps, be worthy the attention of the public to consider, whether any manufacture, which, in order to be carried on successfully requires that cottages and workhouses should be ransacked for poor children; that they should be employed by turns during the greater part of the night and robbed of that rest which, though indispensable to all, is most required by the young; and that numbers of both sexes, of different ages and dispositions, should be collected together in such a manner that the contagion of example cannot but lead to profligacy and debauchery; will add to the sum of individual or national felicity?" *

"In the counties of Derbyshire, Nottinghamshire, and more particularly in Lancashire," says Fielden, "the newly-invented machinery was used in large factories built on the sides of streams capable of turning the water-wheel. Thousands of hands were suddenly required in these places, remote from towns; and Lancashire, in particular, being, till then, comparatively thinly populated and barren, a population was all that she now wanted. The small and nimble fingers of little children being by very far the most in request, the custom instantly sprang up of procuring *apprentices* from the different parish workhouses of London, Birmingham, and elsewhere. Many, many thousands of these little, hapless creatures were sent down into the north, being from the age of 7 to the age of 13 or 14 years old. The custom was for the master to clothe his apprentices and to feed and lodge them in an "apprentice house" near the factory; overseers were appointed to see to the works, whose interest it was to work the children to the utmost, because their pay was in proportion to the quantity of work that they could exact. Cruelty was, of course, the consequence.... In many of the manufacturing districts, but particularly, I am afraid, in the guilty county to which I belong (Lancashire), cruelties

---

* Eden, l.c., Vol. I., Book II., Ch. I., p. 421.

the most heart-rending were practised upon the unoffending and friendless creatures who were thus consigned to the charge of master-manufacturers; they were harassed to the brink of death by excess of labour ... were flogged, fettered and tortured in the most exquisite refinement of cruelty; they were in many cases starved to the bone while flogged to their work and ... even in some instances ... were driven to commit suicide.... The beautiful and romantic valleys of Derbyshire, Nottinghamshire and Lancashire, secluded from the public eye, became the dismal solitudes of torture, and of many a murder. The profits of manufacturers were enormous; but this only whetted the appetite that it should have satisfied, and therefore the manufacturers had recourse to an expedient that seemed to secure to them those profits without any possibility of limit; they began the practice of what is termed "night-working," that is, having tired one set of hands, by working them throughout the day, they had another set ready to go on working throughout the night; the day-set getting into the beds that the night-set had just quitted, and in their turn again, the night-set getting into the beds that the day-set quitted in the morning. It is a common tradition in Lancashire, that the beds *never get cold.*"*

With the development of capitalist production during the manufacturing period, the public opinion of Europe had lost the last remnant of shame and conscience. The nations bragged cynically of every infamy that served them as a means to capitalistic accumulation. Read, *e.g.*, the naïve Annals of Commerce of the

---

*John Fielden, l.c., pp. 5, 6. On the earlier infamies of the factory system, cf. Dr. Aikin (1795), l.c., p. 219, and Gisborne: "Enquiry into the Duties of Men," 1795, Vol. II. When the steam-engine transplanted the factories from the country waterfalls to the middle of towns, the "abstemious" surplus-value maker found the child-material ready to his hand, without being forced to seek slaves from the workhouses. When Sir R. Peel (father of the "minister of plausibility"), brought in his bill for the protection of children, in 1815, Francis Horner, lumen of the Bullion Committee and intimate friend of Ricardo, said in the House of Commons: "It is notorious, that with a bankrupt's effects, a gang, if he might use the word, of these children had been put up to sale, and were advertised publicly as part of the property. A most atrocious instance had been brought before the Court of King's Bench two years before, in which a number of these boys, apprenticed by a parish in London to one manufacturer, had been transferred to another, and had been found by some benevolent persons in a state of absolute famine. Another case more horrible had come to his knowledge while on a [Parliamentary] Committee ... that not many years ago, an agreement had been made between a London parish and a Lancashire manufacturer, by which it was stipulated, that with every 20 sound children one idiot should be taken."

worthy A. Anderson. Here it is trumpeted forth as a triumph of English statecraft that at the Peace of Utrecht, England extorted from the Spaniards by the Asiento Treaty[33] the privilege of being allowed to ply the negro-trade, until then only carried on between Africa and the English West Indies, between Africa and Spanish America as well. England thereby acquired the right of supplying Spanish America until 1743 with 4,800 negroes yearly. This threw, at the same time, an official cloak over British smuggling. Liverpool waxed fat on the slave-trade. This was its method of primitive accumulation. And, even to the present day, Liverpool "respectability" is the Pindar of the slave-trade which—compare the work of Aikin [1795] already quoted—"has coincided with that spirit of bold adventure which has characterised the trade of Liverpool and rapidly carried it to its present state of prosperity; has occasioned vast employment for shipping and sailors, and greatly augmented the demand for the manufactures of the country" (p. 339). Liverpool employed in the slave-trade, in 1730, 15 ships; in 1751, 53; in 1760, 74; in 1770, 96; and in 1792, 132.

Whilst the cotton industry introduced child-slavery in England, it gave in the United States a stimulus to the transformation of the earlier, more or less patriarchal slavery, into a system of commercial exploitation. In fact, the veiled slavery of the wage-workers in Europe needed, for its pedestal, slavery pure and simple in the new world.*

Tantae molis erat,[34] to establish the "eternal laws of Nature" of the capitalist mode of production, to complete the process of separation between labourers and conditions of labour, to transform, at one pole, the social means of production and subsistence into capital, at the opposite pole, the mass of the population into wage-labourers, into "free labouring poor", that artificial product of modern society.** If money, according to

---

* In 1790, there were in the English West Indies ten slaves for one free man, in the French fourteen for one, in the Dutch twenty-three for one. (Henry Broughman: "An Inquiry into the Colonial Policy of the European Powers." Edin, 1803, Vol. II., p. 74.)

** The phrase, "labouring poor," is found in English legislation from the moment when the class of wage-labourers becomes noticeable. This term is used in opposition, on the one hand, to the "idle poor", beggars, etc., on the other to those labourers, who, pigeons not yet plucked, are still possessors of their own means of labour. From the Statute Book it passed into Political Economy, and was handed down by Culpeper, J. Child, etc., to Adam Smith and Eden. After this, one can

Augier,* "comes into the world with a congenital blood-stain on one cheek," capital comes dripping from head to foot, from every pore, with blood and dirt.**

HISTORICAL TENDENCY
OF CAPITALIST ACCUMULATION

What does the primitive accumulation of capital, *i.e.,* its historical genesis, resolve itself into? In so far as it is not immediate transformation of slaves and serfs into wage-labourers, and therefore a mere change of form, it only means the expropriation of the immediate producers, *i.e.,* the dissolution of private property based on the labour of its owner. Private property, as the antithesis to social, collective property, exists only where the means of labour and the external conditions of labour belong to private individuals. But according as these private individuals are labourers or not labourers, private property has a different character. The

---

judge of the good faith of the "execrable political cant-monger," Edmund Burke, when he called the expression, "labouring poor,"—"execrable political cant." This sycophant who, in the pay of the English oligarchy, played the romantic laudator temporis acti against the French Revolution, just as, in the pay of the North American Colonies, at the beginning of the American troubles, he had played the Liberal against the English oligarchy, was an out and out vulgar bourgeois. "The laws of commerce are the laws of Nature, and therefore the laws of God." (E. Burke, "Thoughts and Details on Scarcity," ed. London, 1800, pp. 31, 32.) No wonder that, true to the laws of God and of Nature, he always sold himself in the best market. A very good portrait of this Edmund Burke, during his liberal time, is to be found in the writings of the Rev. Mr. Tucker. Tucker was a parson and a Tory, but, for the rest, an honourable man and a competent political economist. In face of the infamous cowardice of character that reigns to-day, and believes most devoutly in "the laws of commerce," it is our bounden duty again and again to brand the Burkes, who only differ from their successors in one thing—talent.

*Marie Augier: "Du Crédit Public." Paris, 1842.
** "Capital is said by a Quarterly Reviewer to fly turbulence and strife, and to be timid, which is very true; but this is very incompletely stating the question. Capital eschews no profit, or very small profit, just as Nature was formerly said to abhor a vacuum. With adequate profit, capital is very bold. A certain 10 per cent., will ensure its employment anywhere; 20 per cent., certain will produce eagerness; 50 per cent., positive audacity; 100 per cent., will make it ready to trample on all human laws; 300 per cent., and there is not a crime at which it will scruple, nor a risk it will not run, even to the chance of its owner being hanged. If turbulence and strife will bring a profit, it will freely encourage both. Smuggling and the slave-trade have amply proved all that is here stated." (T. J. Dunning, "Trades' Unions and Strikes: their Philosophy and Intention", pp. 35, 36.)

numberless shades, that it at first sight presents, correspond to the intermediate stages lying between these two extremes. The private property of the labourer in his means of production is the foundation of petty industry, whether agricultural, manufacturing, or both; petty industry, again, is an essential condition for the development of social production and of the free individuality of the labourer himself. Of course, this petty mode of production exists also under slavery, serfdom, and other states of dependence. But it flourishes, it lets loose its whole energy, it attains its adequate classical form, only where the labourer is the private owner of his own means of labour set in action by himself: the peasant of the land which he cultivates, the artisan of the tool which he handles as a virtuoso. This mode of production presupposes parcelling of the soil, and scattering of the other means of production. As it excludes the concentration of these means of production, so also it excludes co-operation, division of labour within each separate process of production, the control over, and the productive application of the forces of Nature by society, and the free development of the social productive powers. It is compatible only with a system of production, and a society, moving within narrow and more or less primitive bounds. To perpetuate it would be, as Pecqueur rightly says, "to decree universal mediocrity". At a certain stage of development it brings forth the material agencies for its own dissolution. From that moment new forces and new passions spring up in the bosom of society; but the old social organisation fetters them and keeps them down. It must be annihilated; it is annihilated. Its annihilation, the transformation of the individualised and scattered means of production into socially concentrated ones, of the pigmy property of the many into the huge property of the few, the expropriation of the great mass of the people from the soil, from the means of subsistence, and from the means of labour, this fearful and painful expropriation of the mass of the people forms the prelude to the history of capital. It comprises a series of forcible methods, of which we have passed in review only those that have been epoch-making as methods of the primitive accumulation of capital. The expropriation of the immediate producers was accomplished with merciless Vandalism, and under the stimulus of passions the most infamous, the most sordid, the pettiest, the most meanly odious. Self-earned private property, that is based, so to say, on the fusing together of the isolated, independent labouring-individual with the conditions of his labour, is supplanted by capitalistic private property, which rests on exploitation of the nominally free labour of others, *i.e.,* on wage-labour.*

As soon as this process of transformation has sufficiently decomposed the old society from top to bottom, as soon as the labourers are turned into proletarians, their means of labour into capital, as soon as the capitalist mode of production stands on its own feet, then the further socialisation of labour and further transformation of the land and other means of production into socially exploited and, therefore, common means of production, as well as the further expropriation of private proprietors, takes a new form. That which is now to be expropriated is no longer the labourer working for himself, but the capitalist, exploiting many labourers. This expropriation is accomplished by the action of the immanent laws of capitalistic production itself, by the centralisation of capital. One capitalist always kills many. Hand in hand with this centralisation, or this expropriation of many capitalists by few, develop, on an ever-extending scale, the co-operative form of the labour-process, the conscious technical application of science, the methodical cultivation of the soil, the transformation of the instruments of labour into instruments of labour only usable in common, the economising of all means of production by their use as the means of production of combined, socialised labour, the entanglement of all peoples in the net of the world-market, and with this, the international character of the capitalistic régime. Along with the constantly diminishing number of the magnates of capital, who usurp and monopolise all advantages of this process of transformation, grows the mass of misery, oppression, slavery, degradation, exploitation; but with this too grows the revolt of the working-class, a class always increasing in numbers, and disciplined, united, organised by the very mechanism of the process of capitalist production itself. The monopoly of capital becomes a fetter upon the mode of production, which has sprung up and flourished along with, and under it. Centralisation of the means of production and socialisation of labour at last reach a point where they become incompatible with their capitalist integument. Thus integument is burst asunder. The knell of capitalist private property sounds. The expropriators are expropriated.

---

*"Nous sommes dans une condition tout-à-fait nouvelle de la société ... nous tendons à séparer toute espèce de propriété d'avec toute espèce de travail." (Sismondi: "Nouveaux Principes d'Econ. Polit." t. II., p. 434.)

The capitalist mode of appropriation, the result of the capitalist mode of production, produces capitalist private property. This is the first negation of individual private property, as founded on the labour of the proprietor. But capitalist production begets, with the inexorability of a law of Nature, its own negation. It is the negation of negation. This does not re-establish private property for the producer, but gives him individual property based on the acquisitions of the capitalist era: *i.e.,* on co-operation and the possession in common of the land and of the means of production.

The transformation of scattered private property, arising from individual labour, into capitalist private property is, naturally, a process, incomparably more protracted, violent, and difficult, than the transformation of capitalistic private property, already practically resting on socialised production, into socialised property. In the former case, we had the expropriation of the mass of the people by a few usurpers; in the latter, we have the expropriation of a few usurpers by the mass of the people.*

Karl Marx, *Capital,* Vol. I,
pp. 702-15

---

* The advance of industry, whose involuntary promoter is the bourgeoisie, replaces the isolation of the labourers, due to competition, by their revolutionary combination, due to association. The development of Modern Industry, therefore, cuts from under its, feet, the very foundation on which the bourgeoisie produces and appropriates products. What the bourgeoisie, therefore, produces, above all, are its own grave-diggers. Its fall and the victory of the proletariat are equally inevitable.... Of all the classes, that stand face to face with the bourgeoisie to-day, the proletariat alone is a really revolutionary class. The other classes perish and disappear in the face of Modern Industry, the proletariat is its special and essential product. The lower middle-classes, the small manufacturers, the shopkeepers, the artisan, the peasant, all these fight against the bourgeoisie, to save from extinction their existence as fractions of the middle-class ... they are reactionary, for they try to roll back the wheel of history. Karl Marx und Friedrich Engels, "Manifest der Kommunistischen Partei," London, 1848, pp. 9, 11.

KARL MARX

From
LETTER
TO LUDWIG KUGELMANN
IN HANOVER

London, April 12, 1871

If you look at the last chapter of my *Eighteenth Brumaire*, you will find that I declare: the next French Revolution will no longer attempt to transfer the bureaucratic-military apparatus from one hand to another, but *to smash* it, and this is the precondition for every real people's revolution on the Continent. And this is what our heroic Party comrades in Paris are attempting.[35] What flexibility, what historical initiative, what a capacity for sacrifice in these Parisians! After six months of hunger and ruin, caused by internal treachery even more than by the external enemy, they rise, in the face of the Prussian bayonets, as if there had never been a war between France and Germany and the enemy were not standing at the gates of Paris! History has no comparable example of similar greatness! If they are defeated only their "good nature" will be to blame. They ought to have marched at once on Versailles after the withdrawal first of Vinoy and then of the reactionary section of the Paris National Guard. They missed their opportunity because of moral scruples. They did not want *to start a civil war*, as if that mischievous dwarf Thiers had not already started the civil war with his attempt to disarm Paris! Second mistake: The Central Committee surrendered its power too soon, to make way for the Commune. Again from a too "honourable" scrupulosity! However that may be, the present rising in Paris—even if it be crushed by

140

the wolves, swine, and vile curs of the old society—is the most glorious deed of our Party since the June insurrection in Paris. Compare these Parisians, storming heaven, with the slaves to heaven of the German-Prussian Holy Roman Empire, with its posthumous masquerades reeking of the barracks, the Church, the clod-hopping junkers and above all, of the philistine.

Marx and Engels,
Selected Correspondence,
Moscow, 1975, p. 247

KARL MARX

From
LETTER
TO LUDWIG KUGELMANN
IN HANOVER

[London,] April 17, 1871

How you can compare petty-bourgeois demonstrations *à la* June 13, 1849, etc., with the present struggle in Paris is quite incomprehensible to me.

World history would indeed be very easy to make if the struggle were taken up only on condition that the prospects were unmistakably favourable. It would on the other hand be of a very mystical nature, if "accidents" played no part. These accidents naturally form part of the general course of development and are compensated by other accidents. But acceleration and delay are very much dependent upon such "accidents", including the "accident" of the character of the people who first head the movement.

The decisively unfavourable "accident" this time is by no means to be sought in the general conditions of French society, but in the presence of the Prussians in France and their position right before Paris. Of this the Parisians were well aware. But of this, the bourgeois *canaille* of Versailles were also well aware. Precisely for that reason they presented the Parisians with the alternative of either taking up the fight or succumbing without a struggle. The demoralisation of the working class in the latter case would have been a far greater misfortune than the doom of any number of "leaders". With the struggle in Paris the struggle of the working class against the capitalist class and its state has entered upon a new phase. Whatever the immediate outcome may be, a new point of departure of world-wide importance has been gained.

Marx and Engels,
Selected Correspondence,
Moscow, 1975, p. 248

KARL MARX

From
THE CIVIL WAR
IN FRANCE

**ADDRESS
OF THE GENERAL COUNCIL
OF THE INTERNATIONAL
WORKING MEN'S
ASSOCIATION**[36]

**To all the Members
of the Association
in Europe and
the United States**

I

On the 4th of September, 1870, when the working men of Paris
proclaimed the Republic, which was almost instantaneously acclaimed throughout France, without a single voice of dissent, a
cabal of place-hunting barristers, with Thiers for their statesman
and Trochu for their general, took hold of the Hôtel de Ville. At
that time they were imbued with so fanatical a faith in the mission
of Paris to represent France in all epochs of historical crisis, that,
to legitimate their usurped titles as governors of France, they
thought it quite sufficient to produce their lapsed mandates as
representatives of Paris. In our second address on the late war,
five days after the rise of these men, we told you who they were.[37]
Yet, in the turmoil of surprise, with the real leaders of the working
class still shut up in Bonapartist prisons and the Prussians already
marching upon Paris, Paris bore with their assumption of power,
on the express condition that it was to be wielded for the single
purpose of national defence. Paris, however, was not to be
defended without arming its working class, organising them into
an effective force, and training their ranks by the war itself. But
Paris armed was the Revolution armed. A victory of Paris over the
Prussian aggressor would have been a victory of the French workman over the French capitalist and his State parasites. In this
conflict between national duty and class interest, the Government
of National Defence did not hesitate one moment to turn into a
Government of National Defection.

The first step they took was to send Thiers on a roving tour to all the courts of Europe, there to beg mediation by offering the barter of the Republic for a king. Four months after the commencement of the siege, when they thought the opportune moment had come for breaking the first word of capitulation, Trochu, in the presence of Jules Favre and others of his colleagues, addressed the assembled mayors of Paris in these terms:

> "The first question put to me by my colleagues on the very evening of the 4th of September was this: Paris, can it with any chance of success stand a siege by the Prussian army? I did not hesitate to answer in the negative. Some of my colleagues here present will warrant the truth of my words and the persistence of my opinion. I told them, in these very terms, that, under the existing state of things, the attempt of Paris to hold out a siege by the Prussian army would be a folly. Without doubt, I added, it would be an heroic folly; but that would be all.... The events (managed by himself) have not given the lie to my prevision."

This nice little speech of Trochu was afterwards published by M. Corbon, one of the mayors present....

A master in small state roguery, a virtuoso in perjury and treason, a craftsman in all the petty stratagems, cunning devices, and base perfidies of parliamentary party warfare; never scrupling, when out of office, to fan a revolution, and to stifle it in blood when at the helm of the state; with class prejudices standing him in the place of ideas, and vanity in the place of a heart; his private life as infamous as his public life is odious—even now, when playing the part of a French Sulla, he cannot help setting off the abomination of his deeds by the ridicule of his ostentation.

The capitulation of Paris, by surrendering to Prussia not only Paris, but all France, closed the long-continued intrigues of treason with the enemy, which the usurpers of the 4th of September had begun, as Trochu himself said, on that very same day. On the other hand, it initiated the civil war they were now to wage, with the assistance of Prussia, against the Republic and Paris. The trap was laid in the very terms of the capitulation. At that time above one-third of the territory was in the hands of the enemy, the capital was cut off from the provinces, all communications were disorganised. To elect under such circumstances a real representation of France was impossible, unless ample time were given for preparation. In view of this, the capitulation stipulated that a National Assembly must be elected within eight days; so that in many parts of France

144

the news of the impending election arrived on its eve only. This Assembly, moreover, was, by an express clause of the capitulation, to be elected for the sole purpose of deciding on peace or war, and, eventually, to conclude a treaty of peace. The population could not but feel that the terms of the armistice rendered the continuation of the war impossible, and that for sanctioning the peace imposed by Bismarck, the worst men in France were the best. But not content with these precautions, Thiers, even before the secret of the armistice had been broached to Paris, set out for an electioneering tour through the provinces, there to galvanise back into life the Legitimist party, which now, along with the Orleanists,[38] had to take the place of the then impossible Bonapartists. He was not afraid of them. Impossible as a government of modern France, and, therefore, contemptible as rivals, what party were more eligible as tools of counter-revolution than the party whose action, in the words of Thiers himself (Chamber of Deputies, 5th January, 1833),

"had always been confined to the three resources of foreign invasion, civil war, and anarchy"?

They verily believed in the advent of their long-expected retrospective millennium. There were the heels of foreign invasion trampling upon France; there was the downfall of an empire, and the captivity of a Bonaparte; and there they were themselves. The wheel of history had evidently rolled back to stop at the "Chambre introuvable" of 1816.[39] In the assemblies of the Republic, 1848 to 1851, they had been represented by their educated and trained parliamentary champions; it was the rank and file of the party which now rushed in—all the Pourceaugnacs[a] of France.

As soon as this Assembly of "Rurals" had met at Bordeaux, Thiers made it clear to them that the peace preliminaries must be assented to at once, without even the honours of a Parliamentary debate, as the only condition on which Prussia would permit them to open the war against the Republic and Paris, its stronghold. The counter-revolution had, in fact, no time to lose. The Second Empire had more than doubled the national debt, and plunged all the large towns into heavy municipal debts. The war had fearfully swelled the liabilities, and mercilessly ravaged the resources of the nation. To complete the ruin, the Prussian Shylock was there with

---

[a] *Pourceaugnac*: A character in one of Moliere's comedies, typifying the dull-witted, narrow-minded petty landed gentry.—*Ed.*

his bond for the keep of half a million of his soldiers on French soil, his indemnity of five milliards, and interest at 5 per cent on the unpaid instalments thereof. Who was to pay the bill? It was only by the violent overthrow of the Republic that the appropriators of wealth could hope to shift on the shoulders of its producers the cost of a war which they, the appropriators, had themselves originated. Thus, the immense ruin of France spurred on these patriotic representatives of land and capital, under the very eyes and patronage of the invader, to graft upon the foreign war a civil war—a slaveholders' rebellion.

There stood in the way of this conspiracy one great obstacle — Paris. To disarm Paris was the first condition of success. Paris was therefore summoned by Thiers to surrender its arms. Then Paris was exasperated by the frantic anti-republican demonstrations of the "Rural" Assembly and by Thiers' own equivocations about the legal status of the Republic; by the threat to decapitate and decapitalise Paris; the appointment of Orleanist ambassadors; Dufaure's laws on over-due commercial bills and house-rents,[40] inflicting ruin on the commerce and industry of Paris; Pouyer-Quertier's tax of two centimes upon every copy of every imaginable publication; the sentences of death against Blanqui and Flourens; the suppression of the Republican journals; the transfer of the National Assembly to Versailles; the renewal of the state of siege declared by Palikao, and expired on the 4th of September; the appointment of Vinoy, the *Décembriseur*,[41] as governor of Paris—of Valentin, the imperialist *gendarme*, as its prefect of police—and of Aurelle de Paladines, the Jesuit general, as the commander-in-chief of its National Guard.

And now we have to address a question to M. Thiers and the men of national defence, his understrappers. It is known that, through the agency of M. Pouyer-Quertier, his finance minister, Thiers had contracted a loan of two milliards. Now, is it true, or not, —

1. That the business was so managed that a consideration of several hundred millions was secured for the private benefit of Thiers, Jules Favre, Ernest Picard, Pouyer-Quertier, and Jules Simon? and —

2. That no money was to be paid down until after the "pacification" of Paris[42]?

At all events, there must have been something very pressing in the matter, for Thiers and Jules Favre, in the name of the majority

146

f the Bordeaux Assembly, unblushingly solicited the immediate occupation of Paris by Prussian troops. Such, however, was not the game of Bismarck, as he sneeringly, and in public, told the admiring Frankfort philistines on his return to Germany.

II

Armed Paris was the only serious obstacle in the way of the counter-revolutionary conspiracy. Paris was, therefore, to be disarmed. On this point the Bordeaux Assembly was sincerity itself. If the roaring rant of its Rurals had not been audible enough, the surrender of Paris by Thiers to the tender mercies of the triumvirate of Vinoy the *décembriseur*, Valentin the Bonapartist *gendarme*, and Aurelle de Paladines the Jesuit general, would have cut off even the last subterfuge of doubt. But while insultingly exhibiting the true purpose of the disarmament of Paris, the conspirators asked her to lay down her arms on a pretext which was the most glaring, the most barefaced of lies. The artillery of the Paris National Guard, said Thiers, belonged to the State, and to the State it must be returned. The fact was this: From the very day of the capitulation, by which Bismarck's prisoners had signed the surrender of France, but reserved to themselves a numerous bodyguard for the express purpose of cowing Paris, Paris stood on the watch. The National Guard reorganised themselves and entrusted their supreme control to a Central Committee elected by their whole body, save some fragments of the old Bonapartist formations. On the eve of the entrance of the Prussians into Paris, the Central Committee took measures for the removal to Montmartre, Belleville, and La Villete of the cannon and *mitrailleuses* treacherously abandoned by the *capitulards*[43] in and about the very quarters the Prussians were to occupy. That artillery had been furnished by the subscriptions of the National Guard. As their private property, it was officially recognised in the capitulation of the 28th of January, and on that very title exempted from the general surrender, into the hands of the conqueror, of arms belonging to the government. And Thiers was so utterly destitute of even the flimsiest pretext for initiating the war against Paris, that he had to resort to the flagrant lie of the artillery of the National Guard being State property!

The seizure of her artillery was evidently but to serve as the preliminary to the general disarmament of Paris, and, therefore, of the Revolution of the 4th of September. But that Revolution had become the legal status of France. The Republic, its work, was recognised by the conqueror in the terms of the capitulation. After the capitulation, it was acknowledged by all the foreign Powers; and in its name the National Assembly had been summoned. The Paris working men's Revolution of the 4th of September was the only legal title of the National Assembly seated at Bordeaux, and of its executive. Without it, the National Assembly would at once have to give way to the *Corps Législatif* elected in 1869 by universal suffrage under French, not under Prussian, rule, and forcibly dispersed by the arm of the Revolution. Thiers and his ticket-of-leave men would have had to capitulate for safe conducts signed by Louis Bonaparte, to save them from a voyage to Cayenne. The National Assembly, with its power of attorney to settle the terms of peace with Prussia, was but an incident of that Revolution, the true embodiment of which was still armed Paris, which had initiated it, undergone for it a five months' siege, with its horrors of famine, and made her prolonged resistance, despite Trochu's plan, the basis of an obstinate war of defence in the provinces. And Paris was now either to lay down her arms at the insulting behest of the rebellious slaveholders of Bordeaux, and acknowledged that her Revolution of the 4th of September meant nothing but a simple transfer of power from Louis Bonaparte to his Royal rivals; or she had to stand forward as the self-sacrificing champion of France, whose salvation from ruin, and whose regeneration were impossible, without the revolutionary overthrow of the political and social conditions that had engendered the Second Empire, and, under its fostering care, matured into utter rottenness. Paris, emaciated by a five months' famine, did not hesitate one moment. She heroically resolved to run all the hazards of a resistance against the French conspirators, even with Prussian cannon frowning upon her from her own forts. Still, in its abhorrence of the civil war into which Paris was to be goaded, the Central Committee continued to persist in a merely defensive attitude, despite the provocations of the Assembly, the usurpations of the Executive, and the menacing concentration of troops in and around Paris.

Thiers opened the civil war by sending Vinoy, at the head of a multitude of *sergents-de-ville* and some regiments of the line, upon a nocturnal expedition against Montmartre, there to seize, by surprise, the artillery of the National Guard. It is well known how this attempt broke down before the resistance of the National Guard and the fraternisation of the line with the people. Aurelle de

Paladines had printed beforehand his bulletin of victory, and Thiers held ready the placards announcing his measures of *coup d'état*. Now these had to be replaced by Thiers' appeals, imparting his magnanimous resolve to leave the National Guard in the possession of their arms, with which, he said, he felt sure they would rally round the Government against the rebels. Out of 300,000 National Guards only 300 responded to this summons to rally round little Thiers against themselves. The glorious working men's Revolution of the 18th March took undisputed sway of Paris. The Central Committee was its provisional government. Europe seemed, for a moment, to doubt whether its recent sensational performances of state and war had any reality in them, or whether they were the dreams of a long bygone past.

From the 18th of March to the entrance of the Versailles troops into Paris, the proletarian revolution remained so free from the acts of violence in which the revolutions, and still more the counter-revolutions, of the "better classes" abound, that no facts were left to its opponents to cry out about but the execution of Generals Lecomte and Clément Thomas, and the affair of the Place Vendôme.

One of the Bonapartist officers engaged in the nocturnal attempt against Montmartre, General Lecomte, had four times ordered the 81st line regiment to fire at an unarmed gathering in the Place Pigalle, and on their refusal fiercely insulted them. Instead of shooting women and children, his own men shot him. The inveterate habits acquired by the soldiery under the training of the enemies of the working class are, of course, not likely to change the very moment these soldiers changed sides. The same men executed Clément Thomas.

"General" Clément Thomas, a malcontent ex-quartermaster-sergeant, had, in the latter times of Louis Philippe's reign, enlisted at the office of the republican newspaper *Le National,* there to serve in the double capacity of responsible man-of-straw (*gérant résponsable*) and of duelling bully to that very combative journal. After the revolution of February, the men of the *National* having got into power, they metamorphosed this old quartermaster-sergeant into a general on the eve of the butchery of June, of which he, like Jules Favre, was one of the sinister plotters, and became one of the most dastardly executioners. Then he and his generalship disappeared for a long time, to again rise to the surface on the 1st November, 1870. The day before the Government of Defence, caught at the Hôtel de Ville, had solemnly pledged their parole to Blanqui, Flourens, and other representatives of the working class, to abdicate their usurped power into the hands of a commune to be freely elected by Paris.[44] Instead of keeping their word, they let loose on Paris the Bretons of Trochu, who now replaced the Corsicans of Bonaparte. General Tamisier alone, refusing to sully his name by such a breach of faith, resigned the commandership-in-chief of the National Guard, and in his place Clément Thomas for once became again a general. During the whole of his tenure of command, he made war, not upon the Prussians, but upon the Paris National Guard. He prevented their general armament, pitted the bourgeois battalions against the working men's battalions, weeded out the officers hostile to Trochu's "plan", and disbanded, under the stigma of cowardice, the very same proletarian battalions whose heroism has now astonished their most inveterate enemies. Clément Thomas felt quite proud of having reconquered his June pre-eminence as the personal enemy of the working class of Paris. Only a few days before the 18th of March, he laid before the War Minister, Le Flô, a plan of his own for "finishing of *la fine fleur* ('the cream') of the Paris *canaille*". After Vinoy's rout, he must needs appear upon the scene of action in the quality of an amateur spy. The Central Committee and the Paris working men were as much responsible for the killing of Clément Thomas and Lecomte as the Princess of Wales was for the fate of the people crushed to death on the day of her entrance into London.

The massacre of unarmed citizens in the Place Vendôme is a myth which M. Thiers and the Rurals persistently ignored in the Assembly, entrusting its propagation exclusively to the servants' hall of European journalism. "The men of order", the reactionists of Paris, trembled at the victory of the 18th of March. To them it was the signal of popular retribution at last arriving. The ghosts of the victims assassinated at their hands from the days of June, 1848, down to the 22nd of January, 1871,[45] arose before their faces. Their panic was their only punishment. Even the *sergents-de-ville*, instead of being disarmed and locked up, as ought to have been done, had the gates of Paris flung wide open for their safe retreat to Versailles. The men of order were left not only unarmed, but allowed to rally and quietly to seize more than one stronghold in the very centre of Paris. This indulgence of the Central Committee—this magnanimity of the armed working men—so strangely at variance with the habits of the "Party of Order", the latter misinterpreted as mère symptoms of conscious weakness.

Hence their silly plan to try, under the cloak of an unarmed demonstration, what Vinoy had failed to perform with his cannon and *mitrailleuses*. On the 22nd of March a riotous mob of swells started from the quarters of luxury, all the *petits crevés* in their ranks, and at their head the notorious familiars of the Empire—the Heeckeren, Coëtlogon, Henri de Pène, etc. Under the cowardly pretence of a pacific demonstration, this rabble, secretly armed with the weapons of the bravo, fell into marching order, ill-treated and disarmed the detached patrols and sentries of the National Guards they met with on their progress, and, on debouching from the Rue de la Paix, with the cry of "Down with the Central Committee! Down with the assassins! The National Assembly for ever!" attempted to break through the line drawn up there, and thus to carry by a surprise the headquarters of the National Guard in the Place of Vendôme. In reply to their pistol-shots, the regular *sommations*[46](the French equivalent of the English Riot Act) were made, and, proving ineffective, fire was commanded by the general of the National Guard.[a] One volley dispersed into wild fflight the silly coxcombs, who expected that the mere exhibition of their "respectability" would have the same effect upon the Revolution of Paris as Joshua's trumpets upon the wall of Jericho. The runaways left behind them two National Guards killed, nine severely wounded (among them a member of the Central Committee[b]), and the whole scene of their exploit strewn with revolvers, daggers, and sword-canes, in evidence of the "unarmed" character of their "pacific" demonstration. When, on the 13th of June, 1849, the National Guard made a really pacific demonstration in protest against the felonious assault of French troops upon Rome, Changarnier, then general of the Party of Order, was acclaimed by the National Assembly, and especially by M. Thiers, as the saviour of society, for having launched his troops from all sides upon these unarmed men, to shoot and sabre them down, and to trample them under their horses' feet. Paris, then, was placed under a state of siege. Dufaure hurried through the Assembly new laws of repression. New arrests, new proscriptions—a new reign of terror set in. But the lower orders manage these things otherwise. The Central Committee of 1871 simply ignored the heroes of the "pacific demonstration", so much so that only two days later they were enabled to muster under Admiral Saisset for that *armed*

---

[a] Bergeret.—*Ed.*
[b] Maljournal.—*Ed.*

demonstration, crowned by the famous stampede to Versailles. In their reluctance to continue the civil war opened by Thiers' burglarious attempt on Montmartre, the Central Committee made itself, this time, guilty of a decisive mistake in not at once marching upon Versailles, then completely helpless, and thus putting an end to the conspiracies of Thiers and his Rurals. Instead of this, the Party of Order was again allowed to try its strength at the ballot box, on the 26th of March, the day of the election of the Commune. Then, in the *mairies* of Paris, they exchanged bland words of conciliation with their too generous conquerors, muttering in their hearts solemn vows to exterminate them in due time.

Now look at the reverse of the medal. Thiers opened his second campaign against Paris in the beginning of April. The first batch of Parisian prisoners brought into Versailles was subjected to revolting atrocities, while Ernest Picard, with his hands in his trousers' pockets, strolled about jeering them, and while Mesdames Thiers and Favre, in the midst of their ladies of honour (?), applauded, from the balcony, the outrages of the Versailles mob. The captured soldiers of the line were massacred in cold blood; our brave friend, General Duval, the iron-founder, was shot without any form of trial. Galliffet, the kept man of his wife, so notorious for her shameless exhibitions at the orgies of the Second Empire, boasted in a proclamation of having commanded the murder of a small troop of National Guards, with their captain and lieutenant, surprised and disarmed by his Chasseurs. Vinoy, the runaway, was appointed by Thiers Grand Cross of the Legion of Honour, for his general order to shoot down every soldier of the line taken in the ranks of the Federals. Desmarêst, the gendarme, was decorated for the treacherous butcher-like chopping in pieces of the high-souled and chivalrous Flourens, who had saved the heads of the Government of Defence on the 31st of October, 1870.[47] "The encouraging particulars" of his assassination were triumphantly expatiated upon by Thiers in the National Assembly. With the elated vanity of a parliamentary Tom Thumb, permitted to play the part of a Tamerlane, he denied the rebels against his littleness every right of civilised warfare, up to the right of neutrality for ambulances. Nothing more horrid than that monkey, allowed for a time to give full fling to his tigerish instincts, as foreseen by Voltaire.[48] (See note, p. 35.[49])

After the decree of the Commune of the 7th April, ordering reprisals and declaring it to be its duty "to protect Paris against the cannibal exploits of the Versailles banditti, and to demand an eye for an eye, a tooth for a tooth," Thiers did not stop the barbarous treatment of prisoners, moreover insulting them in his bulletins as follows:—"Never have more degraded countenances of a degraded democracy met in the afflicted gazes of honest men",— honest like Thiers himself and his ministerial ticket-of-leave men. Still the shooting of prisoners was suspended for a time. Hardly, however, had Thiers and his Decembrist generals become aware that the Communal decree of reprisals was but an empty threat, that even their gendarme spies caught in Paris under the disguise of National Guards, that even *sergents-de-ville*, taken with incendiary shells upon them, were spared,—when the wholesale shooting of prisoners was resumed and carried on uninterruptedly to the end. Houses to which National Guards had fled were surrounded by gendarmes, inundated with petroleum (which here occurs for the first time in this war), and then set fire to, the charred corpses being afterwards brought out by the ambulance of the Press at the Ternes. Four National Guards having surrendered to a troop of mounted Chasseurs at Belle Epine, on the 25th of April, were afterwards shot down, one after another, by the captain, a worthy man of Galliffet's. One of his four victims, left for dead, Scheffer, crawled back to the Parisian outposts, and deposed to this fact before a commission of the Commune. When Tolain interpellated the War Minister upon the report of this commission, the Rurals drowned his voice and forbade Le Flô to answer. It would be an insult to their "glorious" army to speak of its deeds. The flippant tone in which Thiers' bulletins announced the bayoneting of the Federals surprised asleep at Moulin Saquet, and the wholesale fusillades at Clamart shocked the nerves even of the not over-sensitive London *Times*. But it would be ludicrous today to attempt recounting the merely preliminary atrocities committed by the bombarders of Paris and the fomenters of a slaveholders' rebellion protected by foreign invasion. Amidst all these horrors, Thiers, forgetful of his parliamentary laments on the terrible responsibility weighing down his dwarfish shoulders, boasts in his bulletin that *l'Assemblée siège paisiblement* (the Assembly continues meeting in peace), and proves by his constant carousals, now with Decembrist generals, now with German princes, that his digestion is not troubled in the least, not even by the ghosts of Lecomte and Clément Thomas.

On the dawn of the 18th of March, Paris arose to the thunderburst of "Vive la Commune!" What is the Commune, that sphinx so tantalising to the bourgeois mind?

"The proletarians of Paris," said the Central Committee in its manifesto of the 18th March, "amidst the failures and treasons of the ruling classes, have understood that the hour has struck for them to save the situation by taking into their own hands the direction of public affairs.... They have understood that it is their imperious duty and their absolute right to render themselves masters of their own destinies, by seizing upon the governmental power."

But the working class cannot simply lay hold of the ready-made state machinery, and wield it for its own purposes.

The centralised State power, with its ubiquitous organs of standing army, police, bureaucracy, clergy, and judicature—organs wrought after the plan of a systematic and hierarchic division of labour,—originates from the days of absolute monarchy, serving nascent middle-class society as a mighty weapon in its struggles against feudalism. Still, its development remained clogged by all manner of mediaeval rubbish, seignorial rights, local privileges, municipal and guild monopolies and provincial constitutions. The gigantic broom of the French Revolution of the eighteenth century swept away all these relics of bygone times, thus clearing simultaneously the social soil of its last hindrances to the superstructure of the modern State edifice raised under the First Empire, itself the offspring of the coalition wars of old semi-feudal Europe against modern France. During the subsequent *régimes* the Government, placed under parliamentary control—that is, under the direct control of the propertied classes—became not only a hotbed of huge national debts and crushing taxes; with its irresistible allurements of place, pelf, and patronage, it became not only the bone of contention between the rival factions and adventurers of the ruling classes; but its political character changed simultaneously with the economic changes of society. At the same pace at which the progress of modern industry developed, widened, intensified the class antagonism between capital and labour, the State power assumed more and more the character of the national power of capital over labour, of a public force organised for social enslavement, of an engine of class despotism. After every revolution marking a progressive phase in the class struggle, the purely repressive character of the State power stands out in bolder and bolder relief. The Revolution of 1830, resulting in the transfer of Government from the landlords to the capitalists, transferred it from the more remote to the more direct antagonists of the working men. The bourgeois Republicans, who, in the name of the Revolution of February, took the State power, used it for the June massacres, in order to convince the working class that "social" republic meant the Republic ensuring their social subjection, and in order to convince the royalist bulk of the bourgeois and landlord class that they might safely leave the cares and emoluments of Government to the bourgeois "Republicans". However, after their one heroic exploit of June, the bourgeois Republicans had, from the front, to fall back to the rear of the "Party of Order"—a combination formed by all the rival fractions and factions of the appropriating class in their now openly declared antagonism to the producing classes. The proper form of their joint-stock Government was the *Parliamentary Republic*, with Louis Bonaparte for its President. Theirs was a *régime* of avowed class terrorism and deliberate insult toward the "vile multitude". If the Parliamentary Republic, as M. Theirs said, "divided them (the different fractions of the ruling class) least," it opened an abyss between that class and the whole body of society outside their spare ranks. The restraints by which their own divisions had under former *régimes* still checked the State power, were removed by their union; and in view of the threatening upheaval of the proletariat, they now used that State power mercilessly and ostentatiously as the national war-engine of capital against labour. In their uninterrupted crusade against the producing masses they were, however, bound not only to invest the Executive with continually increased powers of repression, but at the same time to divest their own parliamentary stronghold—the National Assembly—one by one, of all its own means of defence against the Executive. The Executive, in the person of Louis Bonaparte, turned them out. The natural offspring of the "Party-of-Order" Republic was the Second Empire.

The empire, with the *coup d'état* for its certificate of birth, universal suffrage for its sanction, and the sword for its sceptre, professed to rest upon the peasantry, the large mass of producers not directly involved in the struggle of capital and labour. It professed to save the working class by breaking down Parliamentarism and, with it, the undisguised subserviency of Government to the propertied classes. It professed to save the propertied classes by upholding their economic supremacy over the working class; and, finally, it professed to unite all classes by reviving for all the chimera of national glory. In reality, it was the only form of government possible at a time when the bourgeoisie had already lost, and the working class had not yet acquired, the faculty of ruling the nation. It was acclaimed throughout the world as the saviour of society. Under its sway, bourgeois society, freed from political cares, attained a development unexpected even by itself. Its industry and commerce expanded to colossal dimensions; financial swindling celebrated cosmopolitan orgies; the misery of the masses was set off by a shameless display of gorgeous, meretricious and debased luxury. The State power, apparently soaring high above society, was at the same time itself the greatest scandal of that society and the very hotbed of all its corruptions. Its own rottenness, and the rottenness of the society it had saved, were laid bare by the bayonet of Prussia, herself eagerly bent upon transferring the supreme seat of that *régime* from Paris to Berlin. Imperialism is, at the same time, the most prostitute and the ultimate form of the State power which nascent middle-class society had commenced to elaborate as a means of its own emancipation from feudalism, and which full-grown bourgeois society had finally transformed into a means for the enslavement of labour by capital.

The direct antithesis to the empire was the Commune. The cry of "social republic", with which the revolution of February was ushered in by the Paris proletariat, did but express a vague aspiration after a Republic that was not only to supersede the monarchical form of class rule, but class rule itself. The Commune was the positive form of that Republic.

Paris, the central seat of the old governmental power, and, at the same time, the social stronghold of the French working class, had risen in arms against the attempt of Thiers and the Rurals to restore and perpetuate that old governmental power bequeathed to them by the empire. Paris could resist only because, in consequence of the siege, it had got rid of the army, and replaced it by a National Guard, the bulk of which consisted of working men. This fact was now to be transformed into an institution. The first decree of the Commune, therefore, was the suppression of the standing army, and the substitution for it of the armed people.

The Commune was formed of the municipal councillors, chosen by universal suffrage in the various wards of the town, responsible and revocable at short terms. The majority of its members were naturally working men, or acknowledged representatives of the working class. The Commune was to be a working, not a parliamentary, body, executive and legislative at the same time.

Instead of continuing to be the agent of the Central Government, the police was at once stripped of its political attributes, and turned into the responsible and at all times revocable agent of the Commune. So were the officials of all other branches of the Administration. From the members of the Commune downwards, the public service had to be done at *workmen's wages*. The vested interests and the representation allowances of the high dignitaries of State disappeared along with the high dignitaries themselves. Public functions ceased to be the private property of the tools of the Central Government. Not only municipal administration, but the whole initiative hitherto exercised by the State was laid into the hands of the Commune.

Having once got rid of the standing army and the police, the physical force elements of the old Government, the Commune was anxious to break the spiritual force of repression, the "parson-power," by the disestablishment and disendowment of all churches as proprietary bodies. The priests were sent back to the recesses of private life, there to feed upon the alms of the faithful in imitation of their predecessors, the Apostles. The whole of the educational institutions were opened to the people gratuitously, and at the same time cleared of all interference of Church and State. Thus, not only was education made accessible to all, but science itself freed from the fetters which class prejudice and governmental force had imposed upon it.

The judicial functionaries were to be divested of that sham independence which had but served to mask their abject subserviency to all succeeding governments to which, in turn, they had taken, and broken, the oaths of allegiance. Like the rest of public servants, magistrates and judges were to be elective, responsible, and revocable.

The Paris Commune was, of course, to serve as a model to all the great industrial centres of France. The communal *régime* once established in Paris and the secondary centres, the old centralised Government would in the provinces, too, have to give way to the self-government of the producers. In a rough sketch of national organisation which the Commune had no time to develop, it states clearly that the Commune was to be the political form of even the smallest country hamlet, and that in the rural districts the standing army was to be replaced by a national militia, with an extremely short term of service. The rural communes of every district were to administer their common affairs by an assembly of delegates in the central town, and these district assemblies were again to send

157

deputies to the National Delegation in Paris, each delegate to be at any time revocable and bound by the *mandat impératif* (formal instructions) of his constituents. The few but important functions which still would remain for a central government were not to be suppressed, as has been intentionally mis-stated, but were to be discharged by Communal, and therefore strictly responsible agents. The unity of the nation was not to be broken, but, on the contrary, to be organised by the Communal Constitution and to become a reality by the destruction of the State power which claimed to be the embodiment of that unity independent of, and superior to, the nation itself, from which it was but a parasitic excrescence. While the merely repressive organs of the old governmental power were to be amputated, its legitimate functions were to be wrested from an authority usurping pre-eminence over society itself, and restored to the responsible agents of society. Instead of deciding once in three or six years which member of the ruling class was to misrepresent the people in Parliament, universal suffrage was to serve the people, constituted in Communes, as individual suffrage serves every other employer in the search for the workmen and managers in his business. And it is well known that companies, like individuals, in matters of real business generally know how to put the right man in the right place, and, if they for once make a mistake, to redress it promptly. On the other hand, nothing could be more foreign to the spirit of the Commune than to supersede universal suffrage by hierarchic investiture.

It is generally the fate of completely new historical creations to be mistaken for the counterpart of older and even defunct forms of social life, to which they may bear a certain likeness. Thus, this new Commune, which breaks the modern State power, has been mistaken for a reproduction of the mediaeval Communes, which first preceded, and afterwards became the substratum of, that very State power. The Communal Constitution has been mistaken for an attempt to break up into a federation of small States, as dreamt of by Montesquieu and the Girondins[50], that unity of great nations which, if originally brought about by political force, has now become a powerful coefficient of social production. The antagonism of the Commune against the State power has been mistaken for an exaggerated form of the ancient struggle against over-centralisation. Peculiar historical circumstances may have prevented the classical development, as in France, of the bourgeois form of government, and may have allowed, as in England, to complete the great central State organs by corrupt vestries, jobbing councillors, and ferocious poor-law guardians in the towns, and virtually hereditary magistrates in the counties. The Communal Constitution would have restored to the social body all the forces hitherto absorbed by the State parasite feeding upon, and clogging the free movement of society. By this one act it would have initiated the regeneration of France. The provincial French middle class saw in the Commune an attempt to restore the sway their order had held over the country under Louis Philippe, and which, under Louis Napoleon, was supplanted by the pretended rule of the country over the towns. In reality, the Communal Constitution brought the rural producers under the intellectual lead of the central towns of their districts, and these secured to them, in the working men, the natural trustees of their interests. The very existence of the Commune involved, as a matter of course, local municipal liberty, but no longer as a check upon the, now superseded, State power. It could only enter into the head of a Bismarck, who, when not engaged on his intrigues of blood and iron, always likes to resume his old trade, so befitting his mental calibre, of contributor to *Kladderadatsch* (the Berlin *Punch*), it could only enter into such a head, to ascribe to the Paris Commune aspirations after that caricature of the old French municipal organisation of 1791, the Prussian municipal constitution which degrades the town governments to mere secondary wheels in the police-machinery of the Prussian State. The Commune made that catchword of bourgeois revolutions, cheap government, a reality, by destroying the two greatest sources of expenditure—the standing army and State functionarism. Its very existence presupposed the non-existence of monarchy, which, in Europe at least, is the normal incumbrance and indispensable cloak of class rule. It supplied the Republic with the basis of really democratic institutions. But neither cheap Government nor the "true Republic" was its ultimate aim; they were its mere concomitants.

The multiplicity of interpretations to which the Commune has been subjected, and the multiplicity of interests which construed it in their favour, show that it was a thoroughly expansive political form, while all previous forms of government had been emphatically repressive. Its true secret was this. It was essentially a working-class government, the produce of the struggle of the producing against the appropriating class, the political form at last discovered under which to work out the economic emancipation of labour.

Except on this last condition, the Communal Constitution would have been an impossibility and a delusion. The political rule of the producer cannot coexist with the perpetuation of his social slavery. The Commune was therefore to serve as a lever for uprooting the economical foundations upon which rests the existence of classes, and therefore of class-rule. With labour emancipated, every man becomes a working man, and productive labour ceases to be a class attribute.

It is a strange fact. In spite of all the tall talk and all the immense literature, for the last sixty years, about Emancipation of Labour, no sooner do the working men anywhere take the subject into their own hands with a will, than uprises at once all the apologetic phraseology of the mouthpieces of present society with its two poles of Capital and Wages Slavery (the landlord now is but the sleeping partner of the capitalist), as if capitalist society was still in its purest state of virgin innocence, with its antagonisms still undeveloped, with its delusions still unexploded, with its prostitute realities not yet laid bare. The Commune, they exclaim, intends to abolish property, the basis of all civilisation! Yes, gentlemen, the Commune intended to abolish that class-property which makes the labour of the many the wealth of the few. It aimed at the expropriation of the expropriators. It wanted to make individual property a truth by transforming the means of production, land and capital, now chiefly the means of enslaving and exploiting labour, into mere instruments of free and associated labour.— But this is Communism, "impossible" Communism! Why, those members of the ruling classes who are intelligent enough to perceive the impossibility of continuing the present system—and they are many—have become the obtrusive and full-mouthed apostles of co-operative production. If co-operative production is not to remain a sham and a snare; if it is to supersede the Capitalist system; if united co-operative societies are to regulate national production upon a common plan, thus taking it under their own control, and putting an end to the constant anarchy and periodical convulsions which are the fatality of Capitalist production—what else, gentlemen, would it be but Communism, "possible" Communism?

The working class did not expect miracles from the Commune. They have no ready-made utopias to introduce *par décret du peuple*. They know that in order to work out their own emancipation, and along with it that higher form to which present society is irresistibly tending by its own economical agencies, they will have to pass through long struggles, through a series of historic processes, transforming circumstances and men. They have no ideals to realise, but to set free the elements of the new society with which old collapsing bourgeois society itself is pregnant. In the full consciousness of their historic mission, and with the heroic resolve to act up to it, the working class can afford to smile at the coarse invective of the gentlemen's gentlemen with the pen and ink-horn, and at the didactic patronage of well-wishing bourgeois-doctrinaires, pouring forth their ignorant platitudes and sectarian crotchets in the oracular tone of scientific infallibility.

When the Paris Commune took the management of the revolution in its own hands; when plain working men for the first time dared to infringe upon the Governmental privilege of their "natural superiors", and, under circumstances of unexampled difficulty, performed their work modestly, conscientiously, and efficiently,—performed it at salaries the highest of which barely amounted to one-fifth of what, according to high scientific authority,[a] is the minimum required for a secretary to a certain metropolitan school board,—the old world writhed in convulsions of rage at the sight of the Red Flag, the symbol of the Republic of Labour, floating over the Hôtel de Ville.

And yet, this was the first revolution in which the working class was openly acknowledged as the only class capable of social initiative, even by the great bulk of the Paris middle class—shopkeepers, tradesmen, merchants—the wealthy capitalists alone excepted. The Commune had saved them by a sagacious settlement of that ever-recurring cause of dispute among the middle classes themselves—the debtor and creditor accounts.[51] The same portion of the middle class, after they had assisted in putting down the working men's insurrection of June, 1848, had been at once unceremoniously sacrificed to their creditors[52] by the then Constituent Assembly. But this was not their only motive for now rallying round the working class. They felt that there was but one alternative—the Commune, or the Empire—under whatever name it might reappear. The Empire had ruined them economically by the havoc it made of public wealth, by the wholesale financial swindling it fostered, by the props it lent to the artificially accelerated centralisation of capital, and the concomitant expropriation of their own ranks. It had suppressed them politically, it had shocked them morally by its orgies, it had

---

[a] Professor Huxley. [*Note to the German edition of 1871.*]

insulted their Voltairianism by handing over the education of their children to the *frères Ignorantins*,[53] it had revolted their national feeling as Frenchmen by precipitating them headlong into a war which left only one equivalent for the ruins it made—the disappearance of the Empire. In fact, after the exodus from Paris of the high Bonapartist and capitalist *bohème*, the true middle-class Party of Order came out in the shape of the "Union Républicaine,"[54] enrolling themselves under the colours of the Commune and defending it against the willful misconstruction of Thiers. Whether the gratitude of this great body of the middle class will stand the present severe trial, time must show.

The Commune was perfectly right in telling the peasants that "its victory was their only hope."[55] Of all the lies hatched at Versailles and re-echoed by the glorious European penny-a-liner, one of the most tremendous was that the Rurals represented the French peasantry. Think only of the love of the French peasant for the men to whom, after 1815, he had to pay the milliard of indemnity.[56] In the eyes of the French peasant, the very existence of a great landed proprietor is in itself an encroachment on his conquests of 1789. The bourgeois, in 1848, had burdened his plot of land with the additional tax of forty-five cents in the franc; but then he did so in the name of the revolution; while now he had fomented a civil war against the revolution, to shift on to the peasant's shoulders the chief load of the five milliards of indemnity to be paid to the Prussian. The Commune, on the other hand, in one of its first proclamations, declared that the true originators of the war would be made to pay its cost. The Commune would have delivered the peasant of the blood tax,—would have given him a cheap government,—transformed his present blood-suckers, the notary, advocate, executor, and other judicial vampires, into salaried communal agents, elected by, and responsible to, himself. It would have freed him of the tyranny of the *garde champêtre*, the gendarme, and the prefect; would have put enlightenment by the schoolmaster in the place of stultification by the priest. And the French peasant is, above all, a man of reckoning. He would find it extremely reasonable that the pay of the priest, instead of being extorted by the tax-gatherer, should only depend upon the spontaneous action of the parishioners' religious instincts. Such were the great immediate boons which the rule of the Commune—and that rule alone—held out to the French peasantry. It is, therefore, quite superfluous here to expatiate upon the more complicated but vital problems which the Commune

162

alone was able, and at the same time compelled, to solve in favour of the peasant, *viz.*, the hypothecary debt, lying like an incubus upon his parcel of soil the *prolétariat foncier* (the rural proletariat), daily growing upon it, and his expropriation from it enforced, at a more and more rapid rate, by the very development of modern agriculture and the competition of capitalist farming.

The French peasant had elected Louis Bonaparte president of the Republic; but the Party of Order[57] created the Empire. What the French peasant really wants he commenced to show in 1849 and 1850, by opposing his *maire* to the Government's prefect, his schoolmaster to the Government's priest, and himself to the Government's gendarme. All the laws made by the Party of Order in January and February, 1850, were avowed measures of repression against the peasant.[58] The peasant was a Bonapartist, because the great Revolution, with all its benefits to him, was, in his eyes, personified in Napoleon. This delusion, rapidly breaking down under the Second Empire (and in its very nature hostile to the Rurals), this prejudice of the past, how could it have withstood the appeal of the Commune to the living interests and urgent wants of the peasantry?

The Rurals—this was, in fact, their chief apprehension—knew that three months' free communication of Communal Paris with the provinces would bring about a general rising of the peasants, and hence their anxiety to establish a police blockade around Paris, so as to stop the spread of the rinderpest.

If the Commune was thus the true representative of all the healthy elements of French society, and therefore the truly national Government, it was, at the same time, as a working men's Government, as the bold champion of the emancipation of labour, emphatically international. Within sight of the Prussian army, that had annexed to Germany two French provinces, the Commune annexed to France the working people all over the world.

The Second Empire had been the jubilee of cosmopolitan blacklegism, the rakes of all countries rushing in at its call for a share in its orgies and in the plunder of the French people. Even at this moment the right hand of Thiers is Ganesco, the foul Wallachian, and his left hand is Markóvsky, the Russian spy. The Commune admitted all foreigners to the honour of dying for an immortal cause. Between the foreign war lost by their treason, and the civil war fomented by their conspiracy with the foreign invader, the bourgeoisie had found the time to display their patriotism by organising police-hunts upon the Germans in France. The

Commune made a German working man[a] its Minister of Labour. Thiers, the bourgeoisie, the Second Empire, had continually deluded Poland by loud professions of sympathy, while in reality betraying her to, and doing the dirty work of, Russia. The Commune honoured the heroic sons of Poland[b] by placing them at the head of the defenders of Paris. And, to broadly mark the new era of history it was conscious of initiating, under the eyes of the conquering Prussians, on the one side, and of the Bonapartist army, led by Bonapartist generals, on the other, the Commune pulled down that colossal symbol of martial glory, the Vendôme column.[59]

The great social measure of the Commune was its own working existence. Its special measures could but betoken the tendency of a government of the people by the people. Such were the abolition of the nightwork of journeymen bakers; the prohibition, under penalty, of the employers' practice to reduce wages by levying upon their work-people fines under manifold pretexts,—a process in which the employer combines in his own person the parts of legislator, judge, and executor, and filches the money to boot. Another measure of this class was the surrender, to associations of workmen, under reserve of compensation, of all closed workshops and factories, no matter whether the respective capitalists had absconded or preferred to strike work.

The financial measures of the Commune, remarkable for their sagacity and moderation, could only be such as were compatible with the state of a besieged town. Considering the colossal robberies committed upon the city of Paris by the great financial companies and contractors, under the protection of Haussmann,[c] the Commune would have had an incomparably better title to confiscate their property than Louis Napoleon had against the Orleans family. The Hohenzollern and the English oligarchs, who both have derived a good deal of their estates from Church plunder, were, of course, greatly shocked at the Commune clearing but 8,000 *f.* out of secularisation.

---

[a] Leo Frankel.—*Ed.*
[b] J. Dąbrowski and W. Wróblewski.—*Ed.*
[c] During the Second Empire, Baron Haussmann was Prefect of the Department of the Seine, that is, of the City of Paris. He introduced a number of changes in the layout of the city for the purpose of facilitating the crushing of workers' insurrections.[*Note to the Russian edition of 1905 edited by V. I. Lenin.*]—*Ed.*

While the Versailles Government, as soon as it had recovered some spirit and strength, used the most violent means against the Commune; while it put down the free expression of opinion all over France, even to the forbidding of meetings of delegates from the large towns; while it subjected Versailles and the rest of France to an espionage far surpassing that of the Second Empire; while it burned by its gendarme inquisitors all papers printed at Paris, and sifted all correspondence from and to Paris; while in the National Assembly the most timid attempts to put in a word for Paris were howled down in a manner unknown even to the *Chambre introuvable* of 1816; with the savage warfare of Versailles outside, and its attempts at corruption and conspiracy inside Paris—would the Commune not have shamefully betrayed its trust by affecting to keep up all the decencies and appearances of liberalism as in a time of profound peace? Had the Government of the Commune been akin to that of M. Thiers, there would have been no more occasion to suppress Party-of-Order papers at Paris than there was to suppress Communal papers at Versailles.

It was irritating indeed to the Rurals that at the very same time they declared the return to the church to be the only means of salvation for France, the infidel Commune unearthed the peculiar mysteries of the Picpus nunnery, and of the Church of Saint Laurent.[60] It was a satire upon M. Thiers that, while he showered grand crosses upon the Bonapartist generals in acknowledgement of their mastery in losing battles, signing capitulations, and turning cigarettes at Wilhelmshöhe,[61] the Commune dismissed and arrested its generals whenever they were suspected of neglecting their duties. The expulsion from, and arrest by, the Commune of one of its members[a] who had slipped in under a false name, and had undergone at Lyons six days' imprisonment for simple bankruptcy, was it not a deliberate insult hurled at the forger, Jules Favre, then still the foreign minister of France, still selling France to Bismarck, and still dictating his orders to that paragon Government of Belgium? But indeed the Commune did not pretend to infallibility, the invariable attribute of all governments of the old stamp. It published its doings and sayings, it initiated the public into all its shortcomings.

In every revolution there intrude, at the side of its true agents, men of a different stamp; some of them survivors of and devotees to past revolutions, without insight into the present movement, but

---

[a] Blanchet.—*Ed.*

preserving popular influence by their known honesty and courage, or by the sheer force of tradition; others mere bawlers, who, by dint of repeating year after year the same set of stereotyped declamations against the Government of the day, have sneaked into the reputation of revolutionists of the first water. After the 18th of March, some such men did also turn up, and in some cases contrived to play pre-eminent parts. As far as their power went, they hampered the real action of the working class, exactly as men of that sort have hampered the full development of every previous revolution. They are an unavoidable evil: with time they are shaken off; but time was not allowed to the Commune.

Wonderful, indeed, was the change the Commune had wrought in Paris! No longer any trace of the meretricious Paris of the Second Empire. No longer was Paris the rendezvous of British landlords, Irish absentees,[62] American ex-slaveholders and shoddy men, Russian ex-serfowners, and Wallachian boyards. No more corpses at the morgue, no nocturnal burglaries, scarcely any robberies; in fact, for the first time, since the days of February, 1848, the streets of Paris were safe, and that without any police of any kind.

"We," said a member of the Commune, "hear no longer of assassination, theft and personal assault; it seems indeed as if the police had dragged along with it to Versailles all its Conservative friends."

The *cocottes* had refound the scent of their protectors—the absconding men of family, religion, and, above all, of property. In their stead, the real women of Paris showed again at the surface—heroic, noble, and devoted, like the women of antiquity. Working, thinking, fighting, bleeding Paris—almost forgetful, in its incubation of a new society, of the cannibals at its gates—radiant in the enthusiasm of its historic initiative!

Opposed to this new world at Paris, behold the old world at Versailles—that assembly of the ghouls of all defunct *régimes*, Legitimists and Orleanists, eager to feed upon the carcass of the nation,—with a tail of antediluvian Republicans, sanctioning, by their presence in the Assembly, the slaveholders' rebellion, relying for the maintenance of their Parliamentary Republic upon the vanity of the senile mountebank at its head, and caricaturing 1789 by holding their ghastly meetings in the *Jeu de Paume*.* There it was, this Assembly, the representative of everything dead in

---

Jeu de Paume: The tennis court where the National Assembly of 1789 adopted its famous decisions. [*Note to the German edition of 1871.*]

France, propped up to the semblance of life by nothing but the swords of the generals of Louis Bonaparte. Paris all truth, Versailles all lie; and that lie vented through the mouth of Thiers.

Thiers tells a deputation of the mayors of the Seine-et-Oise,—

"You may rely upon my word, which I have *never* broken!"

He tells the Assembly itself that "it was the most freely elected and most Liberal Assembly France ever possessed"; he tells his motley soldiery that it was "the admiration of the world, and the finest army France ever possessed"; he tells the provinces that the bombardment of Paris by him was a myth:

"If some cannon-shots have been fired, it is not the deed of the army of Versailles, but of some insurgents trying to make believe that they are fighting, while they dare not show their faces."

He again tells the provinces that

"the artillery of Versailles does not bombard Paris, but only cannonades it."

He tells the Archbishop of Paris that the pretended executions and reprisals (!) attributed to the Versailles troops were all moonshine. He tells Paris that he was only anxious "to free it from the hideous tyrants who oppress it," and that, in fact, the Paris of the Commune was "but a handful of criminals."

The Paris of M. Thiers was not the real Paris of the "vile multitude," but a phantom Paris, the Paris of the *francs-fileurs*,[63] the Paris of the Boulevards, male and female—the rich, the capitalist, the gilded, the idle Paris, now thronging with its lackeys, its blacklegs, its literary *bohème*, and its *cocottes* at Versailles, Saint-Denis, Rueil, and Saint-Germain; considering the civil war but an agreeable diversion, eyeing the battle going on through telescopes, counting the rounds of cannon, and swearing by their own honour and that of their prostitutes, that the performance was far better got up than it used to be at the Porte St. Martin. The men who fell were really dead; the cries of the wounded were cries in good earnest; and, besides, the whole thing was so intensely historical.

This is the Paris of M. Thiers, as the emigration of Coblenz[64] was the France of M. de Calonne.

IV

The first attempt of the slaveholders' conspiracy to put down Paris by getting the Prussians to occupy it, was frustrated by Bismarck's refusal. The second attempt, that of the 18th of March, ended in the rout of the army and the flight to Versailles of the Government, which ordered the whole administration to break up and follow in its track. By the semblance of peace negotiations with Paris, Thiers found the time to prepare for war against it. But where to find an army? The remnants of the line regiments were weak in number and unsafe in character. His urgent appeal to the provinces to succour Versailles, by their National Guards and volunteers, met with a flat refusal. Brittany alone furnished a handful of *Chouans*[65] fighting under a white flag, every one of them wearing on his breast the heart of Jesus in white cloth, and shouting *"Vive le Roi!"* (Long live the King!). Thiers was, therefore, compelled to collect, in hot haste, a motley crew, composed of sailors, marines, Pontifical Zouaves, Valentin's gendarmes, and Pietri's *sergents-de-ville* and *mouchards*. This army, however, would have been ridiculously ineffective without the instalments of imperialist war-prisoners, which Bismarck granted in numbers just sufficient to keep the civil war a-going, and keep the Versailles Government in abject dependence on Prussia. During the war itself, the Versailles police had to look after the Versailles army, while the gendarmes had to drag it on by exposing themselves at all posts of danger. The forts which fell were not taken, but bought. The heroism of the Federals convinced Thiers that the resistance of Paris was not to be broken by his own strategic genius and the bayonets at his disposal.

Meanwhile, his relations with the provinces became more and more difficult. Not one single address of approval came in to gladden Thiers and his Rurals. Quite the contrary. Deputations and addresses demanding, in a tone anything but respectful, conciliation with Paris on the basis of the unequivocal recognition of the Republic, the acknowledgement of the Communal liberties, and the dissolution of the National Assembly, whose mandate was extinct, poured in from all sides, and in such numbers that Dufaure, Thiers' Minister of Justice, in his circular of April 23 to the public prosecutors, commanded them to treat "the cry of conciliation" as a crime! In regard, however, of the hopeless prospect held out by his campaign, Thiers resolved to shift his tactics by ordering, all over the country, municipal elections to take place on the 30th of April, on the basis of the new municipal law dictated by himself to the National Assembly. What with the intrigues of his prefects, what with police intimidation, he felt quite sanguine of imparting, by the verdict of the provinces, to the

National Assembly that moral power it had never possessed, and of getting at last from the provinces the physical force required for the conquest of Paris.

His banditti-warfare against Paris, exalted in his own bulletins, and the attempts of his ministers at the establishment, throughout France, of a reign of terror, Thiers was from the beginning anxious to accompany with a little by-play of conciliation, which had to serve more than one purpose. It was to dupe the provinces, to inveigle the middle-class element in Paris, and, above all, to afford the professed Republicans in the National Assembly the opportunity of hiding their treason against Paris behind their faith in Thiers. On the 21st of March, when still without an army, he had declared to the Assembly:

"Come what may, I will not send an army to Paris."

On the 27th March he rose again:

"I have found the Republic an accomplished fact, and I am firmly resolved to maintain it."

In reality, he put down the revolution at Lyons and Marseilles[66] in the name of the Republic while the roars of his Rurals drowned the very mention of its name at Versailles. After this exploit, he toned down the "accomplished fact" into an hypothetical fact. The Orleans princes, whom he had cautiously warned off Bordeaux, were now, in flagrant breach of the law, permitted to intrigue at Dreux. The concessions held out by Thiers in his interminable interviews with the delegates from Paris and the provinces, although constantly varied in tone and colour, according to time and circumstances, did in fact never come to more than the prospective restriction of revenge to the

"handful of criminals implicated in the murder of Lecomte and Clément Thomas,"

on the well-understood premise that Paris and France were unreservedly to accept M. Thiers himself as the best of possible Republics, as he, in 1830, had done with Louis Philippe. Even these concessions he not only took care to render doubtful by the official comments put upon them in the Assembly through his Ministers. He had his Dufaure to act. Dufaure, this old Orleanist lawyer, had always been the justiciary of the state of siege, as now in 1871, under Thiers, so in 1839 under Louis Philippe, and in 1849 under Louis Bonaparte's presidency. While out of office he made a fortune by pleading for the Paris capitalists, and made political capital by pleading against the laws he had himself originated. He now hurried through the National Assembly not only a set of repressive laws which were, after the fall of Paris, to extirpate the last remnants of Republican liberty in France; he foreshadowed the fate of Paris by abridging the, for him, too slow procedure of courts-martial, and by a new-fangled, Draconic code of deportation. The Revolution of 1848, abolishing the penalty of death for political crimes, has replaced it by deportation. Louis Bonaparte did not dare, at least not in theory, to re-establish the *régime* of the guillotine. The Rural Assembly, not yet bold enough even to hint that the Parisians were not rebels, but assassins, had therefore to confine its prospective vengeance against Paris to Dufaure's new code of deportation. Under all these circumstances Thiers himself could not have gone on with his comedy of conciliation, had it not, as he intended it to do, drawn forth shrieks of rage from the Rurals, whose ruminating mind did neither understand the play, nor its necessities of hypocrisy, tergiversation, and procrastination.

In sight of the impending municipal elections of the 30th April, Thiers enacted one of his great conciliation scenes on the 27th April. Amidst a flood of sentimental rhetoric, he exclaimed from the tribune of the Assembly:

"There exists no conspiracy against the Republic but that of Paris, which compels us to shed French blood. I repeat it again and again. Let those impious arms fall from the hands which hold them, and chastisement will be arrested at once by an act of peace excluding only the small number of criminals."

To the violent interruption of the Rurals he replied:

"Gentlemen, tell me, I implore you, am I wrong? Do you really regret that I could have stated the truth that the criminals are only a handful? Is it not fortunate in the midst of our misfortunes that those who have been capable to shed the blood of Clément Thomas and General Lecomte are but rare exceptions?"

France, however, turned a deaf ear to what Thiers flattered himself to be a parliamentary siren's song. Out of 700,000 municipal councillors returned by the 35,000 communes still left to France, the united Legitimists, Orleanists and Bonapartists did not carry 8,000. The supplementary elections which followed were still more decidedly hostile. Thus, instead of getting from the provinces the badly-needed physical force, the National Assembly lost even its last claim to moral force, that of being the expression of the universal suffrage of the country. To complete the discomfiture, the newly chosen municipal councils of all the cities of France openly threatened the usurping Assembly at Versailles with a counter Assembly at Bordeaux.

170

Then the long-expected moment of decisive action had at last come for Bismarck. He peremptorily summoned Thiers to send to Frankfort plenipotentiaries for the definite settlement of peace. In humble obedience to the call of his master, Thiers hastened to despatch his trusty Jules Favre, backed by Pouyer-Quertier. Pouyer-Quertier, an "eminent" Rouen cotton-spinner, a fervent and even servile partisan of the Second Empire, had never found any fault with it save its commercial treaty with England prejudicial to his own shop interest. Hardly installed at Bordeaux as Thiers' Minister of Finance, he denounced that "unholy" treaty, hinted at its near abrogation, and had even the effrontery to try, although in vain (having counted without Bismarck), the immediate enforcement of the old protective duties against Alsace, where, he said, no previous international treaties stood in the way. This man, who considered counter-revolution as a means to put down wages at Rouen, and the surrender of French provinces as a means to bring up the price of his wares in France, was he not *the one* predestined to be picked out by Thiers as the helpmate of Jules Favre in his last and crowning treason?

On the arrival at Frankfort of this exquisite pair of plenipotentiaries, bully Bismarck at once met them with the imperious alternative: Either the restoration of the Empire, or the unconditional acceptance of my own peace terms! These terms included a shortening of the intervals in which the war indemnity was to be paid and the continued occupation of the Paris forts by Prussian troops until Bismarck should feel satisfied with the state of things in France; Prussia thus being recognised as the supreme arbiter in internal French politics! In return for this he offered to let loose, for the extermination of Paris, the captive Bonapartist army, and to lend them the direct assistance of Emperor William's troops. He pledged his good faith by making payment of the first instalment of the indemnity dependent on the "pacification" of Paris. Such a bait was, of course, eagerly swallowed by Thiers and his plenipotentiaries. They signed the treaty of peace on the 10th of May, and had it endorsed by the Versailles Assembly on the 18th.

In the interval between the conclusion of peace and the arrival of the Bonapartist prisoners, Thiers felt the more bound to resume his comedy of conciliation, as his Republican tools stood in sore need of a pretext for blinking their eyes at the preparations for the carnage of Paris. As late as the 8th of May he replied to a deputation of middle-class conciliators:

171

"Whenever the insurgents will make up their minds for capitulation, the gates of Paris shall be flung wide open during a week for all except the murderers of Generals Clément Thomas and Lecomte."

A few days afterwards, when violently interpellated on these promises by the Rurals, he refused to enter into any explanations; not, however, without giving them this significant hint:

"I tell you there are impatient men amongst you, men who are in too great a hurry. They must have another eight days; at the end of these eight days there will be no more danger, and the task will be proportionate to their courage and to their capacities."

As soon as MacMahon was able to assure him that he could shortly enter Paris, Thiers declared to the Assembly that

"he would enter Paris with the *laws* in his hands, and demand a full expiation from the wretches who had sacrificed the lives of soldiers and destroyed public monuments."

As the moment of decision drew near he said—to the Assembly, "I shall be pitiless!"—to Paris, that it was doomed; and to his Bonapartist banditti, that they had State licence to wreak vengeance upon Paris to their hearts' content. At last, when treachery had opened the gates of Paris to General Douay, on the 21st of May, Thiers, on the 22nd, revealed to the Rurals the "goal" of his conciliation comedy, which they had so obstinately persisted in not understanding.

"I told you a few days ago that we were approaching *our goal*; today I come to tell you *the goal* is reached. The victory of order, justice and civilisation is at last won!"

So it was. The civilisation and justice of bourgeois order comes out in its lurid light whenever the slaves and drudges of that order rise against their masters. Then this civilisation and justice stand forth as undisguised savagery and lawless revenge. Each new crisis in the class struggle between the appropriator and the producer brings out this fact more glaringly. Even the atrocities of the bourgeois in June, 1848, vanish before the ineffable infamy of 1871. The self-sacrificing heroism with which the population of Paris—men, women and children—fought for eight days after the entrance of the Versaillese, reflects as much the grandeur of their cause, as the infernal deeds of the soldiery reflect the innate spirit of that civilisation of which they are the mercenary vindicators. A glorious civilisation, indeed, the great problem of which is how to get rid of the heaps of corpses it made after the battle was over!

To find a parallel for the conduct of Thiers and his bloodhounds we must go back to the times of Sulla and the two Triumvirates of Rome. The same wholesale slaughter in cold blood; the same disregard, in massacre, of age and sex; the same system of torturing prisoners; the same proscriptions, but this time of a whole class; the same savage hunt after concealed leaders, lest one might escape; the same denunciations of political and private enemies; the same indifference for the butchery of entire strangers to the feud. There is but this difference, that the Romans had no *mitrailleuses* for the despatch, in the lump, of the proscribed, and that they had not "the law in their hands," nor on their lips the cry of "civilisation."

And after those horrors, look upon the other, still more hideous, face of that bourgeois civilisation as described by its own press!

"With stray shots," writes the Paris correspondent of a London Tory paper, "still ringing in the distance, and untended wounded wretches dying amid the tombstones of Père Lachaise — with 6,000 terror-stricken insurgents wandering in an agony of despair in the labyrinth of the catacombs, and wretches hurried through the streets to be shot down in scores by the *mitrailleuse*—it is revolting to see the *cafés* filled with the votaries of absinthe, billiards, and dominoes; female profligacy perambulating the boulevards, and the sound of revelry disturbing the night from the *cabinets particuliers* of fashionable restaurants."

M. Edouard Hervé writes in the *Journal de Paris*, a Versaillist journal suppressed by the Commune:

"The way in which the population of Paris (!) manifested its satisfaction yesterday was rather more than frivolous, and we fear it will grow worse as time progresses, Paris has now a *fête* day appearance, which is sadly out of place; and, unless we are to be called the *Parisiens de la décadence*, this sort of thing must come to an end."

And then he quotes the passage from Tacitus:

"Yet, on the morrow of that horrible struggle, even before it was completely over, Rome—degraded and corrupt—began once more to wallow in the voluptuous slough which was destroying its body and polluting its soul—*alibi proelia et vulnera*; *alibi balneae popinaeque* (here fights and wounds, there baths and restaurants)."

M. Hervé only forgets to say that the "population of Paris" he speaks of is but the population of the Paris of M. Thiers—the *francs-fileurs* returning in throngs from Versailles, Saint-Denis, Rueil and Saint-Germain—*the* Paris of the "Decline."

In all its bloody triumphs over the self-sacrificing champions of a new and better society, that nefarious civilisation, based upon the enslavement of labour, drowns the moans of its victims in a hue-and-cry of calumny, reverberated by a world-wide echo. The serene working men's Paris of the Commune is suddenly changed into a pandemonium by the bloodhounds of "order." And what does this tremendous change prove to the bourgeois mind of all countries? Why, that the Commune has conspired against civilisation! The Paris people die enthusiastically for the Commune in numbers unequalled in any battle known to history. What does that prove? Why, that the Commune was not the people's own government but the usurpation of a handful of criminals! The women of Paris joyfully give up their lives at the barricades and on the place of execution. What does this prove? Why, that the demon of the Commune has changed them into Megaeras and Hecates! The moderation of the Commune during two months of undisputed sway is equalled only by the heroism of its defence. What does that prove? Why, that for two months the Commune carefully hid, under a mask of moderation and humanity, the blood-thirstiness of its fiendish instincts, to be let loose in the hour of its agony!

The working men's Paris, in the act of its heroic self-holocaust, involved in its flames buildings and monuments. While tearing to pieces the living body of the proletariat, its rulers must no longer expect to return triumphantly into the intact architecture of their abodes. The Government of Versailles cries, "Incendiarism!" and whispers this cue to all its agents, down to the remotest hamlet, to hunt up its enemies everywhere as suspect of professional incendiarism. The bourgeoisie of the whole world, which looks complacently upon the wholesale massacre after the battle, is convulsed by horror at the desecration of brick and mortar!

When governments give state-licences to their navies to "kill, *burn* and destroy," is that a licence for incendiarism? When the British troops wantonly set fire to the Capitol at Washington and to the summer palace of the Chinese Emperor, was that incendiarism? When the Prussians, not for military reasons, but out of the mere spite of revenge, burned down, by the help of petroleum, towns like Châteaudun and innumerable villages, was that incendiarism? When Thiers, during six weeks, bombarded Paris, under the pretext that he wanted to set fire to those houses only in which there were people, was that incendiarism?—In war, fire is an arm as legitimate as any. Buildings held by the enemy are shelled to set them on fire. If their defenders have to retire, they themselves light the flames to prevent the attackers from making use of the buildings. To be burnt down has always been the inevitable fate of all buildings situated in the front of battle of all the regular armies of the world. But in the war of the enslaved against their enslavers, the only justifiable war in history, this is by no means to hold good! The Commune used fire strictly as a means of defence. They used it to stop up to the Versailles troops those long, straight avenues which Haussmann had expressly opened to artillery-fire; they used it to cover their retreat, in the same way as the Versaillese, in their advance, used their shells which destroyed at least as many buildings as the fire of the Commune. It is a matter of dispute, even now, which buildings were set fire to by the defence, and which by the attack. And the defence resorted to fire only then, when the Versaillese troops had already commenced their wholesale murdering of prisoners.—Besides, the Commune had, long before, given full public notice that, if driven to extremities, they would bury themselves under the ruins of Paris, and make Paris a second Moscow, as the Government of Defence, but only as a cloak for its treason, had promised to do. For this purpose Trochu had found them the petroleum. The Commune knew that its opponents cared nothing for the lives of the Paris people, but cared much for their own Paris buildings. And Thiers, on the other hand, had given them notice that he would be implacable in his vengeance. No sooner had he got his army ready on one side, and the Prussians shutting up the trap on the other, than he proclaimed: "I shall be pitiless! The expiation will be complete, and justice will be stern!" If the acts of the Paris working men were vandalism, it was the vandalism of defence in despair, not the vandalism of triumph, like that which the Christians perpetrated upon the really priceless art treasures of heathen antiquity; and even that vandalism has been justified by the historian as an unavoidable and comparatively trifling concomitant to the titanic struggle between a new society arising and an old one breaking down. It was still less the vandalism of Haussmann, razing historic Paris to make place for the Paris of the sightseer!

But the execution by the Commune of the sixty-four hostages, with the Archbishop of Paris at their head! The bourgeoisie and its army in June, 1848, re-established a custom which had long disappeared from the practice of war—the shooting of their defenceless prisoners. This brutal custom has since been more or less strictly adhered to by the suppressors of all popular commotions in Europe and India; thus proving that it constitutes a real "progress of civilisation!" On the other hand, the Prussians, in France, had re-established the practice of taking hostages—innocent men, who, with their lives, were to answer to them for the acts of others. When Thiers, as we have seen, from the very beginning of the conflict, enforced the humane practice of shooting down the Communal prisoners, the Commune, to protect their lives, was obliged to resort to the Prussian practice of securing hostages. The lives of the hostages had been forfeited over and over again by the continued shooting of prisoners on the part of the Versaillese. How could they be spared any longer after the carnage with which MacMahon's praetorians celebrated their entrance into Paris? Was even the last check upon the unscrupulous ferocity of bourgeois governments—the taking of hostages—to be made a mere sham of? The real murderer of Archbishop Darboy is Thiers. The Commune again and again had offered to exchange the archbishop, and ever so many priests in the bargain, against the single Blanqui, then in the hands of Thiers. Thiers obstinately refused. He knew that with Blanqui he would give to the Commune a head; while the archbishop would serve his purpose best in the shape of a corpse. Thiers acted upon the precedent of Cavaignac. How, in June 1848, did not Cavaignac and his men of order raise shouts of horror by stigmatising the insurgents as the assassins of Archbishop Affre! They knew perfectly well that the archbishop had been shot by the soldiers of order. M. Jacquemet, the archbishop's vicar-general, present on the spot, had immediately afterwards handed them in his evidence to that effect.

All this chorus of calumny, which the Party of Order never fail, in their orgies of blood, to raise against their victims, only proves that the bourgeois of our days considers himself the legitimate successor to the baron of old, who thought every weapon in his own hand fair against the plebeian, while in the hands of the plebeian a weapon of any kind constituted in itself a crime.

The conspiracy of the ruling class to break down the Revolution by a civil war carried on under the patronage of the foreign invader—a conspiracy which we have traced from the very 4th of September down to the entrance of MacMahon's praetorians through the gate of St. Cloud—culminated in the carnage of Paris. Bismarck gloats over the ruins of Paris, in which he saw perhaps the first instalment of that general destruction of great cities he had prayed for when still a simple Rural in the Prussian *Chambre introuvable* of 1849. He gloats over the cadavers of the Paris proletariat. For him this is not only the extermination of Revolution, but the extinction of France, now decapitated in reality, and by the French Government itself. With the shallowness characteristic of all successful statesmen, he sees but the surface of this tremendous historic event. Whenever before has history exhibited the spectacle of a conqueror crowning his victory by turning into, not only the gendarme, but the hired bravo of the conquered Government? There existed no war between Prussia and the Commune of Paris. On the contrary, the Commune had accepted the peace preliminaries, and Prussia had announced her neutrality. Prussia was, therefore, no belligerent. She acted the part of a bravo, a cowardly bravo, because incurring no danger; a hired bravo, because stipulating beforehand the payment of her blood-money of 500 millions on the fall of Paris. And thus, at last, came out the true character of the war, ordained by Providence as a chastisement of godless and debauched France by pious and moral Germany! And this unparalleled breach of the law of nations, even as understood by the old-world lawyers, instead of arousing the "civilised" Governments of Europe to declare the felonious Prussian Government, the mere tool of the St. Petersburg Cabinet, an outlaw amongst nations, only incites them to consider whether the few victims who escape the double cordon around Paris are not to be given up to the hangman at Versailles!

That after the most tremendous war of modern times, the conquering and the conquered hosts should fraternise for the common massacre of the proletariat—this unparalleled event does indicate, not, as Bismarck thinks, the final repression of a new society upheaving, but the crumbling into dust of bourgeois society. The highest heroic effort of which old society is still capable is national war; and this is now proved to be a mere governmental humbug, intended to defer the struggle of classes, and to be thrown aside as soon as that class struggle bursts out into civil war. Class-rule is no longer able to disguise itself in a national uniform; the national Governments are *one* as against the proletariat!

After Whit-Sunday, 1871, there can be neither peace nor truce possible between the working men of France and the appropriators of their produce. The iron hand of a mercenary soldiery may keep for a time both classes tied down in common oppression. But the battle must break out again and again in ever growing dimensions, and there can be no doubt as to who will be the victor in the end,—the appropriating few, or the immense working majority. And the French working class is only the advanced guard of the modern proletariat.

While the European governments thus testify, before Paris, to the international character of class-rule, they cry down the International Working Men's Association—the international counter-organisation of labour against the cosmopolitan conspiracy of capital—as the head fountain of all these disasters.

Thiers denounced it as the despot of labour, pretending to be its liberator. Picard ordered that all communications between the French Internationals and those abroad should be cut off; Count Jaubert, Thiers' mummified accomplice of 1835, declares it the great problem of all civilised governments to weed it out. The Rurals roar against it, and the whole European press joins the chorus. An honourable French writer,[a] completely foreign to our Association, speaks as follows:—

> "The members of the Central Committee of the National Guard, as well as the great part of the members of the Commune, are the most active, intelligent, and energetic minds of the International Working Men's Association; ... men who are thoroughly honest, sincere, intelligent, devoted, pure, and fanatical in the *good* sense of the word."

The police-tinged bourgeois mind naturally figures to itself the International Working Men's Association as acting in the manner of a secret conspiracy, its central body ordering, from time to time, explosions in different countries. Our Association is, in fact, nothing but the international bond between the most advanced working men in various countries of the civilised world. Wherever, in whatever shape, and under whatever conditions the class struggle obtains any consistency, it is but natural that members of our Association should stand in the foreground. The soil out of which it grows is modern society itself. It cannot be stamped out by any amount of carnage. To stamp it out, the Governments would have to stamp out the despotism of capital over labour—the condition of their own parasitical existence.

Working men's Paris, with its Commune, will be for ever celebrated as the glorious harbinger of a new society. Its martyrs are enshrined in the great heart of the working class. Its exterminators history has already nailed to that eternal pillory from which all the prayers of their priests will not avail to redeem them.

The General Council:

M. J. Boon, F. Bradnick, G. Butteri, Caihill, Delahaye, William Hales, A. Herman, Colb, F. Lessner, Lochner, J. P. MacDonnell, George Milner, Thomas Mottershead, Ch. Mills, Ch. Marri, Pfänder, Roch, Roshat, Rühl, Sadler, O. Serraillier, Cowell Stepney, Alf, Taylor, William Townshend

---

[a] Evidently Robinet.—*Ed.*

Corresponding Secretaries:

Eugène Dupont, *for France;* Karl Marx, *for Germany and Holland;* F. Engels, *for Belgium and Spain;* Hermann Jung, *for Switzerland;* P. Govaccini, *for Italy;* Zévy Maurice, *for Hungary;* Anton Zabicki, *for Poland;* James Cohn, *for Denmark;* J. G. Eccarius, *for the United States*

Hermann Jung, Chairman
John Weston, Treasurer
George Harris, Financial Secretary
John Hales, General Secretary

256, High Holborn, London,
Western Central, May 30, 1871

Written in April-May 1871

Marx and Engels,
Selected Works in 3 vols.,
Vol. 2, Moscow, 1976,
pp. 202-03, 208-41

KARL MARX

From

FIRST OUTLINE
OF THE CIVIL WAR
IN FRANCE

THE CHARACTER
OF THE COMMUNE

The *Commune*—the reabsorption of the state power by society as its own living forces instead of as forces controlling and subduing it, by the popular masses themselves, forming their own force instead of the organised force of their suppression—the political form of their social emancipation, instead of the artificial force appropriated by their oppressors (their own force opposed to and organised against them) of society wielded for their oppression by their enemies. This form was simple like all great things. The reaction of former revolutions—the time wanted for all historical developments, and in the past always lost in all revolutions in the very days of popular triumph, whenever it had rendered its victorious arms to be turned against itself—[the Commune] first displaced the army by the National Guard.

"For the first time since the 4th September the Republic is liberated from the *government of its enemies*.... In the city [is] a national militia that defends the citizens against the power *(the government) instead of a permanent army that defends the government* against the citizens." (*Proclamation* of Central Committee of 22 March.)[67]

(The people had only to organise this militia on a national scale, to have done away with the standing armies; the first economical *conditio sine qua non* for all social improvements, discarding at once this source of taxes and state debt, and this constant danger of government usurpation of class rule—of the regular class rule or an adventurer pretending to save all classes); at the same time the safest guarantee against foreign aggression and making in fact the costly military apparatus impossible in all other states; the emancipation of the peasant from the blood-tax and [from being] the most fertile source of all state taxation and state debts. Here

180

already [is] the point in which the Commune is a *bait for the peasant*, the first word of his emancipation. With the "in-dependent police" abolished, and its ruffians supplanted by ser-vants of the Commune. The general suffrage, till now abused either for the parliamentary sanction of the Holy State Power, or a play in the hands of the ruling classes, only employed by the people to sanction (choose the instruments of) parliamentary class rule once in many years, adapted to its real purposes, to choose by the Communes their own functionaries of administration and initiation. [Gone is] the delusion as if administration and political governing were mysteries, transcendent functions only to be trusted to the hands of a trained caste—state parasites, richly paid sycophants and sinecurists, in the higher posts, absorbing the intelligence of the masses and turning them against themselves in the lower places of the hierarchy. Doing away with the state hierarchy altogether and replacing the haughteous masters of the people by its always removable servants, a mock responsibility by a real responsibility, as they act continuously under public super-vision. Paid like skilled workmen, 12 pounds a month, the highest salary not exceeding £240 a year, a salary somewhat more than a fifth, according to a great scientific authority, Professor Huxley, [needed] to satisfy a clerk for the Metropolitan School Board. The whole sham of state mysteries and state pretensions was done away [with] by a Commune, mostly consisting of simple working men, organising the defence of Paris, carrying on war against the praetorians of Bonaparte, securing the supplies for that immense town, filling all the posts hitherto divided between government, police, and prefecture, doing their work publicly, simply, under the most difficult and complicated circumstances, and doing it, as Milton did his *Paradise Lost*, for a few pounds, acting in bright daylight, with no pretensions to infallibility, not hiding itself behind circumlocution offices, not ashamed to confess blunders by correcting them. Making in one order the public functions—military, administrative, political—*real workmen's functions*, instead of the hidden attributes of a trained caste; (keeping order in the turbulence of civil war and revolution) (initiating measures of general regeneration). Whatever the merits of the single measures of the Commune, its greatest measure was its own organisation, extemporised with the foreign enemy at one door, and the class enemy at the other, proving by its life its vitality, confirming its theories by its action. Its appearance was a victory over the victors of France. Captive Paris resumed by one bold spring the leadership of Europe, not depending on brute force, but by taking the lead of the social movement, by giving body to the aspirations of the working class of all countries.

With all the great towns organised into Communes after the model of Paris, no government could have repressed the movement by the surprise of sudden reaction. Even by this preparatory step the time of incubation, the guarantee of the movement, won. All France would have been organised into self-working and self-governing communes, the standing army replaced by the popular militias, the army of state parasites removed, the clerical hierarchy displaced by the schoolmasters, the state judge transformed into Communal organs, the suffrage for national representation not a matter of sleight of hand for an all-powerful government, but the deliberate expression of the organised Communes, the state functions reduced to a few functions for general national purposes.

Such is the *Commune—the political form of the social emancipation*, of the liberation of labour from the usurpation (slaveholding) of the monopolists of the means of labour, created by the labourers themselves or forming the gift of nature. As the state machinery and parliamentarism are not the real life of the ruling classes, but only the organised general organs of their dominion, the political guarantees and forms and expressions of the old order of things, so the Commune is not the social movement of the working class and, therefore, of a general regeneration of mankind, but the organised means of action. The Commune does not [do] away with the class struggles, through which the working classes strive for the abolition of all classes and, therefore, of all [class rule] (because it does not represent a peculiar interest. It represents the liberation of "labour", that is, the fundamental and natural condition of individual and social life which only by usurpation, fraud, and artificial contrivances can be shifted from the few upon the many), but it affords the rational medium in which that class struggle can run through its different phases in the most rational and humane way. It could start violent reactions and as violent revolutions. It begins the *emancipation of labour—* its great goal—by doing away with the unproductive and mischievous work of the state parasites, by cutting away the springs which sacrifice an immense portion of the national produce to the feeding of the state monster, on the one side, by doing, on the other, the real work of administration, local and national, for working men's wages. It begins therefore with an immense saving, with economical reform as well as political transformation.

The Communal organisation once firmly established on a national scale, the catastrophes it might still have to undergo would be sporadic slaveholders' insurrections, which, while for a moment interrupting the work of peaceful progress, would only accelerate the movement, by putting the sword into the hand of the Social Revolution.

The working classes know that they have to pass through different phases of class struggle. They know that the superseding of the economical conditions of the slavery of labour by the conditions of free and associated labour can only be the progressive work of time (that economical transformation), that they require not only a change of distribution, but a new organisation of production, or rather the delivery (setting free) of the social forms of production in present organised labour (engendered by present industry) of the trammels of slavery, of their present class character, and their harmonious national and international co-ordination. They know that this work of regeneration will be again and again relented and impeded by the resistance of vested interests and class egotisms. They know that the present "spontaneous action of the natural laws of capital and landed property" can only be superseded by "the spontaneous action of the laws of the social economy of free and associated labour" in a long process of development of new conditions, as was the "spontaneous action of the economic laws of slavery" and the "spontaneous action of the economical laws of serfdom". But they know at the same time that great strides may be [made] at once through the Communal form of political organisation and that the time has come to begin that movement for themselves and mankind.

PEASANTRY

(*War indemnity*.) Even before the instalment of the Commune, the Central Committee had declared through its *Journal Officiel*: "*The greater part of the war indemnity should be paid by the authors of war.*"[68] This is the great "conspiracy against civilisation" the men of order are most afraid of. It is the most practical question. With the Commune victorious, the authors of the war will have to pay its indemnity; with Versailles victorious, the producing masses who have already paid in blood, ruin, and contributions, will have again to pay, and the financial dignitaries will even contrive to make a profit out of the transaction. The liquidation of the war costs is to be decided by the civil war. The Commune represents on this vital point not only the interests of the working class, the petty middle class, in fact, all the middle class with the exception of the *bourgeoisie* (the wealthy capitalists) (the rich landowners and their state parasites). It represents above all the interests of the *French peasantry*. On them the greater part of the war taxes will be shifted, if Thiers and his Rurals are victorious. And people are silly enough to repeat the cry of the Rurals that they—the great landed proprietors—represent the peasant, who is of course, in the naivety of his soul, exceedingly anxious to pay for these good "landowners" the milliards of the war indemnity, who made him already pay the milliard of the Revolution indemnity!

The same men deliberately compromised the Republic of February by the additional 45 centimes tax on the peasant[69], but this they did in the name of the Revolution, in the name of the "provisional government" created by it. It is now in their own name that they wage a civil war against the Communal Republic to shift the war indemnity from their own shoulders upon those of the peasant! He will of course be delighted by it!

The Commune will abolish conscription, the Party of Order will fasten the blood-tax on the peasant. The Party of Order will fasten upon him the tax-collector for the payment of a parasitical and costly state machinery, the Commune will give him a cheap government. The Party of Order will continue [to] grind him down by the townish usurer, the Commune will free him of the incubus of the mortgages lasting upon his plot of land. The Commune will replace the parasitical judiciary body eating the heart of his income—the notary, the bailiff, etc.—[by] Communal agents doing their work at workmen's salaries, instead of enriching themselves out of the peasant's work. It will break down this whole judiciary cobweb which entangles the French peasant and gives abodes to the judiciary bench and mayors of the bourgeois spiders that suck his blood! The Party of Order will keep him under the rule of the gendarme, the Commune will restore him to independent social and political life! The Commune will enlighten him by the rule of the schoolmaster, the Party of Order [will] force upon him stultification by the rule of the priest! But the French peasant is above all a man of reckoning! He will find it exceedingly reasonable that the payment of the clergy will no longer [be] exacted from him by the tax-collector, but will be left to the "spontaneous action" of his religious instincts!

The French peasant had elected Louis Bonaparte President of the Republic, but the Party of Order (during the anonymous regime of the Republic under the Constituent and Legislative Assemblies) was the creator of the Empire! What the French peasant really wants, he commenced to show in 1849 and 1850 by opposing his mayor to the government's prefect, his schoolmaster to the government's parson, himself to the government's gendarme! The nucleus of the reactionary laws of the Party of Order in 1849—and peculiarly in January and February 1850—was specifically directed against the French peasantry! If the French peasant had made Louis Bonaparte President of the Republic, because in his tradition all the benefits he had derived from the first Revolution were fantastically transferred on the first Napoleon, the armed risings of peasants in some departments of France and the gendarme hunting upon them after the coup d'état proved that that delusion was rapidly breaking down! The Empire was founded on the artificially nourished delusions and traditional prejudices [of the peasant]; the Commune would be founded on his living interests and his real wants.

The hatred of the French peasant is centring on the "Rural", the man of the *château*, the man of the milliard of indemnity and the townish capitalist, masqueraded into a landed proprietor, whose encroachment upon him marched never more rapidly than under the Second Empire, partly fostered by artificial state means, partly naturally growing out of the very development of modern agriculture. The Rurals know that three months' rule of the Republican Commune in France would be the signal for the rising of the peasantry and the agricultural proletariat against them. Hence their ferocious hatred of the Commune! What they fear even more than the emancipation of the townish proletariat is the emancipation of the peasants! The peasants would soon acclaim the townish proletariat as their own leaders and seniors. There exists of course in France as in most continental countries a deep antagonism between the townish and rural producers, between the industrial proletariat and the peasantry. The aspiration of the proletariat, the material basis of its movement is labour organised on a grand scale, although now despotically organised, and the means of production centralised, although now centralised in the hands of the monopolist, not only as a means of production, but as a means of the exploitation and enslavement of the producer. What the Proletariat has to do is to transform the present capitalist character of that organised labour and those centralised means of labour, to transform them from the means of class rule and class exploitation into forms of free associated labour and social means of production. On the other hand, the labour of the peasant is insulated and the means of production are parcelled, dispersed. On these economical differences rests super-constructed a whole world of different social and political views. But this peasantry proprietorship has long since outgrown its normal phase, that is, the phase in which it was a reality, a mode of production and a form of property which responded to the economical wants of society and placed the rural producers themselves in normal conditions of life. It has entered its period of decay. On the one side, a large *prolétariat foncier* (rural proletariat) has grown out of it, whose interests are identical with those of the townish wages-labourers. The mode of production itself has become superannuated by the modern progress of agronomy. Lastly—the peasant proprietorship itself has become nominal, leaving to the peasant the delusion of proprietorship, and expropriating him from the fruits of his own labour. The competition of the great farm producers, the blood-tax, the state-tax, the usury of the townish mortgages and the multitudinous pilfering of the judiciary system thrown around him, have degraded him to the position of a Hindoo ryot, while expropriation—even expropriation from his nominal proprietorship—and his degradation into a rural proletarian is an everyday fact. What separates the peasant from the proletarian is, therefore, no longer his real interest, but his delusive prejudice. The Commune, as we have shown, is the only power that can give him immediate great boons even in its present economical conditions; it is the only form of government that can secure to him the transformation of his present economical conditions, rescue him from expropriation by the landlord, on the one hand, save him from grinding, trudging and misery on the pretext of proprietorship, on the other, that can convert his nominal proprietorship of the land into real proprietorship of the fruits of his labour, that can combine for him the profits of modern agronomy, dictated by social wants and every day now encroaching upon him as a hostile agency, without annihilating his position as a really independent producer. Being immediately benefited by the Communal Republic, he would soon confide in it.

That the workmen of Paris have taken the initiative of the present Revolution and in heroic self-sacrifice bear the brunt of this battle is nothing new. It is the striking fact of all French revolutions! It is only a repetition of the past! That the Revolution is made *in the name* and confessedly *for* the popular masses, that is, the producing masses, is a feature this Revolution has in common with all its predecessors. The new feature is that the people, after the first rise, have not disarmed themselves and surrendered their power into the hands of the Republican mountebanks of the ruling classes, that, by the constitution of the *Commune,* they have taken the actual management of their Revolution into their own hands and found at the same time, in case of success, the means to hold it in the hands of the people itself, displacing the state machinery, the governmental machinery of the ruling classes by a governmental machinery of their own. This is their ineffable crime! Workmen infringing upon the governmental privilege of the upper 10,000 and proclaiming their will to break the economical basis of that class despotism, which for its own sake wielded the organised state force of society! It is this that has thrown the respectable classes in Europe as in the United States into the paroxysm of convulsions and accounts for their shrieks of abomination about it being a blasphemy, their fierce appeals to assassination of the people, and the Billingsgate of abuse and calumny from their parliamentary tribunes and their journalistic servants' hall!

The greatest measure of the Commune is its own existence, working, acting under circumstances of unheard-of difficulty! The red flag, hoisted by the Paris Commune, crowns in reality only the government of the workmen of Paris! They have clearly, consciously proclaimed the Emancipation of Labour, and the transformation of Society, as their goal! But the actual "social" character of their Republic consists only in this, that workmen govern the Paris Commune! As to their measures, they must, by the nature of things, be principally confined to the military defence of Paris and its supply!

Some patronising friends of the working class, while hardly dissembling their disgust even at the few measures they consider "socialist", although there is nothing socialist in them except their tendency—express their satisfaction and try to coax genteel sympathies for the Paris Commune by the great discovery that after all workmen are rational men and whenever in power always resolutely turn their back upon socialist enterprises! They have in fact tried to establish in Paris neither a *phalanstère* nor an *Icarie*.[70] Wise men of their generation! These benevolent patronisers, profoundly ignorant of the real aspirations and the real movement of the working classes, forget one thing. All the socialist founders of sects belong to a period in which neither the working classes themselves were sufficiently trained and organised by the march of capitalist society itself to enter as historical agents upon the world's stage, nor were the material conditions of their emancipation sufficiently matured in the old world itself. Their misery existed, but the conditions of their own movement did not yet exist. The utopian founders of sects, while in their criticism of present society clearly describing the goal of the social movement, the super-session of the wages-system with all its economical conditions of class rule, found neither in society itself the material conditions of its transformation, nor in the working class the organised power and the conscience of the movement. They tried to compensate for the historical conditions of the movement by fantastic pictures and plans of a new society in whose propaganda they saw the true means of salvation. From the moment the working men's class movement became real, the fantastic utopias evanesced—not because the working class had given up the end aimed at by these Utopians, but because they had found the real means to realise them—but in their place came a real insight into the historical conditions of the movement and a more and more gathering force of the militant organisation of the working class. But the last two ends of the movement proclaimed by the Utopians are the last ends proclaimed by the Paris Revolution and by the International. Only the means are different and the real conditions of the movement are no longer clouded in utopian fables. These patronising friends of the proletariat, in glossing over the loudly proclaimed socialist tendencies of this Revolution, are therefore but the dupes of their own ignorance. It is not the fault of the Paris proletariat, if for them the utopian creations of the prophets of the working men's movement are still the "Social Revolution", that is to say, if the Social Revolution is for them still "utopian".

"Journal Officiel" of the Central Committee, March 20:

"The proletarians of the capital, amidst the *défaillances*[a] and the treasons of the governing (ruling) classes, have understood (*compris*) that the hour has arrived

---

[a] Insolvencies.— *Ed.*

for them *to save the situation by taking into their own hands the direction (management) of public affairs* (the state business)."

They denounce "the political incapacity and the moral decrepitude of the bourgeoisie" as the source of "the misfortunes of France".

"The workmen, who produce everything and enjoy nothing, who suffer from misery in the midst of their accumulated products, the fruit of their work and their sweat ... *shall they never be allowed to work for their emancipation?*... The proletariat, 'in face of the permanent menace against its rights, of the absolute negation of all its legitimate aspirations, of the ruin of the country and all its hopes, has understood that it was its imperious duty and its absolute right to take into its hands its own destinies and to assure its triumph in seizing the state power (en *s'emparant du pouvoir*)."

It is here plainly stated that the government of the working class is, in the first instance, necessary to save France from the ruin and the corruption impended upon it by the ruling classes, that the dislodgment of these classes from power (of these classes who have lost the capacity of ruling France) is *a necessity of national safety*.

But it is no less clearly stated that government by the working class can only save France and do the national business by working for its *own emancipation,* the conditions of that emancipation being at the same time the conditions of the regeneration of France.

It is proclaimed as a war of labour upon the monopolists of the means of labour, upon capital.

The *chauvinism* of the bourgeoisie is only a vanity, giving a national cloak to all their own pretensions. It is a means, by permanent armies, to perpetuate international struggles, to subjugate in each country the producers by pitching them against their brothers in each other country, a means to prevent the international co-operation of the working classes, the first condition of their emancipation. The true character of that chauvinism (long since become a mere phrase) has come out during the war of defence after Sedan, everywhere paralysed by the chauvinist bourgeoisie, in the capitulation of France, in the civil war carried on under that high priest of chauvinism, Thiers, on Bismarck's sufferance! It came out in the petty police intrigue of the Anti-German League,[71] [in] foreigner-hunting in Paris after the capitulation. It was hoped that the Paris people (and the French people) could be stultified into the passion of national hatred and by factitious outrages upon the foreigner forget its real aspiration and its home betrayers!

How this factitious movement has disappeared (vanished) before the breath of Revolutionary Paris! Loudly proclaiming its international tendencies—because the cause of the producer is every [where] the same and his enemy everywhere the same, whatever his nationality (in whatever national garb)—it proclaimed as a principle the admission of foreigners into the Commune, it even elected a foreign workman[a] (a member of the International) to its Executive, it decreed [the destruction of] the symbol of French chauvinism—the Vendôme Column!

And, while the bourgeois chauvinists have dismembered France, and act under the dictatorship of the foreign invasion, the Paris workmen have beaten the foreign enemy by striking at their own class rulers, have abolished frontiers, conquering the post as the vanguard of the workmen of all nations!

The genuine patriotism of the bourgeoisie—so natural for the real proprietors of the different "national" estates—has faded into a mere sham consequent upon the cosmopolitan character imprinted upon their financial, commercial, and industrial enterprise. Under similar circumstances it would explode in all countries as it did in France.

Written in
April-May 1871

Marx and Engels,
On the Paris Commune,
Moscow, 1976,
pp. 153-61, 164-68

---

[a] Leo Frankel.—*Ed.*

FREDERICK ENGELS

APROPOS
OF WORKING-CLASS
POLITICAL ACTION

REPORTER'S RECORD
OF THE SPEECH MADE
AT THE LONDON CONFERENCE
OF THE INTERNATIONAL
WORKING MEN'S ASSOCIATION,
SEPTEMBER 21, 1871

Complete abstention from political action is impossible. The abstentionist press participates in politics every day. It is only a question of how one does it, and of what politics one engages in. For the rest, to us abstention is impossible. The working-class party functions as a political party in most countries by now, and it is not for us to ruin it by preaching abstention. Living experience, the political oppression of the existing governments compels the workers to occupy themselves with politics whether they like it or not, be it for political or for social goals. To preach abstention to them is to throw them into the embrace of bourgeois politics. The morning after the Paris Commune, which has made proletarian political action an order of the day, abstention is entirely out of the question.

We want the abolition of classes. What is the means of achieving it? The only means is political domination of the proletariat. For all this, now that it is acknowledged by one and all, we are told not to meddle with politics. The abstentionists say they are revolutionaries, even revolutionaries *par excellence*. Yet revolution is a supreme political act and those who want revolution must also want the means of achieving it, that is, political action, which prepares the ground for revolution and provides the workers with the revolutionary training without which they are sure to become the dupes of the Favres and Pyats the morning after the battle. However, our politics must be working-class politics. The workers' party must never be the tagtail of any bourgeois party; it must be independent and have its goal and its own policy.

The political freedoms, the right of assembly and association, and the freedom of the press—those are our weapons. Are we to

191

sit back and abstain while somebody tries to rob us of them? It is said that a political act on our part implies that we accept the existing state of affairs. On the contrary, so long as this state of affairs offers us the means of protesting against it, our use of these means does not signify that we recognise the prevailing order.

Marx and Engels,
Selected Works in 3 vols.,
Vol. 2, Moscow, 1973, pp. 245-46

KARL MARX
FREDERICK ENGELS

From
PREFACE
TO THE GERMAN EDITION
OF THE MANIFESTO
OF THE COMMUNIST PARTY
OF 1872

However much the state of things may have altered during the last twenty-five years, the general principles laid down in this *Manifesto* are, on the whole, as correct today as ever. Here and there some detail might be improved. The practical application of the principles will depend, as the *Manifesto* itself states, everywhere and at all times, on the historical conditions for the time being existing, and, for that reason, no special stress is laid on the revolutionary measures proposed at the end of Section II. That passage would, in many respects, be very differently worded today. In view of the gigantic strides of Modern Industry in the last twenty-five years, and of the accompanying improved and extended party organisation of the working class, in view of the practical experience gained, first in the February Revolution, and then, still more, in the Paris Commune, where the proletariat for the first time held political power for two whole months, this programme has in some details become antiquated. One thing especially was proved by the Commune, *viz.*, that "the working class cannot simply lay hold of the ready-made State machinery, and wield it for its own purposes". (See *The Civil War in France, Address of the General Council of the International Working Men's Association*, London, Truelove, 1871, p. 15, where this point is further developed.) Further, it is self-evident that the criticism of socialist literature is deficient in relation to the present time, because it comes down only to 1847; also, that the remarks on the relation of the Communists to the various opposition parties (Section IV), although in principle still correct, yet in practice are antiquated, because the political situation has been entirely changed, and the

193

progress of history has swept from off the earth the greater portion of the political parties there enumerated.

But, then, the *Manifesto* has become a historical document which we have no longer any right to alter.

London, June 24, 1872

Marx and Engels,
Selected Works in 3 vols.,
Vol. 1, Moscow, 1976,
pp. 98-99

FREDERICK ENGELS

ON AUTHORITY

A number of Socialists have latterly launched a regular crusade against what they call the *principle of authority*.[72] It suffices to tell them that this or that act is *authoritarian* for it to be condemned. This summary mode of procedure is being abused to such an extent that it has become necessary to look into the matter somewhat more closely. Authority, in the sense in which the word is used here, means: the imposition of the will of another upon ours; on the other hand, authority presupposes subordination. Now, since these two words sound bad and the relationship which they represent is disagreeable to the subordinated party, the question is to ascertain whether there is any way of dispensing with it, whether—given the conditions of present-day society—we could not create another social system, in which this authority would be given no scope any longer and would consequently have to disappear. On examining the economic, industrial and agricultural conditions which form the basis of present-day bourgeois society, we find that they tend more and more to replace isolated action by combined action of individuals. Modern industry with its big factories and mills, where hundreds of workers supervise complicated machines driven by steam, has superseded the small workshops of the separate producers; the carriages and wagons of the highways have been substituted by railway trains, just as the small schooners and sailing feluccas have been by steamboats. Even agriculture falls increasingly under the dominion of the machine and of steam, which slowly but relentlessly put in the place of the small proprietors big capitalists, who with the aid of hired workers cultivate vast stretches of land. Everywhere combined action, the complication of processes dependent upon each other, displaces

195

independent action by individuals. But whoever mentions combined action speaks of organisation; now, is it possible to have organisation without authority?

Supposing a social revolution dethroned the capitalists, who now exercise their authority over the production and circulation of wealth. Supposing, to adopt entirely the point of view of the anti-authoritarians, that the land and the instruments of labour had become the collective property of the workers who use them. Will authority have disappeared or will it only have changed its form? Let us see.

Let us take by way of example a cotton spinning mill. The cotton must pass through at least six successive operations before it is reduced to the state of thread, and these operations take place for the most part in different rooms. Furthermore, keeping the machines going requires an engineer to look after the steam-engine, mechanics to make the current repairs, and many other labourers whose business it is to transfer the products from one room to another, and so forth. All these workers, men, women and children, are obliged to begin and finish their work at the hours fixed by the authority of the steam, which cares nothing for individual autonomy. The workers must, therefore, first come to an understanding on the hours of work; and these hours, once they are fixed, must be observed by all, without any exception. Thereafter particular questions arise in each room and at every moment concerning the mode of production, distribution of materials, etc., which must be settled at once on pain of seeing all production immediately stopped; whether they are settled by decision of a delegate placed at the head of each branch of labour or, if possible, by a majority vote, the will of the single individual will always have to subordinate itself, which means that questions are settled in an authoritarian way. The automatic machinery of a big factory is much more despotic than the small capitalists who employ workers ever have been. At least with regard to the hours of work one may write upon the portals of these factories: *Lasciate ogni autonomia, voi che entrate!*[a][73] If man, by dint of his knowledge and inventive genius, has subdued the forces of nature, the latter avenge themselves upon him by subjecting him; in so far as he employs them, to a veritable despotism independent of all social organisation. Wanting to abolish authority in large-scale industry is tantamount to wanting to abolish industry itself, to destroy the power loom in order to return to the spinning wheel.

---

[a] "Leave, ye that enter in, all autonomy behind!"—*Ed.*

Let us take another example—the railway. Here too the co-operation of an infinite number of individuals is absolutely necessary, and this co-operation must be practised during precisely fixed hours so that no accidents may happen. Here, too, the first condition of the job is a dominant will that settles all subordinate questions, whether this will is represented by a single delegate or a committee charged with the execution of the resolutions of the majority of persons interested. In either case there is very pronounced authority. Moreover, what would happen to the first train dispatched if the authority of the railway employees over the Hon. passengers were abolished?

But the necessity of authority, and of imperious authority at that, will nowhere be found more evident than on board a ship on the high seas. There, in time of danger, the lives of all depend on the instantaneous and absolute obedience of all to the will of one.

When I submitted arguments like these to the most rabid anti-authoritarians the only answer they were able to give me was the following: Yes, that's true, but here it is not a case of authority which we confer on our delegates, *but of a commission entrusted*! These gentlemen think that when they have changed the names of things they have changed the things themselves. This is how these profound thinkers mock at the whole world.

We have thus seen that, on the one hand, a certain authority, no matter how delegated, and, on the other hand, a certain subordination, are things which, independently of all social organisation, are imposed upon us together with the material conditions under which we produce and make products circulate.

We have seen, besides, that the material conditions of production and circulation inevitably develop with large-scale industry and large-scale agriculture, and increasingly tend to enlarge the scope of this authority. Hence it is absurd to speak of the principle of authority as being absolutely evil, and of the principle of autonomy as being absolutely good. Authority and autonomy are relative things whose spheres vary with the various phases of the development of society. If the autonomists confined themselves to saying that the social organisation of the future would restrict authority solely to the limits within which the conditions of production render it inevitable, we could understand each other; but they are blind to all facts that make the thing necessary and they passionately fight the word.

Why do the anti-authoritarians not confine themselves to crying out against political authority, the state? All Socialists are agreed that the political state, and with it political authority, will disappear as a result of the coming social revolution, that is, that public functions will lose their political character and be transformed into the simple administrative functions of watching over the true interests of society. But the anti-authoritarians demand that the authoritarian political state be abolished at one stroke, even before the social conditions that gave birth to it have been destroyed. They demand that the first act of the social revolution shall be the abolition of authority. Have these gentlemen ever seen a revolution? A revolution is certainly the most authoritarian thing there is; it is the act whereby one part of the population imposes its will upon the other part by means of rifles, bayonets and cannon—authoritarian means, if such there be at all; and if the victorious party does not want to have fought in vain, it must maintain this rule by means of the terror which its arms inspire in the reactionaries. Would the Paris Commune have lasted a single day if it had not made use of this authority of the armed people against the bourgeois? Should we not, on the contrary, reproach it for not having used it freely enough?

Therefore, either one of two things: either the anti-authoritarians don't know what they are talking about, in which case they are creating nothing but confusion; or they do know, and in that case they are betraying the movement of the proletariat. In either case they serve the reaction.

Written in October
1872- March 1873

Marx and Engels,
Selected Works in 3 vols.,
Vol. 2, Moscow, 1973,
pp. 376-79.

FREDERICK ENGELS

THE BAKUNINISTS AT WORK

**REVIEW OF THE UPRISING
IN SPAIN
IN THE SUMMER OF 1873**

Foreword

A few chronological data may help to make the following review more easily understood.

On February 9, 1873, King Amadeo, tired of wearing the Spanish crown, abdicated, thus becoming the first king ever to go on strike. On the 12th, a Republic was proclaimed, and immediately a new Carlist revolt broke out in the Basque Provinces.

On April 10, a Constituent Assembly was elected which met at the beginning of June, and on June 8 proclaimed a Federal Republic. On the 11th, a new government was formed under Pi y Margall. At the same time a commission was elected to draw up a new constitution, but the radical republicans, the so-called Intransigents, were excluded from it. When the new Constitution was announced on July 3, it did not go far enough for the Intransigents as regards the dismemberment of Spain into "independent cantons". The Intransigents therefore at once organised uprisings in the provinces. Between July 5th and 11th, the Intransigents triumphed in Seville, Córdoba, Granada, Málaga, Cádiz, Alcoy, Murcia, Cartagena, Valencia, etc., and set up an independent cantonal government in each of these towns. On July 18, Pi y Margall resigned and was replaced by Salmeron, who immediately sent troops against the insurgents. The latter were defeated in a few days after slight resistance; by July 26, with the fall of Cádiz, government power was restored throughout Andalusia and, almost simultaneously, Murcia and Valencia were subdued. Only Valencia fought with any energy.

Cartagena alone held out. This naval port, the largest in Spain, which had fallen to the insurgents together with the Navy, was defended on the landward side by a wall and thirteen separate forts, and was thus not easy to take. The government being not at all eager to destroy its own naval base, the "Sovereign Canton of Cartagena" survived until January 11, 1874, the day on which it finally capitulated, since in fact there was absolutely nothing else left for it to do.

All that concerns us here in this whole ignominious insurrection are the even more ignominious actions of the Bakuninist anarchists; only these are presented here in some detail, as a warning example to the contemporary world.

I

Thé report just published by the Hague Commission on the secret Alliance[74] of Mikhail Bakunin* [see the article *El Cagliostro Bakunin* in No. 87 et seq. of *Volksstaat*[75]] has brought to the attention of the labour world the intrigues, villainies and empty phrases by which it was intended to place the proletarian movement in the service of the swollen ambition and selfish designs of a few misunderstood geniuses. Meanwhile, these megalomaniacs have given us the opportunity in Spain to see something of their practical revolutionary activity. Let us see how they put into practice their ultra-revolutionary phrases on anarchy and autonomy, on the abolition of all authority, especially that of the State, and on the immediate and complete emancipation of the workers. We are at last in a position to do so now, since, apart from the newspaper reports on the events in Spain, we have before us the report sent to the Congress of Geneva by the New Madrid Federation of the International.

It is common knowledge that in Spain the schism in the International gave the upper hand to the members of the secret Alliance; the vast majority of Spanish workers joined them. When the Republic was proclaimed in February 1873, the Spanish members of the Alliance found themselves in a serious predicament. Spain is such a backward country industrially that there can be no question of *immediate* and complete emancipation of the working class. Spain will first have to pass through various stages of development and remove a considerable number of

---

* *L'Alliance de la Démocratie Socialiste*, London, 1873. The German edition was published under the title: *Ein Komplott gegen die Internationale* (Buchhandlung des *Vorwärts*). [*Note by Engels to the 1894 edition.*]

obstacles from its path. The Republic offered a chance of passing through these stages in the shortest possible time and quickly surmounting these obstacles. But this chance could only be made use of through the active *political* intervention of the Spanish working class. The working masses sensed this: everywhere they pressed to participate in events, to take advantage of the opportunity to act, instead of leaving the owning classes a clear field for action and intrigues, as had been hitherto the case. The government announced that elections were to be held to the Constituent Cortes. What stand should the International take? The Bakuninist leaders were in a quandary. Continued political inaction became more ridiculous and impossible with every passing day; the workers wanted "action". On the other hand, the members of the Alliance had been preaching for years that it was wrong to participate in any revolution that did not have as its goal the immediate and complete emancipation of the working class; that to undertake any political action implied recognition of the state, the source of all evil; and that, therefore, participation in any form of elections was a crime worthy of death. How they resolved the dilemma is recounted in the above-mentioned Madrid report.

"The same people who rejected the resolution of the General Congress at The Hague on the political action of the working class and trampled on the Rules of the International, thereby introducing division, conflict and disorder within the Spanish Federation; the same people who had the cheek to present us to the workers as ambitious power-seekers, who, under the pretext of bringing the working class to power, wish to seize power themselves; the same people who call themselves autonomists, anarchist revolutionaries, etc., have on this occasion thrown themselves enthusiastically into politics, but into the worst kind, bourgeois politics. They have worked not to give political power to the working class—an idea which they view with horror—but to help a bourgeois faction to gain control, a faction composed of adventurists, and ambitious power-seekers who call themselves Intransigent Republicans.

"On the eve of the general election for the Constituent Cortes, the workers of Barcelona, Alcoy and other places wanted to know what policy they should follow in the parliamentary and other struggles. Two large meetings were held for this purpose, one in Barcelona and the other in Alcoy. At both the Alliance made every effort to oppose a decision being reached on what policy the International" (their own, mark!) "should adopt. It was resolved that *the International, as an Association, should undertake no political action whatsoever; but that its members, as individuals, could act as they wished and join any party that suited them,* according to their famous principle of autonomy! What was the result of the application of such an outlandish doctrine? That the majority of members of the International, including the anarchists, took part in the elections with no programme, no banner, and no candidates, thereby contributing to the fact that almost exclusively bourgeois republicans were elected, with the exception of two or three workers who represent absolutely nothing, whose voice has not once been raised in defence of the interests of our class and who calmly vote for any of the reactionary proposals advanced by the majority."

This is what Bakuninist "political abstention" leads to. In peaceful times when the proletariat knows in advance that the most it can achieve is to get a few deputies into parliament and that it has no chance at all of gaining a parliamentary majority, it may be possible to convince the workers here or there that it is a great revolutionary action to stay at home during elections and, in general, instead of attacking the concrete State in which we live and which oppresses us, to attack an abstract State that exists nowhere, and therefore cannot defend itself. This is a magnificent way of playing the revolutionary for people who are easily disheartened; and just how much the Alliance leaders belong to this kind of people is shown in detail in the report on the Alliance mentioned at the beginning.

However, as soon as events themselves push the proletariat into the foreground, abstentionism becomes a tangible absurdity, and the active intervention of the working class is an unavoidable necessity. This was the case in Spain. The abdication of Amadeo ousted the radical monarchists[76] from power and from the possibility of recovering it in the near future; the Alfonsists[77] were for the time being in even greater disarray; the Carlists, as they almost invariably do, preferred civil war[78] to an election struggle. All these parties abstained in true Spanish style. Only the Federal Republicans, divided into two groups, and the bulk of the workers took part in the elections. Given the tremendous fascination that the name of the International still exerted at the time on the workers of Spain and given the excellent organisation which, at least for practical purposes, the Spanish Section still preserved, it was certain that in the factory districts of Catalonia, in Valencia, in the towns of Andalusia, etc., all the candidates nominated and supported by the International would have achieved a brilliant victory, producing a sufficiently strong minority in the Cortes to decide the issue every time it came to a vote between the two Republican groups. The workers felt this; they felt the time had come to set their still powerful organisation in motion. But the honourable leaders of the Bakuninist school had long been preaching the gospel of unconditional abstention, and could not suddenly reverse course; and so they invented that lamentable way out of having the International abstain as a body, but allowing individual members to vote *as they liked*. The result of this declaration of political bankruptcy was that the workers, as always in such cases, voted for those who appeared to be the most radical, the Intransigents, and thus, feeling themselves more or less responsible for the subsequent steps taken by their deputies, became involved in them.

II

The members of the Alliance could nót possibly persist in the ridiculous position in which their cunning electoral policy had put them; it would have meant the end of their current domination of the International in Spain. They had to act for appearance sake. Salvation lay in a *general strike*.

In the Bakuninist programme, a general strike is the lever for unleashing social revolution. One fine morning, the workers in all the industries of a country, even of the whole world, stop work and, in four weeks at the maximum, oblige the ruling classes to surrender, or to attack the workers, thereby giving the latter the right to defend themselves and use this opportunity to tear down the whole of the old society. The idea is far from new; the French Socialists, and later the Belgian, have ridden this horse repeatedly since 1848. Actually, however, it is originally English-bred. During the rapid and intense development of Chartism among the English workers following the crisis of 1837, the "holy month" of national strike was preached as early as 1839 (see Engels, *The Condition of the Working-Class in England*, Second Edition, p. 234[79]); and the idea so resounded that the factory workers of Northern England tried putting it into practice in July 1842. At the Alliance Congress held in Geneva on September 1, 1873, also a major role was attributed to general strike, although it was recognised by all that a complete organisation of the working class and a full kitty were necessary. This indeed was the problem. On the one hand, the governments, especially if encouraged by political abstentionism, will never allow the organisation or the funds of the workers to go so far; and on the other hand the political actions and abuses of the ruling classes will promote the emancipation of the workers long before the proletariat manages to achieve this ideal organisation and this vast reserve fund. And 'f it did have them, then it would not need to resort to a general strike to achieve its purpose.

Anybody who knows anything at all about the secret intrigues of the Alliance cannot doubt that the idea of using this well-tried method emanated from the Swiss centre. Be that as it may, the Spanish leaders saw it as a means of doing something without turning directly "political" and seized it with delight. Everywhere the miraculous properties of a general strike were being preached and preparations were at once made in Barcelona and Alcoy to begin it.

Meanwhile, political affairs were relentlessly developing towards a crisis. Castelar and company, the old federal republican boasters, were frightened by the movement which had outgrown them; there was nothing left for them to do but to surrender power to Pi y Margall, who attempted to come to an agreement with the Intransigents. Of all the republican officials, Pi was the only Socialist, the only one who understood the necessity for the Republic to rely on the workers. He also at once presented a programme of social measures for immediate implementation. which were not only directly beneficial to the workers, but whose results would entail further steps and would thus at least set the social revolution in motion. But the Bakuninists in the International, who are obliged to reject even the most revolutionary measures when these emanate from the "State", preferred to support the biggest swindlers among the Intransigents rather than a minister. Pi's negotiations with the Intransigents dragged on. The Intransigents began to lose patience; and the most passionate of them began the cantonal uprising in Andalusia. The time had come for the leaders of the Alliance to act too if they did not want merely to be towed along by the bourgeois Intransigents. They thus ordered the general strike.

In Barcelona the following poster, among others, appeared on the walls:

"Workers! We are calling a general strike to show the profound repugnance we feel on seeing the government send in the army against our brother workers, while hardly bothering about the war against the Carlists", etc.

In other words the workers of Barcelona—the most important industrial centre in Spain, which has seen more barricade fighting in its history than any other city in the world—were invited to confront the armed power of the government, not with arms in their hands, but with ... a general strike, with a means that only directly affects individual bourgeois, but not their collective representative—state power. The workers in Barcelona had been able, in the inactivity of peacetime, to listen to the militant phrases of docile men like Alerini, Farga Pellicer and Viñas; but when the time came for action, Alerini, Farga Pellicer and Viñas first announced their famous election programme, then attempted to calm passions, and finally, instead of issuing a call to arms, declared a general strike, provoking the general contempt of the workers.

However, even the weakest of the Intransigents showed more energy than the strongest member of the Alliance. The Alliance and the sections of the International it had deceived lost all their influence, and when these gentlemen called for a general strike, on the pretext of paralysing the government, the workers simply laughed at them. But one thing at least which the activity of the false International achieved was to ensure that Barcelona took no part in the cantonal uprising. In Barcelona the working-class element was strongly represented everywhere, and Barcelona was the only city whose participation could firmly back up this working-class element, thereby giving it the opportunity of eventually becoming master of the whole movement. Moreover, the participation of Barcelona would have made its triumph as good as certain. But Barcelona did not raise a finger; the Barcelona workers, who knew the Intransigents only too well and had been deceived by the Alliance, did nothing, thereby ensuring the ultimate triumph of the Madrid government. All of which did not prevent Alerini and Brousse, members of the Alliance (details about whom are to be found in the report on the Alliance), from declaring in their newspaper *Solidarité révolutionnaire*.[80]

"The revolutionary movement is spreading like wildfire throughout the peninsula.... In Barcelona *nothing has yet happened, but in the market place the revolution is permanent!*"

But it was the revolution of all Alliance, which consists in keeping up an oratorial barrage, and for this reason remains "permanently" in the same "place".

The general strike was on the agenda at the same time in Alcoy. Alcoy is a recently created industrial centre with a population of some 30,000, in which the International, in the Bakuninist form, had only penetrated a year before and at once developed apace. Socialism, in any form, was well received by these workers, who had hitherto remained outside the movement, as is sometimes the case in certain backward places in Germany, where the General Association of German Workers suddenly acquires a large number of ephemeral adherents. Alcoy was thus chosen for the headquarters of the Spanish Bakuninist Federal Commission, and it is this Federal Commission that we are here going to see in action.

On July 7, a workers' meeting voted in support of the general strike, and the following day sent a deputation to the alcalde (mayor), asking him to summon together the factory-owners within twenty-four hours and present them with the workers' demands.

Alcalde Albors, a bourgeois republican, stalled off the workers, sent to Alicante for troops and advised the factory-owners not to give in to the workers' demands, but to barricade themselves in their houses. As for himself, he would remain at his post. After a meeting with the factory-owners—we are following the official report of the Alliance Federal Commission, dated July 14, 1873—the alcalde, who had originally promised the workers to remain neutral, issues a proclamation in which he "insults and slanders the workers and takes the side of the factory-owners, thus destroying the rights and liberty of the strikers and challenging them to do battle". Just how the pious wishes of a mayor could destroy the rights and liberty of the strikers is not made clear. Anyway, the workers led by the Alliance informed the municipal council, via a commission, that if it did not intend to uphold its promised neutrality in the strike, it had better resign to avoid a conflict. The commission was turned away, and as it was leaving the town hall the police fired on the unarmed people peacefully assembled in the square. That was how the struggle began, according to the Alliance report. The people armed themselves, and a battle began that was to last "twenty hours". On one side, the workers, which *Solidarité révolutionnaire* numbers at 5,000; on the other, 32 gendarmes in the town hall, and several other armed individuals, barricaded in four or five houses round the market place, which the people burnt down in good Prussian manner. Eventually, the gendarmes ran out of ammunition and had to surrender.

"There would have been less misfortunes to lament," says the Alliance report, "had not Alcalde Albors deceived the people by pretending to surrender and then treacherously murdering those who entered the town hall, trusting his word; and the alcalde himself would not have perished as he did at the hands of the justly indignant people, had he not fired his revolver point-blank at those who went to arrest him."

What were the casualties in this battle?

"Although it is impossible to calculate exactly the number of dead and wounded" (on the people's side), "they certainly amount to *no less than ten*. On the part of the provokers, there were no less than *fifteen* dead and wounded."

This was the Alliance's first street battle. For twenty hours, 5,000 people fought against 32 gendarmes and a few armed bourgeois, and beat them after the latter had run out of ammunition, losing *ten men* in all. It would appear that the Alliance has successfully taught its followers to be guided by Falstaff's wise words "the better part of valour is discretion".[81]

Naturally the terrible reports in the bourgeois press of factories burnt down for no reason at all, gendarmes shot en masse, people having petrol poured over them and being set ablaze, are pure inventions. The victorious workers, even when led by the Alliance, whose motto is "Break, destroy!", are always far too generous with their defeated opponents to act thus, so that the latter accuse them of all the atrocities they never fail to commit themselves when they are victorious.

And so victory was achieved.

"In Alcoy," *Solidarité révolutionnaire* declares jubilantly, "our friends, numbering 5,000, are masters of the situation."

Let us see what these "masters" did with their "situation".

At this point the Alliance report and the Alliance newspaper leave us completely in the lurch and we have to rely on ordinary press reports. From the latter we learn that a "Committee of Public Safety", that is to say, a revolutionary government, was immediately set up in Alcoy. Although at the Alliance Congress held at Saint-Imier (Switzerland) on September 15, 1872, it was agreed that "any organisation of a political power, so-called provisional or revolutionary power, can only be a new fraud and would be just as dangerous to the proletariat as all existing governments". Moreover, the members of the Spanish Federal Commission, meeting in Alcoy, did their utmost to get the Congress of the Spanish Section of the International to adopt this decision as its own. Yet, in spite of all this, we find Severino Albarracin, a member of that commission, and, according to some reports, its secretary Francisco Tomas, too, becoming members of this provisional and revolutionary government, the Alcoy Committee of Public Safety!

And what did this Committee of Public Safety do? What measures did it adopt to bring about the "immediate and complete emancipation of the workers"? It forbade any man to leave the town, allowing women to do so, provided they ... had a *pass*! The enemies of all authority re-establishing the pass system! What is more, there reigned complete confusion, complete inactivity and complete ineptitude.

Meanwhile, General Velarde was advancing from Alicante with troops. The government had every reason for wishing to put down the local insurrections in the provinces quietly. And the "masters of the situation" in Alcoy had every reason to wish to extricate themselves from a situation in which they were at a loss as to what to do. Thus, deputy Cervera, acting as mediator, had an easy time of it. The Committee of Public Safety resigned, and the troops entered the town on July 12 without encountering the slightest resistance, the only condition made by the Committee of Public Safety being ... general amnesty. The Alliance "masters of the situation" had thus avoided the issue once again. And this marked the end of the Alcoy adventure.

At Sanlúcar de Barrameda, near Cádiz, the Alliance report relates,

"the alcalde closed down the International's premises and by his threats and incessant attacks on the personal rights of the citizens provoked the anger of the workers. A commission demanded of the minister observation of the law and the reopening of the premises which had been arbitrarily closed down. Señor Pi agreed in principle but refused to comply in practice; the workers saw that the government was systematically trying to outlaw their Association, and dismissed the local authorities, replacing them with others who ordered the reopening of the Association's premises".

"In Sanlúcar ... the people are masters of the situation!" *Solidarité révolutionnaire* declares triumphantly. The Aliancistas, who here too, contrary to their anarchist principles, formed a revolutionary government, did not know what to do with their power. They wasted time in empty debates and paper resolutions, and on the 5th of August, after occupying Seville and Cádiz, General Pavía sent a few companies from Soria's brigade to Sanlúcar and ... met with no resistance whatsoever.

Such were the heroic deeds performed by the Alliance where it had no competition.

III

Immediately after the street battle in Alcoy, the Intransigents rose up in Andalusia. Pi y Margall was still in power and engaged in continuous negotiations with the leaders of this party with the object of forming a ministry with them. What, then, was the point of beginning an uprising while negotiations were still in progress? It has not been possible to determine the reason for this haste; one thing is certain, however, and that is that the Intransigents were eager to establish the federal republic in practice as quickly as possible, in order to seize power and the many new governmental posts that would be created in the separate cantons. In Madrid, the Cortes were delaying the dismemberment of Spain too long; and so it was time to take matters into one's own hands and proclaim sovereign cantons everywhere. The attitude hitherto maintained by the members of the International (the Bakuninists), deeply involved since the elections in the actions of the Intransigents, made it possible to count on their support. They had, after all, just seized power in Alcoy by force, and were thus in open conflict with the government. Moreover, the Bakuninists had been preaching for years that all revolutionary action from above was pernicious and that everything should be organised and carried out from below. And here they were with the opportunity to implement the famous principle of autonomy from below, at least in a few towns. It could not be otherwise; the Bakuninist workers swallowed the bait and began to draw the chestnuts from the fire for the Intransigents, only to be rewarded later by their allies, as ever, with kicks and bullets.

What was the position of the Bakuninist International in this whole movement? They helped to give it the character of federalist atomisation and realised their ideal of anarchy as far as was possible. The same Bakuninists who a few months before in Córdoba had pronounced anathema on the establishment of revolutionary governments, declaring such to be treason and a swindle for the workers, now participated in all the municipal revolutionary governments of Andalusia, but always in a minority, so that the Intransigents were able to do exactly as they wished. The latter monopolised the political and military leadership of the movement, dismissing the workers with a few fine speeches or a few resolutions on social reforms of a most crude and ridiculous nature, which anyway only existed on paper. Whenever the Bakuninist leaders requested some real, positive concession, they rejected it scornfully. On being questioned by English newspaper correspondents, the Intransigents who led the movement hastened to declare that they had nothing at all to do with the so-called "members of the International", were in no way responsible for their actions, and that they were keeping its leaders and all the fugitives from the Paris Commune under strict police surveillance. Finally, as we shall see, in Seville, during the battle with the government troops, the Intransigents also fired on their Bakuninist allies.

Thus, within a few days, the whole of Andalusia was in the hands of the armed Intransigents. Seville, Málaga, Granada, Cádiz, etc., fell to them almost without resistance. Each town declared itself an independent canton and set up a revolutionary junta. Murcia, Cartagena and Valencia followed suit. A similar attempt, but of a more pacific nature, was made in Salamanca. Thus the majority of Spain's large cities were in the hands of the insurgents, with the exception of the capital, Madrid—simply a city of luxury, which hardly ever assumes a decisive role—and Barcelona. Had Barcelona revolted, ultimate success would have been almost certain, and at the same time it would have ensured solid support for the worker element in the movement. But we have already seen how in Barcelona the Intransigents were practically powerless and the Bakuninists, although very strong there at the time, chose general strike as a means of *avoiding the issue*. Thus, this time Barcelona was not at its post.

Nevertheless, this insurrection, although begun in a hair-brained manner, would have had a good chance of success if only it had been conducted with some intelligence—if only in the manner of Spanish military revolts, in which the garrison in one town rises, marches to the next town, talks over the garrison there and leads it away with it, and growing like an avalanche, advances on the capital, until a fortunate engagement or the desertion to its side of the troops sent out against it decides the victory. This method was especially suitable to the present occasion. The insurgents had long been organised everywhere into volunteer battalions, whose discipline was, it is true, pathetic, but certainly no worse than that of the remnants of the old, largely demoralised Spanish army. The only troops on which the government could rely were the gen- darmes (*guardias civiles*), and these were scattered all over the country. The main task was thus to prevent the gendarmes from concentrating, and this could only be done by assuming the offensive in the open field. There was little risk involved in this since the government was only able to oppose the volunteers with troops as undisciplined as they themselves. This was the only way to win.

But no. The federalism of the Intransigents and their Bakuninist appendix actually consisted in leaving each city to fend for itself, insisting on the importance not of co-operation with the other towns but separation from them, thus preventing any possibility of a general offensive. What was an unavoidable evil in the German Peasant War and the German uprisings of May 1849—the disunity and isolation of the revolutionary forces, which enabled the same government troops to go around suppressing one revolt after another—was here declared to be the principle of supreme revolutionary wisdom. Bakunin had this satisfaction. Back in September 1870 (in his *Lettres à un français*) he had declared that

210

the only way of driving the Prussians from France by a revolutionary struggle was to abolish all centralised leadership and leave every city, every village, every community to wage war for itself. One had only to oppose the Prussian army with its single command, with the outburst of revolutionary passions, and victory was certain. Faced by the collective intelligence of the French people, finally restored to it, the individual intelligence of Moltke would, naturally, vanish. The French just would not understand that then, but in Spain Bakunin had achieved a brilliant triumph, as we have already seen and shall yet see.

Meanwhile, this rash uprising, sparked off without any motive at all, made it impossible for Pi y Margall to continue negotiations with the Intransigents. He was forced to resign, and was replaced by pure republicans like Castelar, undisguised bourgeois, whose first aim was to crush the workers' movement, which they had formerly made use of but which was now a hindrance to them. One division was formed under the command of General Pavía to be sent against Andalusia, and another, under General Campos, to be sent against Valencia and Cartagena. The nucleus of these divisions were gendarmes drawn from all over Spain, all old soldiers whose discipline was still intact. As was the case in the attacks of the Versailles army on Paris, the gendarmes were once again called upon to hold together the demoralised military forces and to always take the head of the attacking columns, tasks which they accomplished to the best of their abilities. Apart from these, the divisions contained some composite line regiments, so that each of them numbered some 3,000 men. This was all the government could mobilise against the insurgents.

General Pavía set out by July 20. On the 24th, Córdoba was occupied by a detachment of gendarmes and troops of the line under Ripoll. On the 29th, Pavía launched an attack on barricaded Seville which fell to him on the 30th or the 31st (the telegrams are contradictory). Leaving a mobile column to put down the surrounding countryside, he advanced on Cádiz, whose defenders only fought on the approaches to the city, and even then with little spirit, and then, on August 4, allowed themselves to be disarmed without resistance. In the next few days, Pavía disarmed, also without resistance, Sanlúcar de Barrameda, San Roque, Tarifa, Algeciras, and a multitude of other small towns, all of which had set themselves up as independent cantons. At the same time he sent detachments against Málaga and Granada, which surrendered without firing a shot on the 3rd and 8th of August respectively; so that by August 10, in less than a fortnight and almost without a struggle, the whole of Andalusia had been subdued.

On July 26, Martínez Campos mounted his attack on Valencia. Here the insurrection had been started by the workers. When the schism in the Spanish International took place, the real International had obtained the majority in Valencia and the new Spanish Federal Council was transferred there. Shortly after the proclamation of the Republic, when revolutionary battles were clearly imminent, the Bakuninist workers of Valencia, mistrusting the Barcelona leaders who masked appeasement with ultra-revolutionary phrases, promised the real International that they would make common cause with them in all local movements. When the cantonal movement broke out, both immediately struck together and, making use of the Intransigents, dislodged the government's troops. It is not known what the composition of the Valencia junta was; however, from the reports of English press correspondents it is clear that in it, as in the Valencian Volunteers, the workers were definitely in the majority. These same correspondents spoke of the Valencian insurgents with a respect which they were far from according to the other rebels, predominantly Intransigents. They praised their discipline and the order that reigned in the city and predicted protracted resistance and a fierce struggle. They were not mistaken. Valencia, an open city, resisted the attacks of Martínez Campos' division from July 26 to August 8, that is to say, for longer than the whole of Andalusia put together.

In the province of Murcia, the capital of the same name was occupied without resistance. After the fall of Valencia, Martínez Campos marched on Cartagena, one of the best-defended strongholds in Spain, protected on the landward side by a wall and a series of separate forts on the dominating heights. The 3,000 government soldiers, without any siege artillery, were naturally powerless with their light field weapons against the heavy artillery of the forts, and had to limit themselves to laying siege to the city from the landward side. This did not mean much, however, as long as the people of Cartagena dominated the sea with the warships they had captured in the port. The insurgents, who while the struggle had been going on in Valencia and Andalusia had only bothered about themselves, began to think about the outside world after most of the revolts had been quelled, when they began to run short of money and provisions. Only then was an attempt made to march on Madrid, which lay at least 60 German miles away, more than twice as far as, for example, Valencia or Granada! The expedition ended in disaster not far from Cartagena; and the siege put an end to any further attempts at a land sortie. They then took to making attacks with the fleet. And what attacks! There could be no question of inciting the recently subdued coastal towns to a fresh revolt with Cartagenan warships. The Navy of the Sovereign Canton of Cartagena thus limited itself to threatening to bombard most of the coastal towns from Valencia to Málaga—which according to the Cartagenan theory were also sovereign—and when necessary to actually bombarding them, if they failed to bring on board the requested provisions and war contribution in hard cash. While these cities had been up in arms against the government as sovereign cantons, the principle of "every man for himself" reigned in Cartagena! Now that they had been defeated, the principle of "everyone for Cartagena" was proclaimed. That was how the Intransigents of Cartagena and their Bakuninist associates understood federation of sovereign cantons.

In order to reinforce the ranks of the freedom fighters, the government of Cartagena set free 1,800 prisoners from the town gaol, the worst thieves and murderers in all Spain. In the light of the information revealed in the report on the Alliance, there is no doubt at all but that this revolutionary measure was suggested to them by the Bakuninists. The report shows how Bakunin dreams of the "releasing of all evil passions" and how he presents the Russian robber as a model for all true revolutionaries. What is alright for the Russians must do for the Spaniards. The government of Cartagena was acting completely in the spirit of Bakunin when it freed the "evil passions" of 1,800 locked-up thugs, thereby taking demoralisation among its troops to the limit. And when the Spanish Government, instead of pounding its own fortifications to dust, awaited the fall of Cartagena through the internal disintegration of its defenders, it was following a perfectly correct policy.

IV

Let us now take a look at what the report of the New Madrid Federation has to say of the whole of this movement:

"The Congress was due to be held in Valencia on the second Sunday in August. Among other things it had the important task of determining the attitude of the Spanish Federation towards the serious political events taking place in Spain since February. Il, the day on which the Republic was proclaimed. But the scruffy cantonal uprising, so pathetically abortive, in which members of the International took an

213

active part in almost all the insurgent provinces, has not only paralysed the Federal Council, by dispersing most of its members, but has almost completely disorganised the local federations, drawing upon their individual members—and this is the worst part about it—all the hatred and persecution that a clumsily handled and defeated uprising always entails....

"When the cantonal movement broke out and the juntas, or cantonal governments, were set up, those same people" (the Bakuninists) "who cried out so strongly against political power and accused us so violently of authoritarianism, lost no time in joining those governments. And in such important towns as Seville, Cádiz, Sanlúcar de Barrameda, Granada and Valencia many of those members of the International who call themselves anti-authoritarians participated in the cantonal juntas, with no programme other than the autonomy of the province or canton. This is officially proved by the proclamations and other documents issued by the above-mentioned juntas, which bear the names of well-known members of the International.

"Such a flagrant contradiction between theory and practice, between propaganda and action, would not mean much if such behaviour had led, or could have led, to any advantage for our Association, any progress towards the organisation of our forces, or have brought us any nearer the achievement of our basic aim, the emancipation of the working class. But in fact the contrary happened, as it was bound to, in the absence of collective action on the part of the Spanish proletariat, which could have been so easily achieved by acting in the name of the International, in the absence of agreement between the local federations, with the result that the movement was abandoned to individual or local initiative, with no leadership *other than that which could be imposed on it by the mysterious Alliance, which unfortunately still rules the Spanish Section of the International,* and with no programme other than that of our natural enemies, the bourgeois republicans. Thus it was that the cantonal uprising succumbed in a shameful manner, almost without resistance, dragging with it in its fall the prestige and organisation of the Spanish International. There is no excess, crime or act of violence that the republicans today do not lay at the door of the International; we are even reliably informed that in Seville, during the battle, the Intransigents fired on their own allies, members of the International" (Bakuninists). "Reaction, taking clever advantage of our follies, is inciting the republicans to persecute us, at the same time arousing impartial people against us; what they were unable to achieve in the time of Sagasta they are accomplishing now. Today, the name of the International in Spain is abhorred even by the working masses.

"In Barcelona, many workers' sections have withdrawn from the International in protest against the men of the newspaper *Le Federación*" (main organ of the Bakuninists) "and against their inexplicable behaviour; in Jerez, Puerto de Santa Maria and other places, the federations have dissolved themselves; in Loja (Granada Province) the few members of the International that lived there have been expelled by the local population; in Madrid, where the greatest freedom is enjoyed, the Old Federation" (Bakuninist) "shows not the slightest signs of life, while our own is forced to remain inactive and silent in order to avoid taking the blame for other people's sins. In towns in the North the increasingly bitter Carlist war prevents us from undertaking anything. Finally, in Valencia, where the government won after a two-week siege, members who did not flee are forced to remain in hiding. The Federal Council has completely dissolved."

So much for the Madrid report. As we see, it fully coincides with the above historical account.

214

Let us now look at the results of our investigation.

1. As soon as they were confronted with a serious revolutionary situation, the Bakuninists were compelled to throw their whole previous programme overboard. To begin with they sacrificed their dogma of political, and above all electoral, abstention. Then came the turn of anarchy, the abolition of the State; instead of abolishing the State, they tried, on the contrary, to set up a number of new small states. They went on to abandon their principle that the workers must not participate in any revolution that did not have as its aim the immediate and complete emancipation of the proletariat, and took part in a movement whose purely bourgeois character was patently evident. Finally, they trampled underfoot the principle they themselves had only just proclaimed—that the establishment of a revolutionary government is but a new deception and a new betrayal of the working class—by comfortably installing themselves in the government juntas of the separate towns, moreover almost always as an impotent minority, paralysed and politically exploited by the bourgeois.

2. Denying the principles they had always preached, they did so in the most cowardly and false manner and under the pressure of a guilty conscience; neither the Bakuninists themselves nor the masses they led joined the movement with any programme, or any idea at all of what they wanted. What was the natural outcome of this? It was that the Bakuninists either obstructed any movement, as in Barcelona; or found themselves drawn into isolated, unplanned and senseless uprisings, as in Alcoy and Sanlúcar de Barrameda; or that leadership of the insurrection fell into the hands of the bourgeois Intransigents,[82] as happened in the majority of cases. Thus, when it came to action, the ultra-revolutionary cries of the Bakuninists gave way to evasion, uprisings doomed to defeat in advance, or adherence to a bourgeois party which not only subjected the workers to the most shameful political exploitation but even rewarded them with blows.

3. All that remains of the so-called principles of anarchy, free federation of independent groups, etc., is the boundless, senseless disintegration of the revolutionary means of struggle, which enabled the government to subdue one town after another with a handful of troops, practically unresisted.

4. The final outcome of this whole farce is that not only has the once so numerous and well-organised Spanish International—both the false and the authentic—found itself involved in the

collapse of the Intransigents so that it is today *de facto* dissolved, but, moreover, that all sorts of invented crimes without which the philistines of all countries cannot imagine a workers' revolt are being heaped upon it, thereby making impossible, at least for many years to come, the International reorganisation of the Spanish proletariat.

5. In a word, the Spanish Bakuninists have given us an unsurpassed example of how *not* to make a revolution.

Written in September-
October 1873

Frederick Engels,
The Bakuninists at Work,
Moscow, 1971, pp. 5-24

KARL MARX

From
CRITIQUE
OF THE
GOTHA PROGRAMME[83]

LETTER
TO WILHELM BRACKE
IN BRUNSWICK

London, May 5, 1875

Dear Bracke,

When you have read the following critical marginal notes on the Unity Programme, would you be so good as to send them on to Geib and Auer, Bebel and Liebknecht for their perusal. I am exceedingly busy and have to overstep by far the limit of work allowed me by the doctors. Hence it was anything but a "pleasure" to write such a lengthy screed. It was however necessary so that steps taken by me later on would not be misinterpreted by our friends in the Party for whom this communication is intended.

For after the Unity Congress has been held, Engels and I will publish a short statement to the effect that our position is altogether remote from the said programme of principles and that we have nothing to do with it.

This is unavoidable because the opinion—the entirely erroneous opinion—is held abroad and assiduously nurtured by enemies of the Party that we secretly guide from here the movement of what is known as the Eisenach Party.[84] In a Russian book[a] that has recently appeared, Bakunin still makes me responsible, for example, not only for all the programmes, etc., of that party, but even for every step taken by Liebknecht from the day when he started to co-operate with the People's Party.[85]

Apart from this, it is my duty not to give recognition, even by diplomatic silence, to what in my opinion is a quite objectionable programme that demoralises the Party.

Every step of real movement is more important than a dozen

---

[a] M. Bakunin, *State and Anarchy.—Ed.*

217

programmes. If, therefore, it was not possible—and the conditions of the time did not permit it—to go *beyond* the Eisenach programme, one should simply have concluded an agreement for action against the common enemy. But by drawing up a programme of principles (instead of postponing this until the way has been prepared for it by a considerable period of common activity) one sets up before the whole world landmarks by which it measures the level of the Party movement.

The Lassallean leaders[86] came because circumstances forced them to. If at the outset they had been told that haggling about principles was out of the question, they would *have had* to be content with a programme of action or a plan of organisation for common action. Instead of this, one permits them to arrive armed with mandates and recognises these mandates as binding, thus surrendering unconditionally to those who are themselves in need of help. To crown the whole business, they are holding a congress *before* the *Congress of Compromise*, while one's own party is holding its congress *post festum*. One had obviously had a desire to dispose of all criticism by a sleight of hand and to give one's own party no opportunity for reflection. One knows that the mere fact of unification is satisfying to the workers, but it is a mistake to believe that this momentary success is not bought too dearly.

Incidentally, the programme is no good, even apart from its sanctification of the Lassallean articles of faith....

Yours,
Karl Marx

MARGINAL NOTES
TO THE PROGRAMME
OF THE GERMAN
WORKERS' PARTY

I

1. "Labour is the source of all wealth and all culture, *and since* useful labour is possible only in society and through society, the proceeds of labour belong undiminished with equal right to all members of society."

First Part of the Paragraph: "Labour is the source of all wealth and all culture."

Labour is *not the source* of all wealth. *Nature* is just as much the source of use values (and it is surely of such that material wealth consists!) as labour, which itself is only the manifestation of a force of nature, human labour-power. The above phrase is to be found in all children's primers and is correct in so far as it is *implied* that labour is performed with the appurtenant subjects and instruments. But a socialist programme cannot allow such bourgeois phrases to pass over in silence the *conditions* that alone give them meaning. And in so far as man from the beginning behaves towards nature, the primary source of all instruments and subjects of labour, as an owner, treats her as belonging to him, his labour becomes the source of use values, therefore also of wealth. The bourgeois have very good grounds for falsely ascribing *super-natural creative power* to labour; since precisely from the fact that labour depends on nature it follows that the man who possesses no other property than his labour-power must, in all conditions of society and culture, be the slave of other men who have made themselves the owners of the material conditions of labour. He can work only with their permission, hence live only with their permission.

Let us now leave the sentence as it stands, or rather limps. What would one have expected in conclusion? Obviously this:

"Since labour is the source of all wealth, no one in society can appropriate wealth except as the product of labour. Therefore, if he himself does not work, he lives by the labour of others and also acquires his culture at the expense of the labour of others."

Instead of this, by means of the verbal rivet *"and since"* a second proposition is added in order to draw a conclusion from this and not from the first one.

Second Part of the Paragraph: "Useful labour is possible only in society and through society."

According to the first proposition, labour was the source of all wealth and all culture; therefore no society is possible without labour. Now we learn, conversely, that no "useful" labour is possible without society.

One could just as well have said that only in society can useless and even socially harmful labour become a branch of gainful occupation, that only in society can one live by being idle, etc., etc.—in short, one could just as well have copied the whole of Rousseau.

And what is "useful" labour? Surely only labour which produces the intended useful result. A savage—and man was a savage after he had ceased to be an ape—who kills an animal with a stone, who collects fruits, etc., performs "useful" labour.

Thirdly. The Conclusion: "And since useful labour is possible only in society and through society, the proceeds of labour belong undiminished with equal right to all members of society."

A fine conclusion! If useful labour is possible only in society and through society, the proceeds of labour belong to society—and only so much therefrom accrues to the individual worker as is not required to maintain the "condition" of labour, society.

In fact, this proposition has at all times been made use of *by the champions of the state of society prevailing at any given time.* First come the claims of the government and everything that sticks to it, since it is the social organ for the maintenance of the social order; then come the claims of the various kinds of private property, for the various kinds of private property are the foundations of society,

220

etc. One sees that such hollow phrases can be twisted and turned as desired.

The first and second parts of the paragraph have some intelligible connection only in the following wording:

"Labour becomes the source of wealth and culture only as social labour," or, what is the same thing, "in and through society."

This proposition is incontestably correct, for although isolated labour (its material conditions presupposed) can create use values, it can create neither wealth nor culture.

But equally incontestable is this other proposition:

"In proportion as labour develops socially, and becomes thereby a source of wealth and culture, poverty and destitution develop among the workers, and wealth and culture among the non-workers."

This is the law of all history hitherto. What, therefore, had to be done here, instead of setting down general phrases about "labour" and "society," was to prove concretely how in present capitalist society the material, etc., conditions have at last been created which enable and compel the workers to lift this social curse.

In fact, however, the whole paragraph, bungled in style and content, is only there in order to inscribe the Lassallean catchword of the "undiminished proceeds of labour" as a slogan at the top of the party banner. I shall return later to the "proceeds of labour," "equal right," etc., since the same thing recurs in a somewhat different form further on.

> 2. "In present-day society, the instruments of labour are the monopoly of the capitalist class; the resulting dependence of the working class is the cause of misery and servitude in all its forms."

This sentence, borrowed from the Rules of the International, is incorrect in this "improved" edition.

In present-day society the instruments of labour are the monopoly of the landowners (the monopoly of property in land is even the basis of the monopoly of capital) *and* the capitalists. In the passage in question, the Rules of the International do not mention either the one or the other class of monopolists. They speak of the "*monopoliser of the means of labour, that is, the sources of life.*" The addition, "*sources of life,*" makes it sufficiently clear that land is included in the instruments of labour.

The correction was introduced because Lassalle, for reasons now generally known, attacked *only* the capitalist class and not the landowners. In England, the capitalist is usually not even the owner of the land on which his factory stands.

"Promotion of the instruments of labour to the common property" ought obviously to read their "conversion into the common property"; but this only in passing.

What are "*proceeds of labour*"? The product of labour or its value? And in the latter case, is it the total value of the product or only that part of the value which labour has newly added to the value of the means of production consumed?

"Proceeds of labour" is a loose notion which Lassalle has put in the place of definite economic conceptions.

What is "a fair distribution"?

Do not the bourgeois assert that the present-day distribution is "fair"? And is it not, in fact, the only "fair" distribution on the basis of the present-day mode of production? Are economic relations regulated by legal conceptions or do not, on the contrary, legal relations arise from economic ones? Have not also the socialist sectarians the most varied notions about "fair" distribution?

To understand what is implied in this connection by the phrase "fair distribution," we must take the first paragraph and this one together. The latter presupposes a society wherein "the instruments of labour are common property and the total labour is co-operatively regulated," and from the first paragraph we learn that "the proceeds of labour belong undiminished with equal right to all members of society."

"To all members of society"? To those who do not work as well? What remains then of the "undiminished proceeds of labour?" Only to those members of society who work? What remains then of the "equal right" of all members of society?

But "all members of society" and "equal right" are obviously mere phrases. The kernel consists in this, that in this communist society every worker must receive the "undiminished" Lassallean "proceeds of labour."

Let us take first of all the words "proceeds of labour" in the sense of the product of labour; then the co-operative proceeds of labour are the *total social product*.

From this must now be deducted:

"*First*, cover for replacement of the means of production used up.

Secondly, additional portion for expansion of production.

Thirdly, reserve or insurance funds to provide against accidents, dislocations caused by natural calamities, etc.

These deductions from the "undiminished proceeds of labour" are an economic necessity and their magnitude is to be determined according to available means and forces, and partly by computations of probabilities but they are in no way calculable by equity.

There remains the other part of the total product, intended to serve as means of consumption.

Before this is divided among the individuals, there has to be deducted again, from it:

First, the general costs of administration not belonging to production.

This part will, from the outset, be very considerably restricted in comparison with present-day society and it diminishes in proportion as the new society develops.

Secondly, that which is intended for the common satisfaction of needs, such as schools, health services, etc.

From the outset this part grows considerably in comparison with present-day society and it grows in proportion as the new society develops.

Thirdly, funds for those unable to work, etc., in short, for what is included under so-called official poor relief today.

Only now do we come to the "distribution" which the programme, under Lassallean influence, alone has in view in its narrow fashion, namely, to that part of the means of consumption which is divided among the individual producers of the co-operative society.

The "undiminished proceeds of labour" have already unnoticeably become converted into the "diminished" proceeds, although what the producer is deprived of in his capacity as a private individual benefits him directly or indirectly in his capacity as a member of society.

Just as the phrase of the "undiminished proceeds of labour" has disappeared, so now does the phrase of the "proceeds of labour" disappear altogether.

Within the co-operative society based on common ownership of the means of production, the producers do not exchange their products; just as little does the labour employed on the products appear here *as the value* of these products, as a material quality possessed by them, since now, in contrast to capitalist society, individual labour no longer exists in an indirect fashion but directly as a component part of the total labour. The phrase "proceeds of labour," objectionable also today on account of its ambiguity, thus loses all meaning.

What we have to deal with here is a communist society, not as it has *developed* on its own foundations, but, on the contrary, just as it *emerges* from capitalist society; which is thus in every respect, economically, morally and intellectually, still stamped with the birth-marks of the old society from whose womb it emerges. Accordingly, the individual producer receives back from society—after the deductions have been made—exactly what he gives to it. What he has given to it is his individual quantum of labour. For example, the social working day consists of the sum of the individual hours of work; the individual labour time of the individual producer is the part of the social working day contributed by him, his share in it. He receives a certificate from society that he has furnished such and such an amount of labour (after deducting his labour for the common funds), and with this certificate he draws from the social stock of means of consumption as much as costs the same amount of labour. The same amount of labour which he has given to society in one form he receives back in another.

Here obviously the same principle prevails as that which regulates the exchange of commodities, as far as this is exchange of equal values. Content and form are changed, because under the altered circumstances no one can give anything except his labour, and because, on the other hand, nothing can pass to the ownership of individuals except individual means of consumption. But, as far as the distribution of the latter among the individual producers is concerned, the same principle prevails as in the exchange of commodity equivalents: a given amount of labour in one form is exchanged for an equal amount of labour in another form.

Hence, *equal right* here is still in principle—*bourgeois right*, although principle and practice are no longer at loggerheads, while the exchange of equivalents in commodity exchange only exists *on the average* and not in the individual case.

In spite of this advance, this *equal right* is still constantly stigmatised by a bourgeois limitation. The right of the producers is *proportional* to the labour they supply; the equality consists in the fact that measurement is made with an *equal standard*, labour.

But one man is superior to another physically or mentally and so supplies more labour in the same time, or can labour for a longer

224

time; and labour, to serve as a measure, must be defined by its duration or intensity, otherwise it ceases to be a standard of measurement. This *equal* right is an unequal right for unequal labour. It recognises no class differences, because everyone is only a worker like everyone else; but it tacitly recognises unequal individual endowment and thus productive capacity as natural privileges. *It is, therefore, a right of inequality, in its content, like every right.* Right by its very nature can consist only in the application of an equal standard; but unequal individuals (and they would not be different individuals if they were not unequal) are measurable only by an equal standard in so far as they are brought under an equal point of view, are taken from one *definite* side only, for instance, in the present case, are regarded *only as workers* and nothing more is seen in them, everything else being ignored. Further, one worker is married, another not; one has more children than another, and so on and so forth. Thus, with an equal performance of labour, and hence an equal share in the social consumption fund, one will in fact receive more than another, one will be richer than another, and so on. To avoid all these defects, right instead of being equal would have to be unequal.

But these defects are inevitable in the first phase of communist society as it is when it has just emerged after prolonged birth pangs from capitalist society. Right can never be higher than the economic structure of society and its cultural development conditioned thereby.

In a higher phase of communist society, after the enslaving subordination of the individual to the division of labour, and therewith also the antithesis between mental and physical labour, has vanished; after labour has become not only a means of life but life's prime want; after the productive forces have also increased with the all-round development of the individual, and all the springs of co-operative wealth flow more abundantly—only then can the narrow horizon of bourgeois right be crossed in its entirety and society inscribe on its banners: From each according to his ability, to each according to his needs!

I have dealt more at length with the "undiminished proceeds of labour," on the one hand, and with "equal right" and "fair distribution," on the other, in order to show what a crime it is to attempt, on the one hand, to force on our Party again, as dogmas, ideas which in a certain period had some meaning but have now become obsolete verbal rubbish, while again perverting, on the other, the realistic outlook, which it cost so much effort to instil

225

into the Party but which has now taken root in it, by means of ideological nonsense about right and other trash so common among the democrats and French Socialists.

Quite apart from the analysis so far given, it was in general a mistake to make a fuss about so-called *distribution* and put the principal stress on it.

Any distribution whatever of the means of consumption is only a consequence of the distribution of the conditions of production themselves. The latter distribution, however, is a feature of the mode of production itself. The capitalist mode of production, for example, rests on the fact that the material conditions of production are in the hands of non-workers in the form of property in capital and land, while the masses are only owners of the personal condition of production, of labour-power. If the elements of production are so distributed, then the present-day distribution of the means of consumption results automatically. If the material conditions of production are the co-operative property of the workers themselves, then there likewise results a distribution of the means of consumption different from the present one. Vulgar socialism (and from it in turn a section of the democracy) has taken over from the bourgeois economists the consideration and treatment of distribution as independent of the mode of production and hence the presentation of socialism as turning principally on distribution. After the real relation has long been made clear, why retrogress again?

> 4. "The emancipation of labour must be the work of the working class, relatively to which all other classes are *only one reactionary mass*."

The first strophe is taken from the introductory words of the Rules of the International, but "improved." There it is said: "The emancipation of the working class must be the act of the workers themselves"; here, on the contrary, the "working class" has to emancipate—what? "Labour." Let him understand who can.

In compensation, the antistrophe, on the other hand, is a Lassallean quotation of the first water: "relatively to which (the working class) all other classes are *only one reactionary mass*."

In the *Communist Manifesto* it is said: "Of all the classes that stand face to face with the bourgeoisie today, the proletariat alone is a *really revolutionary class*. The other classes decay and finally disappear in the face of Modern Industry; the proletariat is its special and essential product."

The bourgeoisie is here conceived as a revolutionary class—as

226

the bearer of large-scale industry — relatively to the feudal lords and the lower middle class, who desire to maintain all social positions that are the creation of obsolete modes of production. Thus they do not form *together* with the *bourgeoisie* only one reactionary mass.

On the other hand, the proletariat is revolutionary relatively to the bourgeoisie because, having itself grown up on the basis of large-scale industry, it strives to strip off from production the capitalist character that the bourgeoisie seeks to perpetuate. But the *Manifesto* adds that the "lower middle class" is becoming revolutionary "in view of [its] impending transfer into the proletariat."

From this point of view, therefore, it is again nonsense to say that it, together with the bourgeoisie, and with the feudal lords into the bargain, "forms only one reactionary mass" relatively to the working class.

Has one proclaimed to the artisans, small manufacturers, etc., and *peasants* during the last elections: Relatively to us you, together with the bourgeoisie and feudal lords, form only one reactionary mass?

Lassalle knew the *Communist Manifesto* by heart, as his faithful followers know the gospels written by him. If, therefore, he has falsified it so grossly, this has occurred only to put a good colour on his alliance with absolutist and feudal opponents against the bourgeoisie.

In the above paragraph, moreover, his oracular saying is dragged in by main force without any connection with the botched quotation from the Rules of the International. Thus it is here simply an impertinence, and indeed not at all displeasing to Herr Bismarck, one of those cheap pieces of insolence in which the Marat of Berlin[87] deals.

> 5. "The working class strives for its emancipation first of all *within the framework of the present-day national state*, conscious that the necessary result of its efforts, which are common to the workers of all civilised countries, will be the international brotherhood of peoples."

Lassalle, in opposition to the *Communist Manifesto* and to all earlier socialism, conceived the workers' movement from the narrowest national standpoint. He is being followed in this—and that after the work of the International!

It is altogether self-evident that, to be able to fight at all, the working class must organise itself at home *as a class* and that its own country is the immediate arena of its struggle. In so far its class struggle is national, not in substance, but, as the *Communist Manifesto* says, "in form". But the "framework of the present-day national state," for instance, the German Empire, is itself in its turn economically "within the framework" of the world market, politically "within the framework" of the system of states. Every businessman knows that German trade is at the same time foreign trade, and the greatness of Herr Bismarck consists, to be sure, precisely in his pursuing a kind of *international* policy.

And to what does the German workers' party reduce its internationalism? To the consciousness that the result of its efforts will be *"the international brotherhood of peoples"*—a phrase borrowed from the bourgeois League of Peace and Freedom,[88] which is intended to pass as equivalent to the international brotherhood of the working classes in the joint struggle against the ruling classes and their governments. Not a word, therefore, *about the international functions* of the German working class! And it is thus that it is to challenge its own bourgeoisie—which is already linked up in brotherhood against it with the bourgeois of all other countries—and Herr Bismarck's international policy of conspiracy!

In fact, the internationalism of the programme stands *even infinitely below* that of the Free Trade Party. The latter also asserts that the result of its efforts will be "the international brotherhood of peoples." But it also *does* something to make trade international and by no means contents itself with the consciousness—that all peoples are carrying on trade at home.

The international activity of the working classes does not in any way depend on the existence of the *International Working Men's Association*. This was only the first attempt to create a central organ for that activity; an attempt which was a lasting success on account of the impulse which it gave but which was no longer realisable in *its first historical form* after the fall of the Paris Commune.

Bismarck's *Norddeutsche* was absolutely right when it announced, to the satisfaction of its master, that the German Workers' Party had sworn off internationalism in the new programme.

II

"Starting from these basic principles, the German Workers' Party strives by all legal means for the *free state—and—*socialist society: the abolition of the wage system *together with the iron law of wages—and—*exploitation in every form; the elimination of all social and political inequality."

228

I shall return to the "free" state later.

So, in future, the German Workers' Party has got to believe in Lassalle's "iron law of wages"! That this may not be lost, the nonsense is perpetrated of speaking of the "abolition of the wage system" (it should read: system of wage labour) "*together with* the iron law of wages." If I abolish wage labour, then naturally I abolish its laws also, whether they are of "iron" or sponge. But Lassalle's attack on wage labour turns almost solely on this so-called law. In order, therefore, to prove that Lassalle's sect has conquered, the "wage system" must be abolished "*together with* the iron law of wages" and not without it.

It is well known that nothing of the "iron law of wages" is Lassalle's except the word "iron" borrowed from Goethe's "great, eternal iron laws."[89] The word *iron* is a label by which the true believers recognise one another. But if I take the law with Lassalle's stamp on it and, consequently, in his sense, then I must also take it with his substantiation for it. And what is that? As Lange already showed, shortly after Lassalle's death, it is the Malthusian theory of population[90] (preached by Lange himself). But if this theory is correct, then again I *cannot* abolish the law even if I abolish wage labour a hundred times over, because the law then governs not only the system of wage labour but *every* social system. Basing themselves directly on this, the economists have been proving for fifty years and more that socialism cannot abolish poverty, *which has its basis in nature*, but can only make it *general*, distribute it simultaneously over the whole surface of society!

But all this is not the main thing. *Quite apart* from the *false* Lassallean formulation of the law, the truly outrageous retrogression consists in the following:

Since Lassalle's death there has asserted itself in *our* Party the scientific understanding that *wages* are not what they *appear* to be, namely, the *value*, or *price*, *of labour*, but only a masked form for the *value*, or *price*, *of labour-power*. Thereby the whole bourgeois conception of wages hitherto, as well as all the criticism hitherto directed against this conception, was thrown overboard once for all and it was made clear that the wage-worker has permission to work for his own subsistence, that is, *to live*, only in so far as he works for a certain time gratis for the capitalist (and hence also for the latter's co-consumers of surplus value); that the whole capitalist system of production turns on the increase of this gratis labour by extending the working day or by developing the productivity, that is, increasing the intensity of labour-power, etc.; that, consequently, the system of wage labour is a system of slavery, and indeed of a slavery which becomes more severe in proportion as the social productive forces of labour develop, whether the worker receives better or worse payment. And after this understanding has gained more and more ground in our Party, one returns to Lassalle's dogmas although one must have known that Lassalle *did not know* what wages were, but following in the wake of the bourgeois economists took the appearance for the essence of the matter.

It is as if, among slaves who have at last got behind the secret of slavery and broken out in rebellion, a slave still in thrall to obsolete notions were to inscribe on the programme of the rebellion: Slavery must be abolished because the feeding of slaves in the system of slavery cannot exceed a certain low maximum!

Does not the mere fact that the representatives of our Party were capable of perpetrating such a monstrous attack on the understanding that has spread among the mass of our Party prove by itself with what criminal levity and with what lack of conscience they set to work in drawing up this compromise programme!

Instead of the indefinite concluding phrase of the paragraph, "the elimination of all social and political inequality," it ought to have been said that with the abolition of class distinctions all social and political inequality arising from them would disappear of itself.

III

> "The German workers' party, in order *to pave the way to the solution of the social question*, demands the establishment of producers' co-operative societies with *state aid under the democratic control of the toiling people*. The producers' co-operative societies *are to be called into being* for industry and agriculture on such a scale *that the socialist organisation of the total labour will arise from them*."

After the Lassallean "iron law of wages," the physic of the prophet. The way to it is "paved" in worthy fashion. In place of the existing class struggle appears a newspaper scribbler's phrase: "the social *question*," to the "*solution*" of which one "paves the way." Instead of arising from the revolutionary process of transformation of society, the "socialist organisation of the total labour" "arises" from the "state aid" that the state gives to the producers' co-operative societies and which the *state*, not the worker, "*calls into being*." It is worthy of Lassalle's imagination that with state loans one can build a new society just as well as a new railway!

230

From the remnants of a sense of shame, "state aid" has been put—under the democratic control of the "toiling people."

In the first place, the majority of the "toiling people" in Germany consists of peasants, and not of proletarians.

Secondly, "democratic" means in German "*volksherrschaftlich*" ("by the rule of the people"). But what does "control by the rule of the people of the toiling people" mean? And particularly in the case of a toiling people which, through these demands that it puts to the state, expresses its full consciousness that it neither rules nor is ripe for ruling!

It would be superfluous to deal here with the criticism of the recipe prescribed by Buchez in the reign of Louis Philippe *in opposition* to the French Socialists and accepted by the reactionary workers of the *Atelier*. The chief offence does not lie in having inscribed this specific nostrum in the programme, but in taking, in general, a retrograde step from the standpoint of a class movement to that of a sectarian movement.

That the workers desire to establish the conditions for co-operative production on a social scale, and first of all on a national scale, in their own country, only means that they are working to revolutionise the present conditions of production, and it has nothing in common with the foundation of co-operative societies with state aid. But as far as the present co-operative societies are concerned, they are of value *only* in so far as they are the independent creations of the workers and not protégés either of the governments or of the bourgeois.

IV

I come now to the democratic section.

A. *"The free basis of the state."*

First of all, according to II, the German workers' party strives for "the free state."

Free state—what is this?

It is by no means the aim of the workers, who have got rid of the narrow mentality of humble subjects, to set the state free. In the German Empire the "state" is almost as "free" as in Russia. Freedom consists in converting the state from an organ superimposed upon society into one completely subordinate to it, and today, too, the forms of state are more free or less free to the extent that they restrict the "freedom of the state."

The German Workers' Party—at least if it adopts the programme — shows that its socialist ideas are not even skin-deep; in that, instead of treating existing society (and this holds good for any future one) as the *basis* of the existing *state* (or of the future state in the case of future society), it treats the state rather as an independent entity that possesses its own *intellectual, ethical and libertarian bases*.

And what of the riotous misuse which the programme makes of the words "*present-day state*," "*present-day society*," and of the still more riotous misconception it creates in regard to the state to which it addresses its demands?

"Present-day society" is capitalist society, which exists in all civilised countries, more or less free from mediaeval admixture, more or less modified by the particular historical development of each country, more or less developed. On the other hand, the "present-day state" changes with a country's frontier. It is different in the Prusso-German Empire from what it is in Switzerland, and different in England from what it is in the United States. "The present-day state" is, therefore, a fiction.

Nevertheless, the different states of the different civilised countries, in spite of their motley diversity of form, all have this in common, that they are based on modern bourgeois society, only one more or less capitalistically developed. They have, therefore, also certain essential characteristics in common. In this sense it is possible to speak of the "present-day state", in contrast with the future, in which its present root, bourgeois society, will have died off.

The question then arises: what transformation will the state undergo in communist society? In other words, what social functions will remain in existence there that are analogous to present state functions? This question can only be answered scientifically, and one does not get a flea-hop nearer to the problem by a thousandfold combination of the word people with the word state.

Between capitalist and communist society lies the period of the revolutionary transformation of the one into the other. Corresponding to this is also a political transition period in which the state can be nothing but *the revolutionary dictatorship of the proletariat*.

Now the programme does not deal with this nor with the future state of communist society.

Its political demands contain nothing beyond the old democratic litany familiar to all: universal suffrage, direct legislation, popular rights, a people's militia, etc. They are a mere echo of the bourgeois People's Party, of the League of Peace and Freedom. They are all demands which, in so far as they are not exaggerated in fantastic presentation, have already been *realised*. Only the state to which they belong does not lie within the borders of the German Empire, but in Switzerland, the United States, etc. This sort of "state of the future" is *a present-day state*, although existing outside the "framework" of the German Empire.

But one thing has been forgotten. Since the German Workers' Party expressly declares that it acts within "the present-day national state," hence within its own state, the Prusso-German Empire—its demands would indeed otherwise be largely meaningless, since one only demands what one has not got—it should not have forgotten the chief thing, namely, that all those pretty little gewgaws rest on the recognition of the so-called sovereignty of the people and hence are appropriate only in a *democratic republic*.

Since one has not the courage—and wisely so, for the circumstances demand caution—to demand the democratic republic, as the French workers' programmes under Louis Philippe and under Louis Napoleon did, one should not have resorted, either, to the subterfuge, neither "honest" nor decent, of demanding things which have meaning only in a democratic republic from a state which is nothing but a police-guarded military despotism, embellished with parliamentary forms, alloyed with a feudal admixture, already influenced by the bourgeoisie and bureaucratically carpentered, and then to assure this state into the bargain that one imagines one will be able to force such things upon it "by legal means."

Even vulgar democracy, which sees the millennium in the democratic republic and has no suspicion that it is precisely in this last form of state of bourgeois society that the class struggle has to be fought out to a conclusion—even it towers mountains above this kind of democratism which keeps within the limits of what is permitted by the police and not permitted by logic.

That, in fact, by the word "state" is meant the government machine, or the state, so far as it forms a special organism separated from society through division of labour, is shown by the words "the German Workers' Party demands *as the economic basis of the state*: a single progressive income tax," etc. Taxes are the economic basis of the government machinery and of nothing else.

In the state of the future, existing in Switzerland, this demand has been pretty well fulfilled. Income tax presupposes various sources of income of the various social classes, and hence capitalist society. It is, therefore, nothing remarkable that the Liverpool financial reformers, bourgeois headed by Gladstone's brother, are putting forward the same demand as the programme.

> B. "The German workers' party demands as the intellectual and ethical basis of the state:
>
> "1. Universal and *equal elementary education* by the state. Universal compulsory school attendance. Free instruction."

Equal elementary education? What idea lies behind these words? Is it believed that in present-day society (and it is only with this one has to deal) education can be *equal* for all classes? Or is it demanded that the upper classes also shall be compulsorily reduced to the modicum of education—the elementary school—that alone is compatible with the economic conditions not only of the wage-workers but of the peasants as well?

"Universal compulsory school attendance. Free instruction." The former exists even in Germany, the second in Switzerland and in the United States in the case of elementary schools. If in some states of the latter country higher educational institutions are also "free" that only means in fact defraying the cost of the education of the upper classes from the general tax receipts. Incidentally, the same holds good for "free administration of justice" demanded under A, 5. The administration of criminal justice is to be had free everywhere; that of civil justice is concerned almost exclusively with conflicts over property and hence affects almost exclusively the possessing classes. Are they to carry on their litigation at the expense of the national coffers?

The paragraph on the schools should at least have demanded technical schools (theoretical and practical) in combination with the elementary school.

"Elementary education by the state" is altogether objectionable. Defining by a general law the expenditures on the elementary schools, the qualifications of the teaching staff, the branches of instruction, etc., and, as is done in the United States, supervising the fulfilment of these legal specifications by state inspectors, is a very different thing from appointing the state as the educator of the people! Government and Church should rather be equally excluded from any influence on the school. Particularly, indeed, in the Prusso-German Empire (and one should not take refuge in the rotten subterfuge that one is speaking of a "state of the future"; we

234

have seen how matters stand in this respect) the state has need, on the contrary, of a very stern education by the people.

But the whole programme, for all its democratic clang, is tainted through and through by the Lassallean sect's servile belief in the state, or, what is no better, by a democratic belief in miracles, or rather it is a compromise between these two kinds of belief in miracles, both equally remote from socialism.

"*Freedom of science*" says a paragraph of the Prussian Constitution. Why, then, here?

"*Freedom of conscience!*" If one desired at this time of the *Kulturkampf*[91] to remind liberalism of its old catchwords, it surely could have been done only in the following form: Everyone should be able to attend to his religious as well as his bodily needs without the police sticking their noses in. But the workers' party ought at any rate in this connection to have expressed its awareness of the fact that bourgeois "freedom of conscience" is nothing but the toleration of all possible kinds of *religious freedom of conscience*, and that for its part it endeavours rather to liberate the conscience from the witchery of religion. But one chooses not to transgress the "bourgeois" level.

· I have now come to the end, for the appendix that now follows in the programme does not constitute a characteristic component part of it. Hence I can be very brief here.

2. "*Normal working day.*"

In no other country has the workers' party limited itself to such an indefinite demand, but has always fixed the length of the working day that it considers normal under the given circumstances.

3. "Restriction of female labour and prohibition of child labour."

The standardisation of the working day must include the restriction of female labour, in so far as it relates to the duration, intermissions, etc., of the working day: otherwise it could only mean the exclusion of female labour from branches of industry that are especially unhealthy for the female body or are objectionable morally for the female sex. If that is what was meant, it should have been said so.

"*Prohibition of child labour.*" Here it was absolutely essential to state the *age limit*.

A *general prohibition* of child labour is incompatible with the existence of large-scale industry and hence an empty, pious wish.

Its realisation—if it were possible—would be reactionary, since, with a strict regulation of the working time according to the different age groups and other safety measures for the protection of children, an early combination of productive labour with education is one of the most potent means for the transformation of present-day society.

4. "State supervision of factory, workshop and domestic industry."

In consideration of the Prusso-German state it should definitely have been demanded that the inspectors are to be removable only by a court of law; that any worker can have them prosecuted for neglect of duty; that they must belong to the medical profession.

5. "Regulation of prison labour."

A petty demand in a general workers' programme. In any case, it should have been clearly stated that there is no intention from fear of competition to allow ordinary criminals to be treated like beasts, and especially that there is no desire to deprive them of their sole means of betterment, productive labour. This was surely the least one might have expected from Socialists.

6. "An effective liability law."

It should have been stated what is meant by an "effective" liability law.

Be it noted, incidentally, that in speaking of the normal working day the part of factory legislation that deals with health regulations and safety measures, etc., has been overlooked. The liability law only comes into operation when these regulations are infringed.

In short, this appendix also is distinguished by slovenly editing. *Dixi et salvavi animam meam.*[a]

Written in April-
early May 1875

Marx and Engels,
Selected Works in 3 vols.,
Vol. 3, Moscow, 1973,
pp. 13-20

---

[a] I have spoken and saved my soul. —*Ed.*

KARL MARX

TO THE EDITORIAL BOARD OF THE "OTECHESTVENNIYE ZAPISKI"[92]

London [November 1877]

Dear Sir,

The author[a] of the article *Karl Marx Before the Tribunal of Mr. Zhukovsky* is evidently a clever man and if, in my account of primitive accumulation, he had found a single passage to support his conclusions he would have quoted it. In the absence of any such passage he finds himself obliged to seize upon an *incidental remark*, a sort of polemic against a Russian "literary man",[b] published in the appendix to the first German edition of *Kapital*. What do I reproach this writer with? That he discovered the Russian commune not in Russia but in a book written by Haxthausen,[93] Prussian Counsellor of State, and that in his hands the Russian commune only serves as an argument to prove that rotten old Europe must be regenerated by the victory of Pan-Slavism. My estimate of this writer may be right or it may be wrong, but it cannot in any case furnish a clue to my views regarding the efforts "of Russians to find a path of development for their country different from that which Western Europe pursued and still pursues",[c] etc.

In the Afterword to the second German edition of *Kapital*—which the author of the article on Mr. Zhukovsky knows, because he quotes it—I speak of a "great Russian scholar and critic,"[d] with the high consideration he deserves. In his remarkable articles this writer has dealt with the question whether, as her liberal

---

[a] N. K. Mikhailovsky.—*Ed.*

[b] Alexander Herzen.—*Ed.*

[c] This passage from N. K. Mikhailovsky's article is in Russian in Marx's manuscript.—*Ed.*

[d] N. G. Chernyshevsky.—*Ed.*

economists maintain, Russia must begin by destroying the village commune in order to pass to the capitalist regime, or whether, on the contrary, she can without experiencing the tortures of this regime appropriate all its fruits by developing the historical conditions specifically her own. He pronounces in favour of this latter solution. And my honourable critic would have had at least as much reason for inferring from my esteem for this "great Russian scholar and critic" that I shared his views on the question as for concluding from my polemic against the "literary man" and Pan-Slavist that I rejected them.

To conclude, as I am not fond of leaving "anything to guesswork" I shall come straight to the point. In order that I might be specially qualified to estimate the economic development in Russia, I learnt Russian and then for many years studied the official publications and others bearing on this subject. I have arrived at this conclusion: If Russia continues to pursue the path she has followed since 1861, she will lose the finest chance ever offered by history to a people and undergo all the fatal vicissitudes of the capitalist regime.

II

The chapter on primitive accumulation does not claim to do more than trace the path by which, in Western Europe, the capitalist economic system emerged from the womb of the feudal economic system. It therefore describes the historical process which by divorcing the producers from their means of production converts them into wage-workers (proletarians in the modern sense of the word) while it converts the owners of the means of production into capitalists. In that history "all revolutions are epoch-making that act as levers for the capitalist class in course of formation; but, above all, those moments, when great masses of men are forcibly torn from their traditional means of production and of subsistence, suddenly hurled on the labour market. But the basis of this whole development is the expropriation of the peasants. England is so far the only country where this has been carried through completely ... but all the countries of Western Europe are going through the same development", etc. (*Capital*, French edition, p. 315). At the end of the chapter the historical tendency of production is summed up thus: That it "begets, with the inexorability of a law of Nature its own negation"; that it has

238

itself created the elements of a new economic order, since at the same time it provides for an unprecedented expansion of the productive forces of social labour and the universal development of every individual producer; that capitalist property, which actually rests already on a collective mode of production, can only be transformed into social property. At this point I have not furnished any proof, for the good reason that this statement is itself nothing else but a general summary of long expositions previously given in the chapters on capitalist production.

Now what application to Russia could my critic make of this historical sketch? Simply this: If Russia wants to become a capitalist nation after the example of the West-European countries—and during the last few years she has been taking a lot of trouble in this direction—she will not succeed without having first transformed a good part of her peasants into proletarians; and then, once drawn into the whirlpool of the capitalist economy, she will have to endure its inexorable laws like other profane nations. That is all. But that is too little for my critic. He insists on transforming my historical sketch of the genesis of capitalism in Western Europe into an historico-philosophic theory of the general path of development prescribed by fate to all nations, whatever the historical circumstances in which they find themselves, in order that they may ultimately arrive at the economic system which ensures, together with the greatest expansion of the productive powers of social labour, the most complete development of man. But I beg his pardon. (He is doing me too much honour and at the same time slandering me too much.) Let us take an example.

In several parts of *Kapital* I allude to the fate which overtook the plebeians of ancient Rome. They were originally free peasants, each cultivating his own piece of land on his own account. In the course of Roman history they were expropriated. The same movement which divorced them from their means of production and subsistence involved the formation not only of big landed property but also of big money capital. Thus one fine morning there were to be found on the one hand free men, stripped of everything except their labour power, and on the other, the owners of all the acquired wealth ready to exploit this labour. What happened? The Roman proletarians became not wage-labourers but a *mob* of do-nothings more abject than those known as "poor whites" in the South of the United States, and alongside them there developed a mode of production which was not capitalist but based on slavery. Thus events strikingly analogous but taking place in different historical surroundings led to totally different results. By studying each of these forms of evolution separately and then comparing them one can easily find the clue to this phenomenon, but one will never arrive there by using as one's master key a general historico-philosophical theory, the supreme virtue of which consists in being supra-historical.

Written about
November 1877

Marx and Engels,
Selected Correspondence,
Moscow, 1975, pp. 291-94

KARL MARX

From the draft of
a)**THE DEBATE
IN THE REICHSTAG
ON THE LAW
AGAINST SOCIALISTS**[94]

"And when you look a little more closely at these social-democratic doctrines and goals, then *peaceful development is* not *the goal,* as was said previously; rather, *peaceful development is only a stage* which should lead to *final goals,* which can be attained by no other means than that of violence."[95] [Somewhat as the "nationalists" formed a "stage" in bringing about the forcible Prussianisation of Germany; so Herr Eulenburg imagines the path of "blood and iron".]

If one takes the first part of the sentence, it is tautology or nonsense: if Eulenburg has a "goal" or "final goals", then it is these "goals" and not the nature of the development that are "peaceful" or "not peaceful". What Eulenburg really wants to say is that peaceful development towards a goal is only a stage which should lead to the violent development of the goal and, indeed, for Herr Eulenburg, this later transformation of "peaceful" development into "violent" development is in the nature of the goal aspired to. The goal in the given instance is the emancipation of the working class and the overthrow (transformation) of society that this implies. An historical development can remain "peaceful" only so long as no forcible hindrances are placed in its path by those holding power in society at the time. If, for example, in Britain or the United States the working class gained a majority in Parliament or Congress, then it could legally set aside the laws and institutions standing in its way, as far, indeed, as social development required it. Nevertheless, the "peaceful" movement could become a "violent" one on encountering the resistance of those interested in the old state of affairs and if these were crushed by force (as in the American movement[96] and the French Revolution), they would be rebelling against "legal" power.

a) English translation © Progress Publishers 1978

What Eulenburg preaches, however, is *violent reaction* on the part of those holding power against the *development* which *is* "in the peaceful stage" in order to prevent later "violent" conflicts; war-cry of the violent counter-revolution against formerly "peaceful" development. In fact the government tries to crush *by force* development which is clearly inimical to it although *legally* invulnerable. This is the necessary introduction to violent revolutions. It is an old story, but it remains eternally new.[97]

Written in the
second half
of September 1878

Translated from the German

From

INTERVIEW GIVEN
BY KARL MARX
TO THE CORRESPONDENT
OF THE
AMERICAN NEWSPAPER
"CHICAGO TRIBUNE"
IN THE FIRST HALF
OF DECEMBER 1878

"Now," asked your correspondent, "what has Socialism done so far?"

"Two things," he returned. "Socialists have shown the general universal struggle between capital and labor,—

THE COSMOPOLITAN CHARACTER,

in one word,—and consequently tried to bring about an understanding between the workmen in the different countries, which became more necessary as the capitalists became more cosmopolitan in hiring labor, pitting foreign against native labor not only in America, but in England, France, and Germany. International relations sprang up at once between the workingmen in the different countries, showing that Socialism was not merely a local, but an international problem, to be solved by the international action of workmen. The working classes moved spontaneously, without knowing what the ends of the movement will be. The Socialists invent no movement, but merely tell the workmen what its character and its ends will be."

"Which means the overthrowing of the present social system," I interrupted.

"This system of land and capital in the hands of employers, on the one hand," he continued, "and the mere working power in the hands of the laborers to sell as a commodity, we claim is merely an historical phase, which will pass away and give place to

243

A HIGHER SOCIAL CONDITION.

We see everywhere a division of society. The antagonism of the two classes goes hand in hand with the development of the industrial resources of modern countries. From a Socialistic standpoint the means already exist to revolutionize the present historical phase. Upon Trades-Unions, in many countries, have been built political organizations. In America the need of an independent Workingmen's party has been made manifest. They can no longer trust politicians. Rings and cliques have seized upon the Legislature, and politics has been made a trade. But America is not alone in this, only its people are more decisive than Europeans. Things come to the surface quicker. There is less cant and hypocrisy than there is on this side of the ocean."

"The Rev. Joseph Cook, of Boston,—you know him—"

"We heard of him; a very badly informed man upon the subject of Socialism".

"In a lecture lately upon the subject, he said: 'Karl Marx is credited now with saying that, in the United States, and in Great Britain, and perhaps in France, a reform of labor will occur without bloody revolution, but that blood must be shed in Germany, and in Russia, and in Italy and in Austria.'"

"No Socialist," remarked the Doctor, smiling, "need predict that there will be a bloody revolution in Russia, Germany, Austria, and possibly in Italy if the Italians keep on in the policy they are now pursuing. The deeds of the French Revolution may be enacted again in those countries. That is apparent to any political student. But those revolutions will be made by the majority. No revolution can be made by a party,

BUT BY A NATION."

Published in
The Chicago Tribune,
January 5, 1879

FREDERICK ENGELS

From
SOCIALISM:
UTOPIAN AND SCIENTIFIC

Social forces work exactly like natural forces: blindly, forcibly, destructively, so long as we do not understand, and reckon with them. But when once we understand them, when once we grasp their action, their direction, their effects, it depends only upon ourselves to subject them more and more to our own will, and by means of them to reach our own ends. And this holds quite especially of the mighty productive forces of today. As long as we obstinately refuse to understand the nature and the character of these social means of action—and this understanding goes against the grain of the capitalist mode of production and its defenders—so long these forces are at work in spite of us, in opposition to us, so long they master us, as we have shown above in detail.

But when once their nature is understood, they can, in the hands of the producers working together, be transformed from master demons into willing servants. The difference is as that between the destructive force of electricity in the lightning of the storm, and electricity under command in the telegraph and the voltaic arc; the difference between a conflagration, and fire working in the service of man. With this recognition, at last, of the real nature of the productive forces of today, the social anarchy of production gives place to a social regulation of production upon a definite plan, according to the needs of the community and of each individual. Then the capitalist mode of appropriation, in which the product enslaves first the producer, and then the appropriator, is replaced by the mode of appropriation of the products that is based upon the nature of the modern means of production; upon the one hand, direct social appropriation, as means to the maintenance and extension of production—on the other, direct individual appropriation, as means of subsistence and of enjoyment.

Whilst the capitalist mode of production more and more completely transforms the great majority of the population into proletarians, it creates the power which, under penalty of its own destruction, is forced to accomplish this revolution. Whilst it forces on more and more the transformation of the vast means of production, already socialised, into state property, it shows itself the way to accomplishing this revolution. *The proletariat seizes political power and turns the means of production into state property.*

But, in doing this, it abolishes itself as proletariat, abolishes all class distinctions and class antagonisms, abolishes also the state as state. Society thus far, based upon class antagonisms, had need of the state. That is, of an organisation of the particular class which was *pro tempore* the exploiting class, an organisation for the purpose of preventing any interference from without with the existing conditions of production, and, therefore, especially, for the purpose of forcibly keeping the exploited classes in the condition of oppression corresponding with the given mode of production (slavery, serfdom, wage labour). The state was the official representative of society as a whole; the gathering of it together into a visible embodiment. But it was this only in so far as it was the state of that class which itself represented, for the time being, society as a whole: in ancient times, the state of slave-owning citizens; in the Middle Ages, the feudal lords; in our own time, the bourgeoisie. When at last it becomes the real representative of the whole of society, it renders itself unnecessary. As soon as there is no longer any social class to be held in subjection; as soon as class rule, and the individual struggle for existence based upon our present anarchy in production, with the collisions and excesses arising from these, are removed, nothing more remains to be repressed, and a special repressive force, a state, is no longer necessary. The first act by virtue of which the state really constitutes itself the representative of the whole of society—the taking possession of the means of production in the name of society—this is, at the same time, its last independent act as a state. State interference in social relations becomes, in one domain after another, superfluous, and then dies out of itself; the government of persons is replaced by the administration of things, and by the conduct of processes of production. The state is not "abolished." *It dies out.* This gives the measure of the value of the phrase "*a free state*," both as to its justifiable use at times by agitators, and as to its ultimate scientific insufficiency; and also of the demands of the so-called anarchists for the abolition of the state out of hand.

Since the historical appearance of the capitalist mode of production, the appropriation by society of all the means of production has often been dreamed of, more or less vaguely, by individuals, as well as by sects, as the ideal of the future. But it could become possible, could become a historical necessity, only when the actual conditions for its realisation were there. Like every other social advance, it becomes practicable, not by men understanding that the existence of classes is in contradiction to justice, equality, etc., not by the mere willingness to abolish these classes, but by virtue of certain new economic conditions. The separation of society into an exploiting and an exploited class, a ruling and an oppressed class, was the necessary consequence of the deficient and restricted development of production in former times. So long as the total social labour only yields a produce which but slightly exceeds that barely necessary for the existence of all; so long, therefore, as labour engages all or almost all the time of the great majority of the members of society—so long, of necessity, this society is divided into classes. Side by side with the great majority, exclusively bond slaves to labour, arises a class freed from directly productive labour, which looks after the general affairs of society: the direction of labour, state business, law, science, art, etc. It is, therefore, the law of division of labour that lies at the basis of the division into classes. But this does not prevent this division into classes from being carried out by means of violence and robbery, trickery and fraud. It does not prevent the ruling class, once having the upper hand, from consolidating its power at the expense of the working class, from turning its social leadership into an intensified exploitation of the masses.

But if, upon this showing, division into classes has a certain historical justification, it has this only for a given period, only under given social conditions. It was based upon the insufficiency of production. It will be swept away by the complete development of modern productive forces. And, in fact, the abolition of classes in society presupposes a degree of historical evolution at which the existence, not simply of this or that particular ruling class, but of any ruling class at all, and, therefore, the existence of class distinction itself has become an obsolete anachronism. It presupposes, therefore, the development of production carried out to a degree at which appropriation of the means of production and of the products, and, with this, of political domination, of the monopoly of culture, and of intellectual leadership by a particular class of society, has become not only superfluous but economically, politically, intellectually, a hindrance to development.

This point is now reached. Their political and intellectual bankruptcy is scarcely any longer a secret to the bourgeoisie themselves. Their economic bankruptcy recurs regularly every ten years. In every crisis, society is suffocated beneath the weight of its own productive forces and products, which it cannot use, and stands helpless, face to face with the absurd contradiction that the producers have nothing to consume, because consumers are wanting. The expansive force of the means of production bursts the bonds that the capitalist mode of production had imposed upon them. Their deliverance from these bonds is the one precondition for an unbroken, constantly accelerated development of the productive forces, and therewith for a practically unlimited increase of production itself. Nor is this all. The socialised appropriation of the means of production does away, not only with the present artificial restrictions upon production, but also with the positive waste and devastation of productive forces and products that are at the present time the inevitable concomitants of production, and that reach their height in the crises. Further, it sets free for the community at large a mass of means of production and of products, by doing away with the senseless extravagance of the ruling classes of today and their political representatives. The possibility of securing for every member of society, by means of socialised production, an existence not only fully sufficient materially, and becoming day by day more full, but an existence guaranteeing to all the free development and exercise of their physical and mental faculties—this possibility is now for the first time here, but *it is here*.*

With the seizing of the means of production by society,

---

* A few figures may serve to give an approximate idea of the enormous expansive force of the modern means of production, even under capitalist pressure. According to Mr. Giffen, the total wealth of Great Britain and Ireland amounted, in round numbers, in

> 1814 to £ 2,200,000,000.
> 1865 to £ 6,100,000,000.
> 1875 to £ 8,500,000,000.

production of commodities is done away with, and, simultaneously, the mastery of the product over the producer. Anarchy in social production is replaced by systematic, definite organisation. The struggle for individual existence disappears. Then for the first time man, in a certain sense, is finally marked off from the rest of the animal kingdom, and emerges from mere animal conditions of existence into really human ones. The whole sphere of the conditions of life which environ man, and which have hitherto ruled man, now comes under the dominion and control of man, who for the first time becomes the real, conscious lord of Nature, because he has now become master of his own social organisation. The laws of his own social action, hitherto standing face to face with man as laws of Nature foreign to, and dominating him, will then be used with full understanding, and so mastered by him. Man's own social organisation, hitherto confronting him as a necessity imposed by Nature and history, now becomes the result of his own free action. The extraneous objective forces that have hitherto governed history pass under the control of man himself. Only from that time will man himself, more and more consciously, make his own history—only from that time will the social causes set in movement by him have, in the main and in a constantly growing measure, the results intended by him. It is the ascent of man from the kingdom of necessity to the kingdom of freedom.

Let us briefly sum up our sketch of historical evolution.

I. *Mediaeval Society*—Individual production on a small scale. Means of production adapted for individual use; hence primitive, ungainly, petty, dwarfed in action. Production for immediate consumption, either of the producer himself or of his feudal lord. Only where an excess of production over this consumption occurs is such excess offered for sale, enters into exchange. Production of commodities, therefore, only in its infancy. But already it contains within itself, in embryo, *anarchy in the production of society at large.*

II. *Capitalist Revolution*—Transformation of industry, at first by means of simple co-operation and manufacture. Concentration of the means of production, hitherto scattered, into great workshops. As a consequence, their transformation from in-

---

As an instance of the squandering of means of production and of products during a crisis, the total loss in the *German iron industry* alone, in the crisis 1873-78, was given at the second German Industrial Congress (Berlin, February 21, 1878) as £22,750,000 [*Note by Engels.*]

dividual to social means of production—a transformation which does not, on the whole, affect the form of exchange. The old forms of appropriation remain in force. The capitalist appears. In his capacity as owner of the means of production, he also appropriates the products and turns them into commodities. Production has become a *social* act. Exchange and appropriation continue to be *individual* acts, the acts of individuals. *The social product is appropriated by the individual capitalist.* Fundamental contradiction, whence arise all the contradictions in which our present-day society moves, and which modern industry brings to light.

A. Severance of the producer from the means of production. Condemnation of the worker to wage-labour for life. *Antagonism between the proletariat and the bourgeoisie.*

B. Growing predominance and increasing effectiveness of the laws governing the production of commodities. Unbridled competition. *Contradiction between socialised organisation in the individual factory and social anarchy in production as a whole.*

C. On the one hand, perfecting of machinery, made by competition compulsory for each individual manufacturer, and complemented by a constantly growing displacement of labourers. *Industrial reserve army.* On the other hand, unlimited extension of production, also compulsory under competition for every manufacturer. On both sides, unheard-of development of productive forces, excess of supply over demand, over-production, glutting of the markets, crises every ten years, the vicious circle: excess here, of means of production and products—excess there, of labourers, without employment and without means of existence. But these two levers of production and of social well-being are unable to work together, because the capitalist form of production prevents the productive forces from working and the products from circulating, unless they are first turned into capital—which their very superabundance prevents. The contradiction has grown into an absurdity. *The mode of production rises in rebellion against the form of exchange.* The bourgeoisie are convicted of incapacity further to manage their own social productive forces.

D. Partial recognition of the social character of the productive forces forced upon the capitalists themselves. Taking over of the great institutions for production and communication, first by joint-stock companies, later on by trusts, then by the state. The bourgeoisie demonstrated to be a superfluous class. All its social functions are now performed by salaried employees.

III. *Proletarian Revolution*—Solution of the contradictions. The proletariat seizes the public power, and by means of this transforms the socialised means of production, slipping from the hands of the bourgeoisie, into public property. By this act, the proletariat frees the means of production from the character of capital they have thus far borne, and gives their socialised character complete freedom to work itself out. Socialised production upon a predetermined plan becomes henceforth possible. The development of production makes the existence of different classes of society thenceforth an anachronism. In proportion as anarchy in social production vanishes, the political authority of the state dies out. Man, at last the master of his own form of social organisation, becomes at the same time the lord over Nature, his own master—free.

To accomplish this act of universal emancipation is the historical mission of the modern proletariat. To thoroughly comprehend the historical conditions and thus the very nature of this act, to impart to the now oppressed proletarian class a full knowledge of the conditions and of the meaning of the momentous act it is called upon to accomplish, this is the task of the theoretical expression of the proletarian movement, scientific socialism.

Written in January-
the first half
of March 1880

Marx and Engels,
Selected Works in 3 vols.,
Vol. 3, Moscow, 1973,
pp.146-51

KARL MARX

a) INTRODUCTION TO THE PROGRAMME OF THE FRENCH WORKERS' PARTY[98]

Bearing in mind

that emancipation of the class of producers is emancipation of all mankind, irrespective of race, or sex;

that the producers can become free only when they have come into possession of the means of production;

that the means of production can belong to them only in two forms:

1) in an individual form which, as a general phenomenon, has never existed and which is being increasingly eliminated by the advance of industry;

2) in a collective form, the material and intellectual elements of which are being created by the development of capitalist society itself;

bearing in mind

that a collective appropriation of this kind can only result from revolutionary action by the class of producers—the proletariat—organised into an independent political party;

that it is necessary to strive to achieve such an organisation by all means at the disposal of the proletariat, including universal suffrage, which is thus transformed from the instrument of deception it has hitherto been into an instrument of liberation;

---

a) English translation © Progress Publishers 1978

Setting as the ultimate goal of their struggle the return, on the economic level, to collective ownership of all the means of production, French socialist workers have decided *as a means of organisation and struggle* to participate in the elections on the basis of the following *minimum* programme.[a]

Written at
the beginning
of May 1880

Marx/Engels, *Werke*,
Bd. 19, S. 238

---

[a] The programme indicated is not included in the present edition.—*Ed*.

KARL MARX

From
LETTER
TO FERDINAND DOMELA
NIEUWENHUIS
IN THE HAGUE

London, February 22, 1881

The "question" about which you inform me, that of the forthcoming Zurich Congress, seems to me a mistake. What should be done at any definite, given moment of the future, and done *immediately*, depends of course entirely on the given historical conditions in which one has to act. This question however is posed in the *clouds* and therefore is really a phantom problem to which the only answer can be—a *criticism of the question* itself. No equation can be solved unless its terms contain the elements of its solution. Incidentally, the difficulties of a government which has suddenly come into being through a victory of the people have nothing specifically "socialist" about them. On the contrary. Victorious bourgeois politicians at once feel embarrassed by their "victory", whereas Socialists can at least set to work without any embarrassment. One thing you can at any rate be sure of: a socialist government does not come into power in a country unless conditions are so developed that it can immediately take the necessary measures for intimidating the mass of the bourgeoisie sufficiently to gain time—the first *desideratum*—for permanent action.

Perhaps you will refer me to the Paris Commune; but apart from the fact that this was merely the rising of a city under exceptional conditions, the majority of the Commune was by no means socialist, nor could it be. With a modicum of common sense, however, it could have reached a compromise with Versailles useful to the whole mass of the people—the only thing that it was possible to reach at the time. The appropriation of the Bank of France would have been quite enough to put an end with terror to the vaunt of the Versailles people, etc., etc.

The general demands of the French bourgeoisie before 1789 were defined in about the same terms as *mutatis mutandis* the primary immediate demands of the proletariat are today, being pretty uniform in all countries with capitalist production. But had any eighteenth-century Frenchman the faintest idea beforehand, *a priori*, of the manner in which the demands of the French bourgeoisie would be forced through? The doctrinaire and inevitably fantastic anticipation of the programme of action for a revolution of the future only diverts one from the struggle of the present. The dream that the end of the world was near inspired the early Christians in their struggle with the Roman Empire and gave them confidence in victory. Scientific insight into the inevitable disintegration of the dominant order of society, a disintegration which is going on continually before our eyes, and the ever-growing fury into which the masses are lashed by the old ghostly governments, and the enormous positive development of the means of production taking place simultaneously—all this is a sufficient guarantee that as soon as a real proletarian revolution breaks out the conditions of its immediately next *modus operandi* (though it will certainly not be idyllic) will be in existence.

Marx and Engels,
Selected Correspondence,
Moscow, 1975, pp. 317-18

FREDERICK ENGELS

SOCIAL CLASSES—
NECESSARY
AND SUPERFLUOUS

The question has often been asked, in what degree are the different classes of society useful or even necessary? And the answer was naturally a different one for every different epoch of history considered. There was undoubtedly a time when a territorial aristocracy was an unavoidable and necessary element of society. That, however is very, very long ago. Then there was a time when a capitalist middle class, a *bourgeoisie* as the French call it, arose with equally unavoidable necessity, struggled against the territorial aristocracy, broke its political power, and in its turn became economically and politically predominant. But, since classes arose, there never was a time when society could do without a working class. The name, the social status of that class has changed; the serf took the place of the slave, to be in his turn relieved by the free working man—free from servitude but also free from any earthly possessions save his own labour force. But it is plain: whatever changes took place in the upper, non-producing ranks of society, society could not live without a class of producers. This class, then, is necessary under all circumstances—though the time must come, when it will no longer be a class, when it will comprise all society.

Now, what necessity is there at present for the existence of each of these three classes?

The landed aristocracy is, to say the least, economically useless in England, while in Ireland and Scotland it has become a positive nuisance by its depopulating tendencies. To send the people across the ocean or into starvation, and to replace them by sheep or deer—that is all the merit that the Irish and Scotch landlords can

256

lay claim to. Let the competition of American vegetable and animal food develop a little further, and the English landed aristocracy will do the same, at least those that can afford it, having large town estates to fall back upon. Of the rest, American food competition will soon free us. And good riddance—for their political action, both in the Lords and Commons is a perfect national nuisance.

But how about the capitalist middle class, that enlightened and liberal class which founded the British colonial empire and which established British liberty? The class that reformed Parliament in 1831,[99] repealed the Corn Laws, and reduced tax after tax? The class that created and still directs the giant manufactures, and the immense merchant navy, the ever spreading railway system of England? Surely that class must be at least as necessary as the working class which it directs and leads on from progress to progress.

Now the economical function of the capitalist middle class has been, indeed, to create the modern system of steam manufactures and steam communications, and to crush every economical and political obstacle which delayed or hindered the development of that system. No doubt, as long as the capitalist middle class performed this function it was, under the circumstances, a necessary class. But is it still so? Does it continue to fulfil its essential function as the manager and expander of social production for the benefit of society at large? Let us see.

To begin with the means of communication, we find the telegraphs in the hands of the Government. The railways and a large part of the sea-going steamships are owned, not by individual capitalists who manage their own business, but by joint-stock companies whose business is managed for them by *paid employees*, by servants whose position is to all intents and purposes that of superior, better paid workpeople. As to the directors and shareholders, they both know that the less the former interfere with the management, and the latter with the supervision, the better for the concern. A lax and mostly perfunctory supervision is, indeed, the only function left to the owners of the business. Thus we see that in reality the capitalist owners of these immense establishments have no other action left with regard to them, but to cash the half-yearly dividend warrants. The social function of the capitalist here has been transferred to servants paid by wages; but he continues to pocket in his dividends, the pay for those functions though he has ceased to perform them.

But another function is still left to the capitalist, whom the extent of the large undertakings in question has compelled to "retire" from their management. And this function is to speculate with his shares on the Stock Exchange. For want of something better to do, our "retired" or in reality superseded capitalists, gamble to their hearts' content in this temple of mammon. They go there with the deliberate intention to pocket money which they were pretending to earn; though they say, the origin of all property is labour and saving—the origin perhaps, but certainly not the end. What hypocrisy to forcibly close petty gambling houses, when our capitalist society cannot do without an immense gambling house, where millions after millions are lost and won, for its very centre! Here, indeed, the existence of the "retired" shareholding capitalist becomes not only superfluous, but a perfect nuisance.

What is true for railways and steamshipping is becoming more and more true every day for all large manufacturing and trading establishments. "Floating"—transforming large private concerns into limited companies—has been the order of the day for the last ten years and more. From the large Manchester warehouses of the City to the ironworks and coalpits of Wales and the North and the factories of Lancashire, everything has been, or is being, floated. In all Oldham there is scarcely a cotton mill left in private hands; nay, even the retail tradesman is more and more superseded by "co-operative stores", the great majority of which are co-operative in name only—but of that another time. Thus we see that by the very development of the system of capitalist's production the capitalist is superseded quite as much as the handloom-weaver. With this difference, though, that the handloom-weaver is doomed to slow starvation, and the superseded capitalist to slow death from overfeeding. In this they generally are both alike, that neither knows what to do with himself.

This, then, is the result: the economical development of our actual society tends more and more to concentrate, to socialise production into immense establishments which cannot any longer be managed by single capitalists. All the trash of "the eye of the master", and the wonders it does, turns into sheer nonsense as soon as an undertaking reaches a certain size. Imagine "the eye of the master" of the London and North Western Railway! But what the master cannot do the workman, the wages-paid servants of the Company, *can* do, and do it successfully.

Thus the capitalist can no longer lay claim to his profits as "wages of supervision", as he supervises nothing. Let us remember that when the defenders of capital drum that hollow phrase into our ears.

But we have attempted to show, in our last week's issue, that the capitalist class had also become unable to manage the immense productive system of this country; that they on the one hand expanded production so as to periodically flood all the markets with produce, and on the other became more and more incapable of holding their own against foreign competition. Thus we find that, not only can we manage very well without the interference of the capitalist class in the great industries of the country, but that their interference is becoming more and more a nuisance.

Again we say to them, "Stand back! Give the working class the chance of a turn."

Written on
August 1-2, 1881

Frederick Engels,
The Wages System,
Moscow, 1975, pp. 48-51

FREDERICK ENGELS

From
LETTER
TO KARL KAUTSKY
IN VIENNA

London, September 12, 1882

... You ask me what the English workers think about colonial policy. Well, exactly the same as they think about politics in general: the same as the bourgeois think. There is no workers' party here, there are only Conservatives and Liberal-Radicals, and the workers are cheerfully consuming their share of England's monopoly of the world market and the colonies. In my opinion the colonies proper, i.e., the countries occupied by a European population—Canada, the Cape, Australia—will all become independent; on the other hand, the countries inhabited by a native population, which are simply subjugated—India, Algeria, the Dutch, Portuguese and Spanish possessions—must be taken over for the time being by the proletariat and led as rapidly as possible towards independence. How this process will develop is difficult to say. India will perhaps, indeed very probably, make a revolution, and as a proletariat in process of self-emancipation cannot conduct any colonial wars, India would have to be given a free hand; things would, of course, not pass off without all sorts of destruction, but that sort of thing is inseparable from all revolutions. The same might also happen elsewhere, e.g., in Algeria and Egypt, and would certainly be the best thing *for us*. We shall have enough to do at home. A reorganised Europe and North America will have such colossal power and provide such an example that the semi-civilised countries will automatically follow in their wake; they will be pushed in that direction even by economic needs alone. It seems to me that we can only make rather futile hypotheses about the social and political phases that these countries will then have to pass through before they likewise arrive at socialist organisation. One thing alone is certain: the victorious proletariat can force no blessings of any kind upon any foreign nation without undermining its own victory by so doing. This does not of course exclude defensive wars of various kinds.

Marx and Engels,
Selected Correspondence,
Moscow, 1975, pp. 330-31

FREDERICK ENGELS

From
ON THE OCCASION
OF KARL MARX'S DEATH

Marx and I, ever since 1845,[100] have held the view that *one* of the final results of the future proletarian revolution will be the gradual dissolution and ultimate disappearance of that political organisation called *the State*; an organisation the main object of which has ever been to secure, by armed force, the economical subjection of the working majority to the wealthy minority. With the disappearance of a wealthy minority the necessity for an armed repressive State-force disappears also. At the same time we have always held, that in order to arrive at this and the other, far more important ends of the social revolution of the future, the proletarian class will first have to possess itself of the organised political force of the State and with this aid stamp out the resistance of the Capitalist class and re-organise society. This is stated already in the *Communist Manifesto* of 1847, end of Chapter II.

The anarchists reverse the matter. They say, that the Proletarian revolution has to *begin* by abolishing the political organisation of the State. But after the victory of the Proletariat, the only organisation the victorious working class finds ready-made for use is that of the State. It may require adaptation to the new functions. But to destroy that at such a moment would be to destroy the only organism by means of which the victorious working class can exert its newly conquered power, keep down its capitalist enemies and carry out that economic revolution of society without which the whole victory must end in a defeat and in a massacre of the working class like that after the Paris Commune.

Does it require my express assertion that Marx opposed these anarchist absurdities from the very first day that they were started in their present form by Bakunin? The whole internal history of the International Working Men's Association is there to prove it.

Written on May 12, 1883

Marx, Engels, Lenin, *Anarchism and Anarcho-Syndicalism,* Moscow, 1974, p. 173

FREDERICK ENGELS

From
LETTER
TO EDUARD BERNSTEIN
IN ZURICH

Eastborne, August 27, 1883

In the discussion of the question of a "republic", especially in France, the fundamentals of our standpoint are not expressed clearly enough[101] in *Sozialdemokrat*, namely:

...The part played by the Bonapartist monarchy (the characteristic features of which have been set forth by Marx in *The Eighteenth Brumaire* and by me in *The Housing Question*, II, and elsewhere) in the class struggle between proletariat and bourgeoisie is similar to the part the old absolute monarchy played in the struggle between feudalism and bourgeoisie. But just as this struggle could not be fought out under the old absolute monarchy but only in a constitutional one (England, France 1789-1792 and 1815-1830), so that between bourgeoisie and proletariat can only be fought out in a republic. If therefore favourable conditions and a revolutionary past helped the French to overthrow Bonaparte[a] and set up a bourgeois republic, the French possess the advantage over us, who are still floundering in a hotchpotch of semi-feudalism and Bonapartism, in that they already possess the form in which the struggle must be fought out whereas we still have to *conquer* it. Politically they are a whole stage ahead of us. The result of a monarchist restoration in France would therefore be that the struggle for the restoration of the *bourgeois* republic would again be put on the order of the day. But the continuing existence of the republic on the other hand signifies increased intensification of the *direct* unconcealed class struggle between proletariat and bourgeoisie until a crisis is reached.

---

[a] Louis Napoleon Bonaparte III.—*Ed.*

In our country too the first and direct result of the revolution with regard to the *form* can and *must* be nothing but the *bourgeois* republic. But this will be here only a brief transitional period because fortunately we do not have a purely republican bourgeois party. The bourgeois republic, headed perhaps by the Progressive Party,[102] will enable us in the beginning to *win over the great masses of the workers to revolutionary socialism*. This will be done in one or two years and will lead to the utter exhaustion and self-destruction of all intermediate parties that may still exist apart from our Party. Only then can we successfully take over.

The big mistake the Germans make is to think that the revolution is something that can be made overnight. As a matter of fact it is a process of development of the masses that takes several years even under conditions accelerating this process. Any revolution completed overnight removed only a reaction that was hopeless at the very start (1830) or led directly to the opposite of what had been aspired to (1848, France).

Marx and Engels,
Selected Correspondence,
Moscow, 1975, pp. 342-43

FREDERICK ENGELS

From
LETTER
TO EDUARD BERNSTEIN
IN ZURICH

London, January 1, 1884

As to your former inquiry concerning the passage in the preface of the *Manifesto* taken from *Der Bürgerkrieg in Frankreich* [*The Civil War in France*] you will most likely agree with the reply given in the original (*Der Bürgerkrieg...*, p. 19 et seq.). I am sending you a copy in case you do not have one there. It is simply a question of showing that the victorious proletariat must first refashion the old bureaucratic, administratively centralised state power before it can use it for its own purposes; whereas *all* bourgeois republicans since 1848 inveighed against this machinery so long as they were in the opposition, but once they were in the government they took it over without altering it and used it partly against the reaction but still more against the proletariat. That in *The Civil War* the *instinctive* tendencies of the Commune were put down to its credit as more or less deliberate plans was justified and even necessary under the circumstances.

Marx and Engels,
Selected Correspondence,
Moscow, 1975, p. 345

FREDERICK ENGELS

From
THE ORIGIN
OF THE FAMILY,
PRIVATE PROPERTY
AND THE STATE

Because the state arose from the need to hold class antagonisms in check, but because it arose, at the same time, in the midst of the conflict of these classes, it is, as a rule, the state of the most powerful, economically dominant class, which, through the medium of the state, becomes also the politically dominant class, and thus acquires new means of holding down and exploiting the oppressed class. Thus, the state of antiquity was above all the state of the slave owners for the purpose of holding down the slaves, as the feudal state was the organ of the nobility for holding down the peasant serfs and bondsmen, and the modern representative state is an instrument of exploitation of wage-labour by capital. By way of exception, however, periods occur in which the warring classes balance each other so nearly that the state power, as ostensible mediator, acquires, for the moment, a certain degree of independence of both. Such was the absolute monarchy of the seventeenth and eighteenth centuries, which held the balance between the nobility and the class of burghers; such was the Bonapartism of the First, and still more of the Second French Empire, which played off the proletariat against the bourgeoisie and the bourgeoisie against the proletariat. The latest performance of this kind, in which ruler and ruled appear equally ridiculous, is the new German Empire of the Bismarck nation: here capitalists and workers are balanced against each other and equally cheated for the benefit of the impoverished Prussian cabbage junkers.

In most of the historical states, the rights of citizens are, besides, apportioned according to their wealth, thus directly expressing the fact that the state is an organisation of the possessing class for its protection against the non-possessing class. It was so already in the Athenian and Roman classification according to property. It was so in the mediaeval feudal state, in which the alignment of political power was in conformity with the amount of land owned. It is seen in the electoral qualifications of the modern representative states. Yet this political recognition of property distinctions is by no means essential. On the contrary, it marks a low stage of state development.

The highest form of the state, the democratic republic, which under our modern conditions of society is more and more becoming an inevitable necessity, and is the form of state in which alone the last decisive struggle between proletariat and bourgeoisie can be fought out—the democratic republic officially knows nothing any more of property distinctions. In it wealth exercises its power indirectly, but all the more surely. On the one hand, in the form of the direct corruption of officials, of which America provides the classical example; on the other hand, in the form of an alliance between government and Stock Exchange, which becomes the easier to achieve the more the public debt increases and the more joint-stock companies concentrate in their hands not only transport but also production itself, using the Stock Exchange as their centre. The latest French republic as well as the United States is a striking example of this; and good old Switzerland has contributed its share in this field. But that a democratic republic is not essential for this fraternal alliance between government and Stock Exchange is proved by England and also by the new German Empire, where one cannot tell who was elevated more by universal suffrage, Bismarck or Bleichröder. And lastly, the possessing class rules directly through the medium of universal suffrage. As long as the oppressed class, in our case, therefore, the proletariat, is not yet ripe to emancipate itself, it will in its majority regard the existing order of society as the only one possible and, politically, will form the tail of the capitalist class, its extreme Left wing. To the extent, however, that this class matures for its self-emancipation, it constitutes itself as its own party and elects its own representatives, and not those of the capitalists. Thus, universal suffrage is the gauge of the maturity of the working class. It cannot and never will be anything more in the present-day state; but that is sufficient. On the day the thermometer of universal suffrage registers boiling point among the workers, both they and the capitalists will know what to do.

The state, then, has not existed from all eternity. There have been societies that did without it, that had no idea of the state and state power. At a certain stage of economic development, which was necessarily bound up with the split of society into classes, the state became a necessity owing to this split. We are now rapidly approaching a stage in the development of production at which the existence of these classes not only will have ceased to be a necessity, but will become a positive hindrance to production. They will fall as inevitably as they arose at an earlier stage. Along with them the state will inevitably fall. Society, which will reorganise production on the basis of a free and equal association of the producers, will put the whole machinery of state where it will then belong: into the museum of antiquities, by the side of the spinning-wheel and the bronze axe.

Written at the end
of March-May 26, 1884

Marx and Engels,
Selected Works in 3 vols.,
Vol. 3, Moscow, 1973,
pp. 328-30

FREDERICK ENGELS

From
PREFACE
TO THE ENGLISH EDITION
OF THE
FIRST VOLUME
OF "CAPITAL"

"Das Kapital" is often called, on the Continent, "the Bible of the working-class." That the conclusions arrived at in this work are daily more and more becoming the fundamental principles of the great working-class movement, not only in Germany and Switzerland, but in France, in Holland and Belgium, in America, and even in Italy and Spain, that everywhere the working-class more and more recognises, in these conclusions, the most adequate expression of its condition and of its aspirations, nobody acquainted with that movement will deny. And in England, too, the theories of Marx, even at this moment, exercise a powerful influence upon the socialist movement which is spreading in the ranks of "cultured" people no less than in those of the working-class. But that is not all. The time is rapidly approaching when a thorough examination of England's economic position will impose itself as an irresistible national necessity. The working of the industrial system of this country, impossible without a constant and rapid extension of production, and therefore of markets, is coming to a dead stop. Free-trade has exhausted its resources; even Manchester doubts this its quondam economic gospel.* Foreign

---

* At the quarterly meeting of the Manchester Chamber of Commerce, held this afternoon, a warm discussion took place on the subject of Free-trade. A resolution was moved to the effect that "having waited in vain 40 years for other nations to follow the Free-trade example of England, this Chamber thinks the time has now arrived to reconsider that position." The resolution was rejected by a majority of one only, the figures being 21 for, and 22 against.—*Evening Standard*, Nov. 1, 1886.

industry, rapidly developing, stares English production in the face everywhere, not only in protected, but also in neutral markets, and even on this side of the Channel. While the productive power increases in a geometric, the extension of markets proceeds at best in an arithmetic ratio. The decennial cycle of stagnation, prosperity, over-production and crisis, ever recurrent from 1825 to 1867, seems indeed to have run its course; but only to land us in the slough of despond of a permanent and chronic depression. The sighed-for period of prosperity will not come; as often as we seem to perceive its heralding symptoms, so often do they again vanish into air. Meanwhile, each succeeding winter brings up afresh the great question, "what to do with the unemployed"; but while the number of the unemployed keeps swelling from year to year, there is nobody to answer that question; and we can almost calculate the moment when the unemployed losing patience will take their own fate into their own hands. Surely, at such a moment, the voice ought to be heard of a man whose whole theory is the result of a lifelong study of the economic history and condition of England, and whom that study led to the conclusion that, at least in Europe, England is the only country where the inevitable social revolution might be effected entirely by peaceful and legal means. He certainly never forgot to add that he hardly expected the English ruling classes to submit, without a "pro-slavery rebellion," to this peaceful and legal revolution.[103]

Dated November 5, 1886

Karl Marx, *Capital*, Vol. I, pp. 16-17

FREDERICK ENGELS

From
[a] INTRODUCTION TO
SIGISMUND BORKHEIM'S
PAMPHLET
"TO THE MEMORY
OF THE FLAG-WAVING
GERMAN PATRIOTS.
1806–1807"

Ultimately no war for a Prussia-Germany is any longer possible other than a world war and, indeed, a world war of a hitherto undreamed-of extent and violence. Eight to ten million soldiers will throttle each other and in doing so strip Europe bare, as no swarm of locusts has ever done. The devastation of the Thirty Years War compressed into three to four years and spread over the entire continent; famine, pestilence and a general relapse into barbarism both by the troops and the mass of the people as a result of acute distress; irretrievable disorder in our artificial mechanism in trade, industry and credit, ending in general bankruptcy; the collapse of old states and their traditional state wisdom to such an extent that crowns will roll by the dozen on the pavement and there will be no-one to pick them up; the absolute impossibility of foreseeing how all this will end and who will emerge victorious from the struggle; only one outcome is absolutely sure—general exhaustion and the creation of conditions for the ultimate victory of the working class.

That is the prospect when the system of mutual outbidding in armaments, which is being carried to extremes, finally bears its inevitable fruit. This, my princes and statesmen, is where you have brought old Europe in your wisdom. And when nothing more remains for you than to begin the last great war dance we shall not

[a] English translation © Progress Publishers 1978

object. The war may well drive us into the background for the moment; it may snatch away from us some of the positions we have conquered. But when you have unleashed forces which you will never again be able to fetter, then let events take their course: at the end of the tragedy you will be ruined and the victory of the proletariat will either have been achieved or will all the same be inevitable.

Dated December 15, 1887

Marx/Engels, *Werke*, Bd. 21, S. 350-51

FREDERICK ENGELS

From
a) LETTER
TO GERSON TRIER
IN COPENHAGEN
[DRAFT]

London, December 18, 1889

I shall start with a point on which I do *not* agree with you.

You reject on principle any and every collaboration, even the most transient, with other parties. I am enough of a revolutionary not to renounce even this means if in the given circumstances it is more advantageous or at least less harmful.

We are agreed on this: that the proletariat cannot conquer political power, the only door to the new society, without violent revolution. For the proletariat to be strong enough to win on- the decisive day it must—and Marx and I have advocated this ever since 1847—form a separate party distinct from all others and opposed to them, a conscious class party.

But that does not mean that this party cannot at certain moments use other parties for its purposes. Nor does this mean that it cannot temporarily support the measures of other parties if these measures either are directly advantageous to the proletariat or progressive as regards economic development or political freedom. I would support anyone waging a real struggle in Germany for the abolition of primogeniture and other feudal survivals, the bureaucracy, protective tariffs, the Anti-Socialist Law, and restrictions on the right of assembly and of association. If our German Progressive Party or your Danish *Venstre* were real radical-bourgeois parties and did not simply consist of wretched windbags who take to the bushes at the first threat of a Bismarck or Estrup, I would by no means be *unconditionally* opposed to any and every temporary collaboration with them for definite purposes.

---

a) English translation © Progress Publishers 1978

274

It is also collaboration when our deputies cast their votes for a proposal which was submitted by another party—and they have to do that often enough. But I am for this only if the advantage to us is direct or if the historical development of the country in the direction of the economic and political revolution is indisputable and worth while; and provided that the proletarian class character of the Party is not jeopardised thereby. For me this is the absolute limit. You can find this policy set forth as early as 1847 in the *Communist Manifesto*; we pursued it in 1848, in the International, everywhere.

To digress from the question of morality (it is beside the point here and I therefore leave it aside) for me, as a revolutionary, any means which leads to the goal is suitable, including both the most violent and the most pacific.

Such a policy requires perspicacity and character, but what policy does not? It exposes us to the danger of corruption, the anarchists and friend Morris say. Yes, if the working class consists of simpletons, weak-willed people and, quite simply, venal rabble, then the best we can do is clear off home immediately, since there is nothing for the proletariat and all of us to do on the political stage. The proletariat, like all other parties, learns most quickly from its own mistakes and no one can completely protect it from these mistakes.

Therefore, you are, I think, incorrect to elevate a question that is above all purely tactical to the level of a matter of principle. And I see here in essence only a tactical question. But a tactical mistake, too, can under certain circumstances lead to the violation of principles.

Marx/Engels, *Werke*,
Bd. 37, S. 326-27

Translated from the German

FREDERICK ENGELS

From
INTRODUCTION TO "THE CIVIL WAR IN FRANCE" BY KARL MARX

If today, after twenty years, we look back at the activity and historical significance of the Paris Commune of 1871, we shall find it necessary to make a few additions to the account given in *The Civil War in France*.

The members of the Commune were divided into a majority, the Blanquists, who had also been predominant in the Central Committee of the National Guard; and a minority, members of the International Working Men's Association, chiefly consisting of adherents of the Proudhon school of socialism. The great majority of the Blanquists were at that time Socialists only by revolutionary, proletarian instinct; only a few had attained greater clarity on principles, through Vaillant, who was familiar with German scientific socialism. It is therefore comprehensible that in the economic sphere much was left undone which, according to our view today, the Commune ought to have done. The hardest thing to understand is certainly the holy awe with which they remained standing respectfully outside the gates of the Bank of France. This was also a serious political mistake. The bank in the hands of the Commune—this would have been worth more than ten thousand hostages. It would have meant the pressure of the whole of the French bourgeoisie on the Versailles government in favour of peace with the Commune. But what is still more wonderful is the correctness of much that nevertheless was done by the Commune, composed as it was of Blanquists and Proudhonists. Naturally, the Proudhonists were chiefly responsible for the economic decrees of the Commune, both for their praiseworthy and their unpraiseworthy aspects; as the Blanquists were for its political commissions and omissions. And in both cases the irony of history willed—as is usual when doctrinaires come to the helm—that both did the opposite of what the doctrines of their school prescribed.

Proudhon, the Socialist of the small peasant and master-craftsman, regarded association with positive hatred. He said of it that there was more bad than good in it; that it was by nature sterile, even harmful, because it was a fetter on the freedom of the worker; that it was a pure dogma, unproductive and burdensome, in conflict as much with the freedom of the worker as with economy of labour; that its disadvantages multiplied more swiftly than its advantages; that, as compared with it, competition, division of labour and private property were economic forces. Only in the exceptional cases—as Proudhon called them—of large-scale industry and large establishments, such as railways, was the association of workers in place. (See *General Idea of the Revolution, 3rd sketch.*)

By 1871, large-scale industry had already so much ceased to be an exceptional case even in Paris, the centre of artistic handicrafts, that by far the most important decree of the Commune instituted an organisation of large-scale industry and even of manufacture which was not only to be based on the association of the workers in each factory, but also to combine all these associations in one great union; in short, an organisation which, as Marx quite rightly says in *The Civil War*, must necessarily have led in the end to communism, that is to say, the direct opposite of the Proudhon doctrine. And, therefore, the Commune was the grave of the Proudhon school of socialism. Today this school has vanished from French working-class circles; here, among the Possibilists[104] no less than among the "Marxists", Marx's theory now rules unchallenged. Only among the "radical" bourgeoisie are there still Proudhonists.

The Blanquists fared no better. Brought up in the school of conspiracy, and held together by the strict discipline which went with it, they started out from the viewpoint that a relatively small number of resolute, well-organised men would be able, at a given favourable moment, not only to seize the helm of state, but also by a display of great, ruthless energy, to maintain power until they succeeded in sweeping the mass of the people into the revolution and ranging them round the small band of leaders. This involved, above all, the strictest, dictatorial centralisation of all power in the hands of the new revolutionary government. And what did the

Commune, with its majority of these same Blanquists, actually do? In all its proclamations to the French in the provinces, it appealed to them to form a free federation of all French Communes with Paris, a national organisation which for the first time was really to be created by the nation itself. It was precisely the oppressing power of the former centralised government, army, political police, bureaucracy, which Napoleon had created in 1798 and which since then had been taken over by every new government as a welcome instrument and used against its opponents—it was precisely this power which was to fall everywhere, just as it had already fallen in Paris.

From the very outset the Commune was compelled to recognise that the working class, once come to power, could not go on managing with the old state machine; that in order not to lose again its only just conquered supremacy, this working class must, on the one hand, do away with all the old repressive machinery previously used against it itself, and, on the other, safeguard itself against its own deputies and officials, by declaring them all, without exception, subject to recall at any moment. What had been the characteristic attribute of the former state? Society had created its own organs to look after its common interests, originally through simple division of labour. But these organs, at whose head was the state power, had in the course of time, in pursuance of their own special interests, transformed themselves from the servants of society into the masters of society. This can be seen, for example, not only in the hereditary monarchy, but equally so in the democratic republic. Nowhere do "politicians" form a more separate and powerful section of the nation than precisely in North America. There, each of the two major parties which alternately succeed each other in power is itself in turn controlled by people who make a business of politics, who speculate on seats in the legislative assemblies of the Union as well as of the separate states, or who make a living by carrying on agitation for their party and on its victory are rewarded with positions. It is well known how the Americans have been trying for thirty years to shake off this yoke, which has become intolerable, and how in spite of it all they continue to sink ever deeper in this swamp of corruption. It is precisely in America that we see best how there takes place this process of the state power making itself independent in relation to society, whose mere instrument, it was originally intended to be. Here there exists no dynasty, no nobility, no standing army, beyond the few men keeping watch on the Indians, no bureaucracy with permanent posts or the right to pensions. And nevertheless we find here two great gangs of political speculators, who alternately take possession of the state power and exploit it by the most corrupt means and for most corrupt ends—and the nation is powerless against these two great cartels of politicians, who are ostensibly its servants, but in reality dominate and plunder it.

Against this transformation of the state and the organs of the state from servants of society into masters of society—an inevitable transformation in all previous states—the Commune made use of two infallible means. In the first place, it filled all posts—administrative, judicial and educational—by election on the basis of universal suffrage of all concerned, subject to the right of recall at any time by the same electors. And, in the second place, all officials, high or low, were paid only the wages received by other workers. The highest salary paid by the Commune to anyone was 6,000 francs. In this way an effective barrier to place-hunting and careerism was set up, even apart from the binding mandates to delegates to representative bodies which were added besides.

This shattering [*Sprengung*] of the former state power and its replacement by a new and truly democratic one is described in detail in the third section of *The Civil War*. But it was necessary to dwell briefly here once more on some of its features, because in Germany particularly the superstitious belief in the state has been carried over from philosophy into the general consciousness of the bourgeoisie and even of many workers. According to the philosophical conception, the state is the "realisation of the idea", or the Kingdom of God on earth, translated into philosophical terms, the sphere in which eternal truth and justice is or should be realised. And from this follows a superstitious reverence for the state and everything connected with it, which takes root the more readily since people are accustomed from childhood to imagine that the affairs and interests common to the whole of society could not be looked after otherwise than as they have been looked after in the past, that is, through the state and its lucratively positioned officials. And people think they have taken quite an extraordinarily bold step forward when they have rid themselves of belief in hereditary monarchy and swear by the democratic republic. In reality, however, the state is nothing but a machine for the oppression of one class by another, and indeed in the democratic republic no less than in the monarchy; and at best an evil inherited by the proletariat after its victorious struggle for class supremacy, whose worst sides the victorious proletariat, just like the Commune, cannot avoid having to lop off at once as much as possible until such time as a generation reared in new, free social conditions is able to throw the entire lumber of the state on the scrap heap.

Of late, the Social-Democratic philistine has once more been filled with wholesome terror at the words: Dictatorship of the Proletariat. Well and good, gentlemen, do you want to know what this dictatorship looks like? Look at the Paris Commune. That was the Dictatorship of the Proletariat.

London on the twentieth
anniversary of the
Paris Commune,
March 18, 1891

Marx and Engels,
Selected Works in 3 vols.,
Vol. 2, Moscow, 1973,
pp. 185-89

FREDERICK ENGELS

From
A CRITIQUE
OF THE DRAFT
SOCIAL-DEMOCRATIC
PROGRAMME
OF 1891

The political demands of the draft have one great fault. It *lacks* precisely what should have been said. If all the 10 demands were granted we should indeed have more diverse means of achieving our main political aim, but the aim itself would in no wise have been achieved. As regards the rights being granted to the people and their representatives, the imperial constitution is, strictly speaking, a copy of the Prussian constitution of 1850, a constitution whose articles are extremely reactionary and give the government all the real power, while the chambers are not even allowed to reject taxes; a constitution, which proved during the period of the conflict[105] that the government could do anything it liked with it. The rights of the Reichstag are the same as those of the Prussian chamber and this is why Liebknecht called this Reichstag the fig-leaf of absolutism. It is an obvious absurdity to wish "to transform all the instruments of labour into common property" on the basis of this constitution and the system of small states sanctioned by it, on the basis of the "union" between Prussia and Reuss-Greiz-Schleiz-Lobenstein,[106] in which one has as many square miles as the other has square inches.

To touch on that is dangerous, however. Nevertheless, somehow or other, the thing has to be attacked. How necessary this is shown precisely at the present time by opportunism, which is gaining ground in a large section of the Social-Democratic press. Fearing a renewal of the Anti-Socialist Law, or recalling all manner of over-hasty pronouncements made during the reign of that law, they now want the Party to find the present legal order in Germany

281

adequate for putting through all Party demands by peaceful means. These are attempts to convince oneself and the Party that "present-day society is developing towards socialism" without asking oneself whether it does not thereby just as necessarily outgrow the old social order and whether it will not have to burst this old shell by force, as a crab breaks its shell, and also whether in Germany, in addition, it will not have to smash the fetters of the still semi-absolutist, and moreover indescribably confused political order. One can conceive that the old society may develop peacefully into the new one in countries where the representatives of the people concentrate all power in their hands, where, if one has the support of the majority of the people, one can do as one sees fit in a constitutional way: in democratic republics such as France and the U.S.A., in monarchies such as Britain, where the imminent abdication of the dynasty in return for financial compensation is discussed in the press daily and where this dynasty is powerless against the people. But in Germany where the government is almost omnipotent and the Reichstag and all other representative bodies have no real power, to advocate such a thing in Germany, when, moreover, there is no need to do so, means removing the fig-leaf from absolutism and becoming oneself a screen for its nakedness.

In the long run such a policy can only lead one's own Party astray. They push general, abstract political questions into the foreground, thereby concealing the immediate concrete questions, which at the moment of the first great events, the first political crisis automatically pose themselves. What can result from this except that at the decisive moment the Party suddenly proves helpless and that uncertainty and discord on the most decisive issues reign in it because these issues have never been discussed? Must there be a repetition of what happened with protective tariffs, which were declared to be a matter of concern only to the bourgeoisie, not affecting the interests of the workers in the least, that is, a matter on which everyone could vote as he wished? Are not many people now going to the opposite extreme and are they not, in contrast to the bourgeoisie, who have become addicted to protective tariffs, rehashing the economic distortions of Cobden and Bright and preaching them as the purest socialism—this Manchesterism unadulterated?[107] This forgetting of the great, the principal considerations for the momentary interests of the day, this struggling and striving for the success of the moment regardless of later consequences, this sacrifice of the future of the movement for its present, may be "honestly" meant, but it is and remains opportunism, and "honest" opportunism is perhaps the most dangerous of all!

Which are these ticklish, but very significant points?

First. If one thing is certain it is that our Party and the working class can only come to power under the form of a democratic republic. This is even the specific form for the dictatorship of the proletariat, as the Great French Revolution has already shown. It would be inconceivable for our best people to become ministers under an emperor, as Miquel. It would seem that from a legal point of view it is inadvisable to include the demand for a republic directly in the programme, although this was possible even under Louis Philippe in France, and is now in Italy. But the fact that in Germany it is not permitted to advance even a republican party programme openly, proves how totally mistaken is the belief that a republic, and not only a republic, but also communist society, can be established in a cosy, peaceful way.

However, the question of the republic could possibly be passed by. What, however, in my opinion should and could be included is the demand for *the concentration of all political power in the hands of the people's representatives*. That would suffice for the time being if it is impossible to go any further.

Second. The reconstitution of Germany. On the one hand, the system of small states must be abolished—just try to revolutionise society while there are the Bavarian-Württemberg reservation rights [108]—and the map of present-day Thuringia, for example, is such a sorry sight. On the other hand, Prussia must cease to exist and must be broken up into self-governing provinces for the specific Prussianism to stop weighing on Germany. The system of small states and Prussianism are the two sides of the antithesis now gripping Germany in a vice, in which one side must always serve as the excuse and justification for the existence of the other.

What should take its place? In my view, the proletariat can only use the form of the one and indivisible republic. In the gigantic territory of the United States, the federal republic is still, on the whole, a necessity, although in the Eastern states it is already becoming a hindrance. It would be a step forward in Britain where the two islands are peopled by four nations and in spite of a single Parliament three different systems of legislation already exist side by side. In little Switzerland, it has long been a hindrance, tolerable only because Switzerland is content to be a purely passive member of the European state system. For Germany, federalisation on the Swiss model would be an enormous step backward. Two points distinguish a union state from a completely unified state: first, that each member state, each canton, has its own civil and criminal legislative and judicial system, and, second, that alongside a popular chamber there is also a federal chamber in which each canton, whether large or small, votes as such. The first we have luckily overcome and we shall not be so childish as to reintroduce it, the second we have in the Bundesrat and we could do very well without it, since our "federal state" generally constitutes a transition to a unified state. The revolution from above of 1866 and 1870 must not be reversed but supplemented and improved by a movement from below.

So, then, a unified republic. But not in the sense of the present French Republic, which is nothing but the Empire established in 1798 without the Emperor[109] From 1792 to 1798 each French department, each commune, enjoyed complete self-government on the American model, and this is what we too must have. How self-government is to be organised and how we can manage without a bureaucracy has been shown to us by America and the First French Republic, and is being shown even today by Australia, Canada, and the other English colonies. And a provincial and communal self-government of this type is far freer than, for instance, Swiss federalism, under which, it is true, the canton is very independent in relation to the federation, but is also independent in relation to the district and the commune. The cantonal governments appoint the district governors and prefects, which is unknown in English-speaking countries and which we want to abolish here as resolutely in the future as the Prussian Landräte and Regierungsräte.

Probably few of these points should be included in the programme. I mention them also mainly to describe the system in Germany where such matters cannot be discussed openly, and to emphasise the self-deception of those who wish to transform such a system in a legal way into communist society. Further, to remind the Party Executive that there are other important political questions besides direct legislation by the people and the gratuitous administration of justice without which we can also ultimately get by. In the generally unstable conditions these questions may become urgent at any time and what will happen then if they have not been discussed by us beforehand and no agreement has been reached on them?

However, what can be included in the programme and can, at least indirectly, serve as a hint of what may not be said directly is the following demand:

"Complete self-government in the provinces, districts and communes through officials elected by universal suffrage. The abolition of all local and provincial authorities appointed by the state."

Written between
June 18 and 29, 1891

Marx and Engels,
Selected Works in 3 vols.,
Vol. 3, Moscow, 1973,
pp. 433-37

a) REPLY
TO GIOVANNI BOVIO[110]

In an article printed in the *Tribune* on 2 February, the illustrious Giovanni Bovio reproves the Italian republican deputies, who recently went over to the monarchist camp, for treating with contempt the question of the form of government. This does not concern me greatly: what concerns me is that he uses my article on German socialism (*Critica Sociale*, January 16, 1892) to cast the same reproach at the German Socialists in general and at me in particular.

Here is what he says:

"From this, moreover, it can be seen what mistake and why is being made by the Socialists who, with Frederick Engels, talk about the Socialists coming to power in the near future, but do not define what power. Engels manages to determine by arithmetical means (and figures in history always seemed good evidence to me) the not-so-distant future when the Socialist Party will gain the majority in the German parliament. Well argued: and then?"

"It will take over power."

"Even better: but what power? Will it be royal power, or republican power, or will the party return to Weitling's utopia, left behind by the *Communist Manifesto* as far back as in January 1848?"

"The form does not matter to us."

"Really?... But one can only talk of power when it has concrete form. It may be considered that the new substance, the new idea, will itself create the form and will produce it out of itself, but it cannot and must not be ignored."

To this I reply that I totally reject the illustrious Bovio's interpretation.

First of all, I certainly did not say that "the Socialist Party will gain the majority and will take over power". On the contrary, I stressed that there was a ten-to-one chance that our rulers would

---

a) English translation © Progress Publishers 1978

apply force against us long before that, and this would take us from the arena of parliamentary struggle into the revolutionary arena. But let us continue.

"It will take over power — but what power? Will it be royal power, or republican power, or will the party return to Weitling's utopia, left behind by the *Communist Manifesto* as far back as in January 1848?"

Here I will permit myself to use an expression from the illustrious Bovio himself. One must indeed be a "hermit" to have the slightest doubt concerning the nature of that power.

The whole of governmental, aristocratic and bourgeois Germany accuses our friends in the Reichstag of being republicans and revolutionaries.

For forty years, Marx and I have repeatedly affirmed that for us the democratic republic is the only political form under which the struggle between the working class and the capitalist class can at first acquire a universal character and then be climaxed by the decisive victory of the proletariat.

The illustrious Bovio is not, of course, so naive as to imagine that any German emperor will appoint his ministers from among the Socialist Party and that, even if he wished to do this, he would accept conditions presupposing his abdication—without which those ministers could not hope for their party's support. Incidentally, to tell the truth, his apprehension that we might "return to Weitling's utopia" makes me think that the naivety of this man who has been taking part in a dialogue with me is indeed considerable.

Or does the illustrious Bovio, in mentioning Weitling, perhaps wish to say that the German Socialists attribute to *social* form no more importance than, in his opinion, they attach to *political*? In this case, he is again mistaken. He should have a sufficient idea of German socialism to know that German socialism demands the socialisation of all the means of production. In what way will this economic revolution be accomplished? This will depend on the circumstances under which our party seizes power, on the moment when it happens, and on the means of its achievement. As Bovio himself declares, "the new substance, the new idea, will itself create the form and will produce it out of itself". And, if, say, tomorrow, as a result of some unexpected turn of events, our party should be called to power, I know very well what I would propose as a programme of action.

"Form does not matter to us?"

I consider it essential to declare that neither I nor any of the German Socialists ever said this or anything of the kind; it was only said by the illustrious Bovio. And I would like to know by what right he attributes such "sciocchezza"[a] to us.

Incidentally, if the illustrious Bovio had waited until he had read the second half of my article (*Critica Sociale*, February 1), he might have saved himself the trouble of confusing the German revolutionary Socialists with the Italian monarchist republicans.

February 6, 1892

Frederick Engels
Translated from the Italian

---

[a] Folly.—*Ed.*

FREDERICK ENGELS

From
LETTER
TO PAUL LAFARGUE
AT LE PERREUX

London, November 12, 1892

The fruits of your peregrinations through France begin to ripen, and all of us are pleased to see the progress made in France. Do you realise now what a splendid weapon you in France have had in your hands for forty years in universal suffrage; if only people had known how to use it! It's slower and more boring than the call to revolution, but it's ten times more sure, and what is even better, it indicates with the most perfect accuracy the day when a call to armed revolution has to be made; it's even ten to one that universal suffrage, intelligently used by the workers, will drive the rulers to overthrow legality, that is, to put us in the most favourable position to make the revolution. We should reach a new stage in the 1893 elections, and then there will be that union between Socialists of different shades of opinions of which Liebknecht never stops talking. That union will come about as soon as there is a score of Socialists in the Chamber; if our people have—as I hope—a majority, they will be able to dictate terms. In the meantime, go on with your "victories and conquests", and you will find that it is the Germans who will applaud you the most warmly.

Frederick Engels, Paul and
Laura Lafargue, *Correspondence*,
Vol. 3, Moscow,
1963, pp. 211-12

FREDERICK ENGELS

From
[a)] GREETINGS
TO THE INTERNATIONAL
CONGRESS OF THE
STUDENTS-SOCIALISTS[111]

London, December 19, 1893

The bourgeois revolution of the past demanded of the universities only lawyers as the best raw material for their politician, the emancipation of the working class will also call for doctors, engineers, chemists, agronomists and other specialists; for it is a matter of gaining control not only of the political machine, but of all social production, and solid knowledge will be needed instead of fine-sounding phrases.

Marx and Engels,
Collected Works, Vol. 22,
Russian edition, p. 432

Translated from the French

FREDERICK ENGELS

From
AFTERWORD
TO THE WORK
"ON SOCIAL RELATIONS
IN RUSSIA"

It is not only possible but inescapable that once the proletariat wins out and the means of production pass into common ownership among the West-European nations, the countries which have just managed to make a start on capitalist production, and where tribal institutions or relics of them are still intact, will be able to use these relics of communal ownership and the corresponding popular customs as a powerful means of considerably shortening their advance to socialist society and largely sparing themselves the sufferings and the struggles through which we in Western Europe have to make our way. But an inevitable condition of this is the example and active support of the hitherto capitalist West. Only when the capitalist economy has been overcome at home and in the countries of its prime, only when the retarded countries have seen from their example "how it's done", how the productive forces of modern industry are made to work as social property for society as a whole—only then will the retarded countries be able to start on this abbreviated process of development. But then their success will be assured. And this applies not only to Russia but to all countries at the pre-capitalist stage of development. However, this will be relatively easiest done in Russia, where a part of the native population has already assimilated the intellectual fruits of capitalist development, which will make it possible, in a period of revolution, to carry out her social transformation almost simultaneously with that of the West.

Marx and I said as much on January 21, 1882, in the Preface to the Russian Edition of the *Manifesto of the Communist Party*, in a translation by Plekhanov. We wrote:

"But in Russia we find, face to face with the rapidly developing capitalist swindle and bourgeois landed property, just beginning to develop, more than half the land owned in common by the peasants. Now the question is: can the Russian *obshchina*, though greatly undermined, yet a form of the primeval common ownership of land, pass directly to the higher form of communist common ownership? Or, on the contrary, must it first pass through the same process of dissolution as constitutes the historical evolution of the West?

"The only answer to that possible today is this: If the Russian Revolution becomes the signal for a proletarian revolution in the West, so that both complement each other, the present Russian common ownership of land may serve as the starting point for a communist development."

I do not undertake to say whether this community is still sufficiently intact to become, when the occasion arises, and in combination with a revolution in Western Europe, the starting point for communist development, as Marx and I had still hoped in 1882. This much, however, is certain: if anything of this community is to be salvaged, the first requirement is the overthrow of the tsarist despotism, a revolution in Russia. The Russian revolution will not only wrest the greater part of the nation, the peasants, from their isolation in the villages, constituting their *mir*, their universe; it will not only lead the peasants out into the large arena, where they will come to know the outside world and with it their own selves, their own condition, and the means of escape from their present misery—the Russian revolution will also give a fresh impulse to the labour movement in the West, creating for it new and better conditions for struggle and thereby advancing the victory of the modern industrial proletariat, a victory without which present-day Russia, whether on the basis of the community or of capitalism, cannot achieve a socialist transformation of society.

Written in the
first half of
January 1894

Marx and Engels,
Selected Works in 3 vols.,
Vol. 2, Moscow, 1973,
pp. 403-04, 409-10

FREDERICK ENGELS

From
FUTURE
ITALIAN REVOLUTION
AND SOCIALIST PARTY

Ever since 1848 the tactics that have brought the Socialists the greatest successes were those set down in the *Communist Manifesto*:

"In the various stages of development which the struggle of the working class against the bourgeoisie has to pass through, the Socialists always and everywhere represent the interests of the movement as a whole.... They fight for the attainment of the immediate aims, for the enforcement of the momentary interests of the working class; but in the movement of the present, they also represent and take care of the future of that movement."

They therefore take an active part in every phase of development of the struggle between the two classes without ever losing sight of the fact that these phases are just so many stages leading to the supreme great goal: the conquest of political power by the proletariat as a means for reorganising society. Their place is by the side of those fighting to obtain immediate benefits in the interests of the working class. They accept all these political or social benefits, but merely *as payments on account*. Hence they consider every revolutionary or progressive movement as a step in the direction in which they themselves are travelling. It is their special mission to impel the other revolutionary parties onward and, should one of them be victorious, to safeguard the interests of the proletariat. Those tactics, which never lose sight of the grand objective, spare Socialists the disappointment that inevitably will befall the other and less clear-sighted parties, be they pure republicans or sentimental Socialists, who mistake what is a mere stage for the final terminus of their forward march.

293

Let us apply all this to Italy.

The victory of the disintegrating petty bourgeoisie and of the peasantry may therefore possibly bring on a ministry of the "converted" republicans. That will get us universal suffrage and considerably greater freedom of movement (press, assembly, association, abolition of police surveillance, etc.)—new arms not to be disdained.

Or it will bring us a bourgeois republic with the same people and some Mazzinists among them. That would considerably increase our liberty and our field of action, at least for the time being. And Marx said that the bourgeois republic is the sole political form in which the struggle between the proletariat and the bourgeoisie can be fought to a finish, to say nothing of the repercussions this would have in Europe.

Hence the victory of the present revolutionary movement is bound to make us stronger and place us in a more favourable *environment*. We should commit the greatest error if we were to stand aside, if in our conduct *vis-à-vis* "related" parties we were to confine ourselves to purely negative criticism. A moment may come when it will be our duty to co-operate with them in a positive way. What moment might that be?

Evidently it is not our business directly to prepare a movement which, strictly speaking, is not a movement of the class we represent. If the republicans and radicals believe the hour for action has struck, let them give free rein to their impetuosity. As for ourselves we have been deceived too often by the high-sounding promises of these gentlemen to let ourselves be taken in once more. Neither their proclamations nor their conspiracies need move us in the least. If we are obliged to support every *real* popular movement we are no less obliged to see that the scarcely formed nucleus of our proletarian Party is not sacrificed in vain and that the proletariat is not decimated in futile local revolts.

But if on the contrary the movement is genuinely national our people will not stay in hiding nor will they need a password and our participation in this movement is a matter of course. At such time however it must be clearly understood, and we must loudly proclaim it, that we are participating *as an independent party*, allied for the moment with radicals and republicans but wholly distinct from them; that we entertain no illusions whatever as to the result of the struggle in case of victory; that far from satisfying us this result will only mean to us another stage won, a new base of operations for further conquests; that on the very day of victory our ways will part; that from that day on we shall constitute the *new opposition* to the new government, an opposition that is not reactionary but progressive, the opposition of the extreme Left, which will press on to new conquests beyond the ground already gained.

After the common victory we might be offered some seats in the new government, but they will always be a *minority. That is the greatest danger.* After February 1848 the French socialist democrats (of the *Réforme*, Ledru-Rollin, Louis Blanc, Flocon, etc.) made the mistake of accepting such posts. Constituting a minority in the government they voluntarily shared the responsibility for all the infamies and treachery which the majority, composed of pure Republicans, committed against the working class, while their presence in the government completely paralysed the revolutionary action of the working class which they claimed they represented.

In all the above I have merely given you my personal opinion because you asked me to, and I have done so with the greatest hesitation. As far as the general tactics are concerned I have experienced their efficacy all my life. They have never failed me. But as regards their application to present conditions in Italy, that is another matter; that must be decided on the spot, by those who are in the thick of events.

Written on
January 26, 1894

Marx and Engels,
Selected Works in 3 vols.,
Vol. 3, Moscow, 1976,
pp. 454-56

FREDERICK ENGELS

From
LETTER
TO PAUL LAFARGUE
IN PARIS

London, March 6, 1894

With respect to the proletariat the republic differs from the monarchy only in that it is the *ready-for-use* political form for the future rule of the proletariat. You are at an advantage compared with us in already having it; we for our part shall have to spend twenty-four hours to make it. But a republic, like every other form of government, is determined by its content; so long as it is a form of *bourgeois* rule it is as hostile to us as any monarchy (except that the *forms* of this hostility are different). It is therefore a wholly baseless illusion to regard it as essentially socialist in form or to entrust socialist tasks to it while it is dominated by the bourgeoisie. We shall be able to wrest concessions from it but never to put in its charge the execution of what is our own concern, even if we should be able to control it by a minority strong enough to change into the majority overnight....

Marx and Engels,
Selected Correspondence,
Moscow, 1975, p. 447

FREDERICK ENGELS

From
THE PEASANT QUESTION
IN FRANCE AND GERMANY

What, then, is our attitude towards the small peasantry? How shall we have to deal with it on the day of our accession to power?

To begin with, the French programme is absolutely correct in stating: that we foresee the inevitable doom of the small peasant but that it is not our mission to hasten it by any interference on our part.

Secondly, it is just as evident that when we are in possession of state power we shall not even think of forcibly expropriating the small peasants (regardless of whether with or without compensation), as we shall have to do in the case of the big landowners. Our task relative to the small peasant consists, in the first place, in effecting a transition of his private enterprise and private possession to co-operative ones, not forcibly but by dint of example and the proffer of social assistance for this purpose. And then of course we shall have ample means of showing to the small peasant prospective advantages that must be obvious to him even today.

Almost twenty years ago the Danish Socialists, who have only one real city in their country—Copenhagen—and therefore have to rely almost exclusively on peasant propaganda outside of it, were already drawing up such plans. The peasants of a village or parish—there are many big individual homesteads in Denmark—were to pool their land to form a single big farm in order to cultivate it for common account and distribute the yield in proportion to the land, money and labour contributed. In Denmark small landed property plays only a secondary role. But if we apply this idea to a region of small holdings we shall find that if these are pooled and the aggregate area cultivated on a large scale, part of the labour-power employed hitherto is rendered superfluous. It is precisely this saving of labour that represents one of the main advantages of large-scale farming. Employment can be found for this labour-power in two ways. Either additional land taken from big estates in the neighbourhood is placed at the disposal of the peasant co-operative or the peasants in question are provided with the means and the opportunity of engaging in industry as an accessory calling, primarily and as far as possible for their own use. In either case their economic position is improved and simultaneously the general social directing agency is assured the necessary influence to transform the peasant co-operative to a higher form, and to equalise the rights and duties of the co-operative as a whole as well as of its individual members with those of the other departments of the entire community. How this is to be carried out in practice in each particular case will depend upon the circumstances of the case and the conditions under which we take possession of political power. We may thus possibly be in a position to offer these co-operatives yet further advantages: assumption of their entire mortgage indebtedness by the national bank with a simultaneous sharp reduction of the interest rate; advances from public funds for the establishment of large-scale production (to be made not necessarily or primarily in money but in the form of required products: machinery, artificial fertiliser, etc.), and other advantages.

The main point is and will be to make the peasants understand that we can save, preserve their houses and fields for them only by transforming them into co-operative property operated co-operatively. It is precisely the individual farming conditioned by individual ownership that drives the peasants to their doom. If they insist on individual operation they will inevitably be driven from house and home and their antiquated mode of production superseded by capitalist large-scale production. That is how the matter stands. Now we come along and offer the peasants the opportunity of introducing large-scale production themselves, not for account of the capitalists but for their own, common account. Should it really be impossible to make the peasants understand that this is in their own interest, that it is the sole means of their salvation?

Neither now nor at any time in the future can we promise the small-holding peasants to preserve their individual property and individual enterprise against the overwhelming power of capitalist production. We can only promise them that we shall not interfere in their property relations by force, against their will. Moreover, we can advocate that the struggle of the capitalists and big landlords against the small peasants should be waged from now on with a minimum of unfair means and that direct robbery and cheating, which are practised only too often, be as far as possible prevented. In this we shall succeed only in exceptional cases. Under the developed capitalist mode of production nobody can tell where honesty ends and cheating begins. But always it will make a considerable difference whether public authority is on the side of the cheater or the cheated. We of course are decidedly on the side of the small peasant; we shall do everything at all permissible to make his lot more bearable, to facilitate his transition to the co-operative should he decide to do so, and even to make it possible for him to remain on his small holding for a protracted length of time to think the matter over, should he still be unable to bring himself to this decision. We do this not only because we consider the small peasant living by his own labour as virtually belonging to us, but also in the direct interest of the Party. The greater the number of peasants whom we can save from being actually hurled down into the proletariat, whom we can win to our side while they are still peasants, the more quickly and easily the social transformation will be accomplished. It will serve us nought to wait with this transformation until capitalist production has developed everywhere to its utmost consequences, until the last small handicraftsman and the last small peasant have fallen victim to capitalist large-scale production. The material sacrifice to be made for this purpose in the interest of the peasants and to be defrayed out of public funds can, from the point of view of capitalist economy, be viewed only as money thrown away, but it is nevertheless an excellent investment because it will effect a perhaps tenfold saving in the cost of the social reorganisation in general. In this sense we can, therefore, afford to deal very liberally with the peasants. This is not the place to go into details, to make concrete proposals to that end; here we can deal only with general principles.

Accordingly we can do no greater disservice to the Party as well as to the small peasants than to make promises that even only create the impression that we intend to preserve the small holdings permanently. It would mean directly to block the way of the peasants to their emancipation and to degrade the Party to the level of rowdy anti-Semitism. On the contrary, it is the duty of our Party to make clear to the peasants again and again that their position is absolutely hopeless as long as capitalism holds sway, that it is absolutely impossible to preserve their small holdings for them as such, that capitalist large-scale production is absolutely sure to run over their impotent antiquated system of small production as a train runs over a pushcart. If we do this we shall act in conformity with the inevitable trend of economic development, and this development will not fail to bring our words home to the small peasants.

Incidentally, I cannot leave this subject without expressing my conviction that the authors of the Nantes programme are also essentially of my opinion. Their insight is much too great for them not to know that areas now divided into small holdings are also bound to become common property. They themselves admit that small-holding ownership is destined to disappear. The report of the National Council drawn up by Lafargue and delivered at the Congress of Nantes likewise fully corroborates this view. It has been published in German in the Berlin *Sozialdemokrat* of October 18 of this year. The contradictory nature of the expressions used in the Nantes programme itself betrays the fact that what the authors actually say is not what they want to say. If they are not understood and their statements misused, as actually has already happened, that is of course their own fault. At any rate, they will have to elucidate their programme and the next French congress revise it thoroughly.

We now come to the bigger peasants. Here as a result of the divisions of inheritance as well as of indebtedness and forced sales of land we find a variegated pattern of intermediate stages, from small-holding peasant to big peasant proprietor, who has retained his old patrimony intact or even added to it. Where the middle peasant lives among small-holding peasants his interests and views will not differ greatly from theirs; he knows from his own experience how many of his kind have already sunk to the level of small peasants. But where middle and big peasants predominate and the operation of the farms requires, generally, the help of male and female servants it is quite a different matter. Of course a workers' party has to fight, in the first place, on behalf of the wage-workers, that is, for the male and female servantry and the day labourers. It is unquestionably forbidden to make any promises to the peasants which include the continuance of the wage slavery of the workers. But as long as the big and middle peasants continue to exist as such they cannot manage without wage-workers. If it would, therefore, be downright folly on our part to hold out prospects to the small-holding peasants of continuing permanently to be such, it would border on treason were we to promise the same to the big and middle peasants.

We have here again the parallel case of the handicraftsmen in the cities. True, they are more ruined than the peasants but there still are some who employ journeymen in addition to apprentices or for whom apprentices do the work of journeymen. Let those of these master craftsmen who want to perpetuate their existence as such cast in their lot with the anti-Semites until they have convinced themselves that they get no help in that quarter either. The rest, who have realised that their mode of production is inevitably doomed, are coming over to us and, moreover, are ready in future to share the lot that is in store for all other workers. The same applies to the big and middle peasants. It goes without saying that we are more interested in their male and female servants and day labourers than in them themselves. If these peasants want to be guaranteed the continued existence of their enterprises we are in no position whatever to assure them of that. They must then take their place among the anti-Semites, peasant leaguers and similar parties who derive pleasure from promising everything and keeping nothing. We are economically certain that the big and middle peasant must likewise inevitably succumb to the competition of capitalist production and the cheap overseas corn, as is proved by the growing indebtedness and the everywhere evident decay of these peasants as well. We can do nothing against this decay except recommend here too the pooling of farms to form co-operative enterprises, in which the exploitation of wage-labour will be eliminated more and more, and their gradual transformation into branches of the great national producers' co-operative with each branch enjoying equal rights and duties can be instituted. If these peasants realise the inevitability of the doom of their present mode of production and draw the necessary conclusions they will come to us and it will be incumbent upon us to facilitate to the best of our ability also their transition to the changed mode of production. Otherwise we shall have to abandon them to their fate and address ourselves to their wage-workers, among whom we shall not fail to find sympathy. Most likely we shall be able to abstain here as well from resorting to forcible expropriation, and as for the rest to count on future economic developments making also these harder pates amenable to reason.

Only the big landed estates present a perfectly simple case. Here we are dealing with undisguised capitalist production and no scruples of any sort need restrain us. Here we are confronted by rural proletarians in masses and our task is clear. As soon as our Party is in possession of political power it has simply to expropriate the big landed proprietors just like the manufacturers in industry. Whether this expropriation is to be compensated for or not will to a great extent depend not upon us but the circumstances under which we obtain power, and particularly upon the attitude adopted by these gentry, the big landowners, themselves. We by no means consider compensation as impermissible in any event; Marx told me (and how many times!) that in his opinion we would get off cheapest if we could buy out the whole lot of them. But this does not concern us here. The big estates thus restored to the community are to be turned over by us to the rural workers who are already cultivating them and are to be organised into co-operatives. They are to be assigned to them for their use and benefit under the control of the community. Nothing can as yet be stated as to the terms of their tenure. At any rate the transformation of the capitalist enterprise into a social enterprise is here fully prepared for and can be carried into execution overnight, precisely as in Mr. Krupp's or Mr. von Stumm's factory. And the example of these agricultural co-operatives would convince also the last of the still resistant small-holding peasants, and surely also many big peasants, of the advantages of co-operative, large-scale production.

Thus we can open up prospects here before the rural proletarians as splendid as those facing the industrial workers, and it can be only a question of time, and of only a very short time, before we win over to our side the rural workers of Prussia east of the Elbe. But once we have the East-Elbe rural workers a different wind will blow at once all over Germany. The actual semi-servitude of the East-Elbe rural workers is the main basis of the domination of Prussian Junkerdom and thus of Prussia's specific overlordship in Germany. It is the Junkers east of the Elbe who have created and preserved the specifically Prussian character of the bureaucracy as well as of the body of army officers—the Junkers, who are being reduced more and more to ruin by their indebtedness, impoverishment and parasitism at state and private cost and for that very reason cling the more desperately to the dominion which they exercise; the Junkers, whose haughtiness, bigotry and arrogance have brought the German Reich of the Prussian nation within the country into such hatred—even when every allowance is made for the fact that at present this Reich is inevitable as the sole form in which national unity can now be attained—and abroad so little respect despite its brilliant victories. The power of these junkers is grounded on the fact that within the compact territory of the seven old Prussian provinces—that is, approximately one-third of the entire territory of the Reich—they have at their disposal the landed property, which here brings with it both social and political power. And not only the landed property but, through their beet-sugar refineries and liquor distilleries, also the most important industries of this area. Neither the big landowners of the rest of Germany nor the big industrialists are in a similarly favourable position. Neither of them have a compact kingdom at their disposal. Both are scattered over a wide stretch of territory and compete among themselves and with other social elements surrounding them for economic and political predominance. But the economic foundation of this domination of the Prussian Junkers is steadily deteriorating. Here too indebtedness and impoverishment are spreading irresistibly despite all state assistance (and since Frederick II this item is included in every regular Junker budget). Only the actual semi-serfdom sanctioned by law and custom and the resulting possibility of the unlimited exploitation of the rural workers, still barely keep the drowning Junkers above water. Sow the seed of Social-Democracy among these workers, give them the courage and cohesion to insist upon their rights, and the glory of the Junkers will be at an end. The great reactionary power, which to Germany represents the same barbarous, predatory element as Russian tsardom does to the whole of Europe, will collapse like a pricked bubble. The "picked regiments" of the Prussian army will become Social-Democratic which will result in a shift in power that is pregnant with an entire upheaval. But for this reason it is of vastly greater importance to win the rural proletariat east of the Elbe than the small peasants of Western Germany or yet the middle peasants of Southern Germany. It is here, in East-Elbe Prussia, that the decisive battle of our cause will have to be fought and for this very reason both government and Junkerdom will do their utmost to prevent our gaining access here. And should, as we are threatened, new violent measures be resorted to to impede the spread of our Party, their primary purpose will be to protect the East-Elbe rural proletariat from our propaganda. It's all the same to us. We shall win it nevertheless.

Written between
November 15
and 22, 1894

Marx and Engels,
Selected Works in 3 vols.
Vol. 3, Moscow, 1973,
pp. 469-76

FREDERICK ENGELS

INTRODUCTION TO "THE CLASS STRUGGLES IN FRANCE 1848 TO 1850"[112]

The work here republished was Marx's first attempt to explain a section of contemporary history by means of his materialist conception, on the basis of the given economic situation. In the *Communist Manifesto*, the theory was applied in broad outline to the whole of modern history; in the articles by Marx and myself in the *Neue Rheinische Zeitung*, it was constantly used to interpret political events of the day. Here, on the other hand, the question was to demonstrate the inner causal connection in the course of a development which extended over some years, a development as critical, for the whole of Europe, as it was typical; hence, in accordance with the conception of the author, to trace political events back to effects of what were, in the final analysis, economic causes.

If events and series of events are judged by current history, it will never be possible to go back to the *ultimate* economic causes. Even today, when the specialised press concerned provides such rich material, it still remains impossible even in England to follow day by day the movement of industry and trade in the world market and the changes which take place in the methods of production in such a way as to be able to draw a general conclusion, for any point of time, from these manifold, complicated and ever-changing factors, the most important of which, into the bargain, generally operate a long time in secret before they suddenly make themselves violently felt on the surface. A clear survey of the economic history of a given period can never be obtained contemporaneously, but only subsequently, after a collecting and sifting of the material has taken place. Statistics are a necessary auxiliary means here, and they always lag behind. For this reason, it is only too often necessary, in current history, to treat this, the most decisive, factor as constant, and the economic situation existing at the beginning of the period concerned as given and unalterable for the whole period, or else to take notice of only such changes in this situation as arise out of the patently manifest events themselves, and are, therefore, likewise patently manifest. Hence, the materialist method has here quite often to limit itself to tracing political conflicts back to the struggles between the interests of the existing social classes and fractions of classes created by the economic development, and to prove the particular political parties to be the more or less adequate political expression of these same classes and fractions of classes.

It is self-evident that this unavoidable neglect of contemporaneous changes in the economic situation, the very basis of all the processes to be examined, must be a source of error. But all the conditions of a comprehensive presentation of current history unavoidably include sources of error—which, however, keeps nobody from writing current history.

When Marx undertook this work, the source of error mentioned was even more unavoidable. It was simply impossible during the period of the Revolution of 1848-49 to follow up the economic transformations taking place at the same time or even to keep them in view. It was the same during the first months of exile in London, in the autumn and winter of 1849-50. But that was just the time when Marx began this work. And in spite of these unfavourable circumstances, his exact knowledge both of the economic situation in France before, and of the political history of that country after the February Revolution made it possible for him to give a picture of events which laid bare their inner connections in a way never attained ever since, and which later brilliantly stood the double test applied by Marx himself.

The first test resulted from the fact that after the spring of 1850 Marx once again found leisure for economic studies, and first of all took up the economic history of the last ten years. Thereby what he had hitherto deduced, half *a priori*, from gappy material, became absolutely clear to him from the facts themselves, namely, that the world trade crisis of 1847 had been the true mother of the February and March Revolutions, and that the industrial prosperity, which had been returning gradually since the middle of 1848 and attained full bloom in 1849 and 1850, was the revitalising force of the newly strengthened European reaction. That was decisive. Whereas in the first three articles (which appeared in the

305

January, February and March issues of the *Neue Rheinische Zeitung. Politisch-ökonomische Revue*, Hamburg, 1850) there was still the expectation of an early new upsurge of revolutionary energy, the historical review written by Marx and myself for the last issue, a double issue (May to October), which was published in the autumn of 1850, breaks once and for all with these illusions: "A new revolution is possible only in consequence of a new crisis. It is, however, just as certain as this crisis." But that was the only essential change which had to be made. There was absolutely nothing to alter in the interpretation of events given in the earlier chapters, or in the causal connections established therein, as the continuation of the narrative from March 10 up to the autumn of 1850 in the review in question proves. I have, therefore, included this continuation as the fourth article in the present new edition.

The second test was even more severe. Immediately after Louis Bonaparte's *coup d'état* of December 2, 1851, Marx worked out anew the history of France from February 1848 up to this event, which concluded the revolutionary period for the time being. (*The Eighteenth Brumaire of Louis Bonaparte*. Third edition, Hamburg, Meissner, 1885.) In this pamphlet the period depicted in our present publication is again dealt with, although more briefly. Compare this second presentation, written in the light of the decisive event which happened over a year later, with ours and it will be found that the author had very little to change.

What, besides, gives our work quite special significance is the circumstance that it was the first to express the formula in which, by common agreement, the workers' parties of all countries in the world briefly summarise their demand for economic transformation: the appropriation of the means of production by society. In the second chapter, in connection with the "right to work", which is characterised as "the first clumsy formula wherein the revolutionary demands of the proletariat are summarised," it is said: "But behind the right to work stands the power over capital; behind the power over capital, the *appropriation of the means of production*, their subjection to the associated working class and, therefore, the abolition of wage-labour as well as of capital and of their mutual relations." Thus, here, for the first time, the proposition is formulated by which modern workers' socialism is equally sharply differentiated both from all the different shades of feudal, bourgeois, petty-bourgeois, etc., socialism and also from the confused community of goods of utopian and of spontaneous workers' communism. If, later, Marx extended the formula to include appropriation of the means of exchange, this extension, which in any case was self-evident after the *Communist Manifesto*, only expressed a corollary to the main proposition. A few wiseacres in England have of late added that the "means of distribution" should also be handed over to society. It would be difficult for these gentlemen to say what these economic means of distribution are, as distinct from the means of production and exchange; unless *political* means of distribution are meant, taxes, poor relief, including the *Sachsenwald*[113] and other endowments. But, first, these are already now means of distribution in possession of society in the aggregate, either of the state or of the community, and secondly, it is precisely the abolition of these that we desire.

* * *

When the February Revolution broke out, all of us, as far as our conceptions of the conditions and the course of revolutionary movements were concerned, were under the spell of previous historical experience, particularly that of France. It was, indeed, the latter which had dominated the whole of European history since 1789, and from which now once again the signal had gone forth for general revolutionary change. It was, therefore, natural and unavoidable that our conceptions of the nature and the course of the "social" revolution proclaimed in Paris in February 1848, of the revolution of the proletariat, should be strongly coloured by memories of the prototypes of 1789 and 1830. Moreover, when the Paris uprising found its echo in the victorious insurrections in Vienna, Milan and Berlin; when the whole of Europe right up to the Russian frontier was swept into the movement; when thereupon in Paris, in June, the first great battle for power between the proletariat and the bourgeoisie was fought; when the very victory of its class so shook the bourgeoisie of all countries that it fled back into the arms of the monarchist-feudal reaction which had just been overthrown—there could be no doubt for us, under the circumstances then obtaining, that the great decisive combat had commenced, that it would have to be fought out in a single, long and vicissitudinous period of revolution, but that it could only end in the final victory of the proletariat.

After the defeats of 1849 we in no way shared the illusions of the vulgar democracy grouped around the future provisional governments *in partibus*. This vulgar democracy reckoned on a speedy

307

and finally decisive victory of the "people" over the "tyrants"; we looked to a long struggle, after the removal of the "tyrants", among the antagonistic elements concealed within this "people" itself. Vulgar democracy expected a renewed outbreak any day; we declared as early as autumn 1850 that at least the *first* chapter of the revolutionary period was closed and that nothing was to be expected until the outbreak of a new world economic crisis. For which reason we were excommunicated, as traitors to the revolution, by the very people who later, almost without exception, made their peace with Bismarck—so far as Bismarck found them worth the trouble.

But history has shown us too to have been wrong, has revealed our point of view of that time to have been an illusion. It has done even more: it has not merely dispelled the erroneous notions we then held; it has also completely transformed the conditions under which the proletariat has to fight. The mode of struggle of 1848 is today obsolete in every respect, and this is a point which deserves closer examination on the present occasion.

All revolutions up to the present day have resulted in the displacement of one definite class rule by another; but all ruling classes up to now have been only small minorities in relation to the ruled mass of the people. One ruling minority was thus over-thrown; another minority seized the helm of state in its stead and refashioned the state institutions to suit its own interests. This was on every occasion the minority group qualified and called to rule by the given degree of economic development; and just for that reason, and only for that reason, it happened that the ruled majority either participated in the revolution for the benefit of the former or else calmly acquiesced in it. But if we disregard the concrete content in each case, the common form of all these revolutions was that they were minority revolutions. Even when the majority took part, it did so—whether wittingly or not—only in the service of a minority; but because of this, or even simply because of the passive, unresisting attitude of the majority, this minority acquired the appearance of being the representative of the whole people.

As a rule, after the first great success, the victorious minority divided; one half was satisfied with what had been gained, the other wanted to go still further, and put forward new demands, which, partly at least, were also in the real or apparent interest of the great mass of the people. In individual cases these more radical demands were actually forced through, but often only for the moment; the more moderate party would regain the upper hand, and what had last been won would wholly or partly be lost again; the vanquished would then shriek of treachery or ascribe their defeat to accident. In reality, however, the truth of the matter was largely this: the achievements of the first victory were only safeguarded by the second victory of the more radical party; this having been attained, and, with it, what was necessary for the moment, the radicals and their achievements vanished once more from the stage.

All revolutions of modern times, beginning with the great English Revolution of the seventeenth century, showed these features, which appeared inseparable from every revolutionary struggle. They appeared applicable, also, to the struggle of the proletariat for its emancipation; all the more applicable, since precisely in 1848 there were but a very few people who had any idea at all of the direction in which this emancipation was to be sought. The proletarian masses themselves, even in Paris, after the victory, were still absolutely in the dark as to the path to be taken. And yet the movement was there, instinctive, spontaneous, irrepressible. Was not this just the situation in which a revolution had to succeed, led, true, by a minority, but this time not in the interest of the minority, but in the veriest interest of the majority? If, in all the longer revolutionary periods, it was so easy to win the great masses of the people by the merely plausible false representations of the forward-thrusting minorities, why should they be less susceptible to ideas which were the truest reflection of their economic condition, which were nothing but the clear, rational expression of their needs, of needs not yet understood but merely vaguely felt by them? To be sure, this revolutionary mood of the masses had almost always, and usually very speedily, given way to lassitude or even to a revulsion of feeling as soon as illusion evaporated and disappointment set in. But here it was not a question of false representations, but of giving effect to the highest special interests of the great majority itself, interests which, true, were at that time by no means clear to this great majority, but which soon enough had to become clear to it in the course of giving practical effect to them, by their convincing obviousness. And when, as Marx showed in his third article, in the spring of 1850, the development of the bourgeois republic that arose out of the "social" Revolution of 1848 had even concentrated real power in the hands of the big bourgeoisie—monarchistically inclined as it was into the bargain—and, on the other hand, had grouped all the other social classes, peasantry as well as petty bourgeoisie, round the proletariat, so that, during and after the common victory, not they but the proletariat grown wise by experience had to become the decisive factor—was there not every prospect then of turning the revolution of the minority into a revolution of the majority?

History has proved us, and all who thought like us, wrong. It has made it clear that the state of economic development on the Continent at that time was not, by a long way, ripe for the elimination of capitalist production; it has proved this by the economic revolution which, since 1848, has seized the whole of the Continent, and has caused big industry to take real root in France, Austria, Hungary, Poland and, recently, in Russia, while it has made Germany positively an industrial country of the first rank—all on a capitalist basis, which in the year 1848, therefore, still had great capacity for expansion. But it is just this industrial revolution which has everywhere produced clarity in class relations, has removed a number of intermediate forms handed down from the period of manufacture and in Eastern Europe even from guild handicraft, has created a genuine bourgeoisie and a genuine large-scale industrial proletariat and has pushed them into the foreground of social development. However, owing to this, the struggle between these two great classes, a struggle which, apart from England, existed in 1848 only in Paris and, at the most, in a few big industrial centres, has spread over the whole of Europe and reached an intensity still inconceivable in 1848. At that time the many obscure evangels of the sects, with their panaceas; today the *one* generally recognised, crystal-clear theory of Marx, sharply formulating the ultimate aims of the struggle. At that time the masses, sundered and differing according to locality and nationality, linked only by the feeling of common suffering, undeveloped, helplessly tossed to and fro from enthusiasm to despair; today the *one* great international army of Socialists, marching irresistibly on and growing daily in number, organisation, discipline, insight and certainty of victory. If even this mighty army of the proletariat has still not reached its goal, if, far from winning victory by one mighty stroke, it has slowly to press forward from position to position in a hard, tenacious struggle, this only proves, once and for all, how impossible it was in 1848 to win social transformation by a simple surprise attack.

A bourgeoisie split into two dynastic-monarchist sections, a bourgeoisie, however, which demanded, above all, peace and security for its financial operations, faced by a proletariat vanquished, indeed, but still always a menace, a proletariat round which petty bourgeois and peasants grouped themselves more and more—the continual threat of a violent outbreak, which, nevertheless, offered absolutely no prospect of a final solution—such was the situation, as if specially created for the *coup d'état* of the third, the pseudo-democratic pretender, Louis Bonaparte. On December 2, 1851, by means of the army, he put an end to the tense situation and secured Europe domestic tranquillity in order to confer upon it the blessing of a new era of wars. The period of revolutions from below was concluded for the time being; there followed a period of revolutions from above.

The reversion to the empire in 1851 gave new proof of the unripeness of the proletarian aspirations of that time. But it was itself to create the conditions under which they were bound to ripen. Internal tranquillity ensured the full development of the new industrial boom; the necessity of keeping the army occupied and of diverting the revolutionary currents outwards produced the wars in which Bonaparte, under the pretext of asserting "the principle of nationality"[114] sought to hook annexations for France. His imitator, Bismarck, adopted the same policy for Prussia; he made his *coup d'état*, his revolution from above, in 1866, against the German Confederation and Austria, and no less against the Prussian *Konfliktskammer*.[a] But Europe was too small for two Bonapartes and the irony of history so willed it that Bismarck overthrew Bonaparte, and King William of Prussia not only established the little German empire, but also the French republic. The general result, however, was that in Europe the independence and internal unity of the great nations, with the exception of Poland, had become a fact. Within relatively modest limits, it is true, but, for all that, on a scale large enough to allow the development of the working class to proceed without finding national complications any longer a serious obstacle. The grave-diggers of the Revolution of 1848 had become the executors of its will. And alongside of them already rose threateningly the heir of 1848, the proletariat, in the shape of the *International*.

After the war of 1870-71, Bonaparte vanishes from the stage and Bismarck's mission is fulfilled, so that he can now sink back again into the ordinary *Junker*. The period, however, is brought to a close

---

[a] *Konfliktskammer*, that is, the Prussian Chamber then in conflict with the government.—*Ed.*

by the Paris Commune. An underhand attempt by Thiers to steal the cannon of the Paris National Guard called forth a victorious rising. It was shown once more that in Paris none but a proletarian revolution is any longer possible. After the victory power fell, quite of itself and quite undisputed, into the hands of the working class. And once again it was proved how impossible even then, twenty years after the time described in our work, this rule of the working class still was. On the one hand, France left Paris in the lurch, looked on while it bled profusely from the bullets of MacMahon; on the other hand, the Commune was consumed in unfruitful strife between the two parties which split it, the Blanquists (the majority) and the Proudhonists (the minority), neither of which knew what was to be done. The victory which came as a gift in 1871 remained just as unfruitful as the surprise attack of 1848.

It was believed that the militant proletariat had been finally buried with the Paris Commune. But, completely to the contrary, it dates its most powerful resurgence from the Commune and the Franco-Prussian War. The recruitment of the whole of the population able to bear arms into armies that henceforth could be counted only in millions, and the introduction of fire-arms, projectiles and explosives of hitherto undreamt-of efficacy, created a complete revolution in all warfare. This revolution, on the one hand, put a sudden end to the Bonapartist war period and ensured peaceful industrial development by making any war other than a world war of unheard-of cruelty and absolutely incalculable outcome an impossibility. On the other hand, it caused military expenditure to rise in geometrical progression and thereby forced up taxes to exorbitant levels and so drove the poorer classes of people into the arms of socialism. The annexation of Alsace-Lorraine, the immediate cause of the mad competition in armaments, was able to set the French and German bourgeoisie chauvinistically at each other's throats; for the workers of the two countries it became a new bond of unity. And the anniversary of the Paris Commune became the first universal day of celebration of the whole proletariat.

The war of 1870-71 and the defeat of the Commune transferred the centre of gravity of the European workers' movement for the time being from France to Germany, as Marx had foretold. In France it naturally took years to recover from the blood-letting of May 1871. In Germany, on the other hand, where industry — fostered, in addition, in positively hothouse fashion by the blessing of the French milliards[115]— developed more and more rapidly,

Social-Democracy experienced a still more rapid and enduring growth. Thanks to the intelligent use which the German workers made of the universal suffrage introduced in 1866, the astonishing growth of the party is made plain to all the world by incontestable figures: 1871, 102,000; 1874, 352,000; 1877, 493,000 Social-Democratic votes. Then came recognition of this advance by high authority in the shape of the Anti-Socialist Law; the party was temporarily broken up, the number of votes dropped to 312,000 in 1881. But that was quickly overcome, and then, under the pressure of the Exceptional Law, without a press, without a legal organisation and without the right of combination and assembly, rapid expansion really began: 1884, 550,000; 1887, 763,000; 1890, 1,427,000 votes. Thereupon the hand of the state was paralysed. The Anti-Socialist Law disappeared; socialist votes rose to 1,787,000, over a quarter of all the votes cast. The government and the ruling classes had exhausted all their expedients—uselessly, purposelessly, unsuccessfully. The tangible proofs of their impotence, which the authorities, from night watchman to the imperial chancellor, had had to accept—and that from the despised workers!—these proofs were counted in millions. The state was at the end of its tether, the workers only at the beginning of theirs.

But, besides, the German workers rendered a second great service to their cause in addition to the first, a service performed by their mere existence as the strongest, best disciplined and most rapidly growing Socialist Party. They supplied their comrades in all countries with a new weapon, and one of the sharpest, when they showed them how to make use of universal suffrage.

There had long been universal suffrage in France, but it had fallen into disrepute through the misuse to which the Bonapartist government had put it. After the Commune there was no workers' party to make use of it. It also existed in Spain since the republic, but in Spain boycott of elections was ever the rule of all serious opposition parties. The experience of the Swiss with universal suffrage was also anything but encouraging for a workers' party. The revolutionary workers of the Latin countries had been wont to regard the suffrage as a snare, as an instrument of government trickery. It was otherwise in Germany. The *Communist Manifesto* had already proclaimed the winning of universal suffrage, of democracy, as one of the first and most important tasks of the militant proletariat, and Lassalle had again taken up this point. Now, when Bismarck found himself compelled to introduce this

313

franchise as the only means of interesting the mass of the people in his plans, our workers immediately took it in earnest and sent August Bebel to the first, constituent Reichstag. And from that day on, they have used the franchise in a way which has paid them a thousandfold and has served as a model to the workers of all countries. The franchise has been, in the words of the French Marxist programme, *transformé, de moyen de duperie qu'il a été jusqu'ici, en instrument d'émancipation*—transformed by them from a means of deception, which it was before, into an instrument of emancipation. And if universal suffrage had offered no other advantage than that it allowed us to count our numbers every three years; that by the regularly established, unexpectedly rapid rise in the number of our votes it increased in equal measure the workers' certainty of victory and the dismay of their opponents, and so became our best means of propaganda; that it accurately informed us concerning our own strength and that of all hostile parties, and thereby provided us with a measure of proportion for our actions second to none, safeguarding us from untimely timidity as much as from untimely foolhardiness—if this had been the only advantage we gained from the suffrage, it would still have been much more than enough. But it did more than this by far. In election agitation it provided us with a means, second to none, of getting in touch with the mass of the people where they still stand aloof from us; of forcing all parties to defend their views and actions against our attacks before all the people; and, further, it provided our representatives in the Reichstag with a platform from which they could speak to their opponents in parliament, and to the masses without, with quite other authority and freedom than in the press or at meetings. Of what avail was their Anti-Socialist Law to the government and the bourgeoisie when election campaigning and socialist speeches in the Reichstag continually broke through it?

With this successful utilisation of universal suffrage, however, an entirely new method of proletarian struggle came into operation, and this method quickly developed further. It was found that the state institutions, in which the rule of the bourgeoisie is organised, offer the working class still further opportunities to fight these very state institutions. The workers took part in elections to particular Diets, to municipal councils and to trades courts; they contested with the bourgeoisie every post in the occupation of which a sufficient part of the proletariat had a say. And so it happened that the bourgeoisie and the government came to be much more afraid of the legal than of the illegal action of the workers' party, of the results of elections than of those of rebellion.

For here, too, the conditions of the struggle had essentially changed. Rebellion in the old style, street fighting with barricades, which decided the issue everywhere up to 1848, was to a considerable extent obsolete.

Let us have no illusions about it: a real victory of an insurrection over the military in street fighting, a victory as between two armies, is one of the rarest exceptions. And the insurgents counted on it just as rarely. For them it was solely a question of making the troops yield to moral influences which, in a fight between the armies of two warring countries, do not come into play at all or do so to a much smaller extent. If they succeed in this, the troops fail to respond, or the commanding officers lose their heads, and the insurrection wins. If they do not succeed in this, then, even where the military are in the minority, the superiority of better equipment and training, of single leadership, of the planned employment of the military forces and of discipline makes itself felt. The most that an insurrection can achieve in the way of actual tactical operations is the proper construction and defence of a single barricade. Mutual support, the disposition and employment of reserves—in short, concerted and co-ordinated action of the individual detachments, indispensable even for the defence of one section of a town, not to speak of the whole of a large town, will be attainable only to a very limited extent, and most of the time not at all. Concentration of the military forces at a decisive point is, of course, out of question here. Hence passive defence is the prevailing form of fighting; the attack will rise here and there, but only by way of exception, to occasional thrusts and flank assaults; as a rule, however, it will be limited to occupation of positions abandoned by retreating troops. In addition, the military have at their disposal artillery and fully equipped corps of trained engineers, resources of war which, in nearly every case, the insurgents entirely lack. No wonder, then, that even the barricade fightings conducted with the greatest heroism—Paris, June 1848; Vienna, October 1848; Dresden, May 1849—ended in the defeat of the insurrection as soon as the leaders of the attack, unhampered by political considerations, acted from the purely military standpoint, and their soldiers remained reliable.

The numerous successes of the insurgents up to 1848 were due to a great variety of causes. In Paris, in July 1830 and February 1848, as in most of the Spanish street fighting, a citizens' guard stood

315

between the insurgents and the military. This guard either sided directly with the insurrection, or else by its lukewarm, indecisive attitude caused the troops likewise to vacillate, and supplied the insurrection with arms into the bargain. Where this citizens' guard opposed the insurrection from the outset, as in June 1848 in Paris, the insurrection was vanquished. In Berlin in 1848, the people were victorious partly through a considerable accession of new fighting forces during the night and the morning of [March] the 19th, partly as a result of the exhaustion and bad victualling of the troops, and, finally, partly as a result of the paralysis that was seizing the command. But in all cases the fight was won because the troops failed to respond, because the commanding officers lost the faculty to decide or because their hands were tied.

Even in the classic time of street fighting, therefore, the barricade produced more of a moral than a material effect. It was a means of shaking the steadfastness of the military. If it held out until this was attained, victory was won; if not, there was defeat. This is the main point, which must be kept in view, likewise, when the chances of possible future street fighting are examined.

Already in 1849, these chances were pretty poor. Everywhere the bourgeoisie had thrown in its lot with the governments, "culture and property" had hailed and feasted the military moving against insurrection. The spell of the barricade was broken; the soldier no longer saw behind it "the people," but rebels, agitators, plunderers, levellers, the scum of society; the officer had in the course of time become versed in the tactical forms of street fighting, he no longer marched straight ahead and without cover against the improvised breastwork, but went round it through gardens, yards and houses. And this was now successful, with a little skill, in nine cases out of ten.

But since then there have been very many more changes, and all in favour of the military. If the big towns have become considerably bigger, the armies have become bigger still. Paris and Berlin have, since 1848, grown less than fourfold, but their garrisons have grown more than that. By means of the railways, these garrisons can, in twenty-four hours, be more than doubled, and in forty-eight hours they can be increased to huge armies. The arming of this enormously increased number of troops has become incomparably more effective. In 1848 the smooth-bore, muzzle-loading percussion gun, today the small-calibre, breech-loading magazine rifle, which shoots four times as far, ten times as accurately and ten times as fast as the former. At that time the

316

relatively ineffective round shot and grape-shot of the artillery; today the percussion shells, of which one is sufficient to demolish the best barricade. At that time the pick-axe of the sapper for breaking through firewalls; today the dynamite cartridge.

On the other hand, all the conditions of the insurgents' side have grown worse. An insurrection with which all sections of the people sympathise will hardly recur; in the class struggle all the middle strata will probably never group themselves round the proletariat so exclusively that in comparison the party of reaction gathered round the bourgeoisie will well-nigh disappear. The "people", therefore, will always appear divided, and thus a most powerful lever, so extraordinarily effective in 1848, is gone. If more soldiers who have seen service came over to the insurrectionists, the arming of them would become so much the more difficult. The hunting and fancy guns of the munitions shops—even if not previously made unusable by removal of part of the lock by order of the police — are far from being a match for the magazine rifle of the soldier, even in close fighting. Up to 1848 it was possible to make the necessary ammunition oneself out of powder and lead; today the cartridges differ for each gun, and are everywhere alike only in one point, namely, that they are a complicated product of big industry, and therefore not to be manufactured *ex tempore*, with the result that most guns are useless as long as one does not possess the ammunition specially suited to them. And, finally, since 1848 the newly built quarters of the big cities have been laid out in long, straight, broad streets, as though made to give full effect to the new cannon and rifles. The revolutionist would have to be mad who himself chose the new working-class districts in the North or East of Berlin for a barricade fight.

Does that mean that in the future street fighting will no longer play any role? Certainly not. It only means that the conditions since 1848 have become far more unfavourable for civilian fighters and far more favourable for the military. In future, street fighting can, therefore, be victorious only if this disadvantageous situation is compensated by other factors. Accordingly, it will occur more seldom in the beginning of a great revolution than in its further progress, and will have to be undertaken with greater forces. These, however, may then well prefer, as in the whole great French Revolution or on September 4 and October 31, 1870, in Paris, the open attack to the passive barricade tactics.

Does the reader now understand why the powers that be positively want to get us to go where the guns shoot and the sabres

317

slash? Why they accuse us today of cowardice, because we do not betake ourselves without more ado into the street, where we are certain of defeat in advance? Why they so earnestly implore us to play for once the part of cannon fodder?

The gentlemen pour out their prayers and their challenges for nothing, for absolutely nothing. We are not so stupid. They might just as well demand from their enemy in the next war that he should accept battle in the line formation of old Fritz,[a] or in the columns of whole divisions à la Wagram and Waterloo, and with the flint-lock in his hands at that. If conditions have changed in the case of war between nations, this is no less true in the case of the class struggle. The time of surprise attacks, of revolutions carried through by small conscious minorities at the head of unconscious masses, is past. Where it is a question of a complete transformation of the social organisation, the masses themselves must also be in it, must themselves already have grasped what is at stake, what they are going in for, body and soul. The history of the last fifty years has taught us that. But in order that the masses may understand what is to be done, long, persistent work is required, and it is just this work that we are now pursuing, and with a success which drives the enemy to despair.

In the Latin countries, also, it is being realised more and more that the old tactics must be revised. Everywhere the German example of utilising the suffrage, of winning all posts accessible to us, has been imitated; everywhere the unprepared launching of an attack has been relegated to the background. In France, where for more than a hundred years the ground has been undermined by revolution after revolution, where there is not a single party which has not done its share in conspiracies, insurrections and all other revolutionary actions; in France, where, as a result, the government is by no means sure of the army and where, in general, the conditions for an insurrectionary *coup de main* are far more favourable than in Germany—even in France the Socialists are realising more and more that no lasting victory is possible for them, unless they first win the great mass of the people, that is, in this case, the peasants. Slow propaganda work and parliamentary activity are recognised here, too, as the immediate tasks of the party. Successes were not lacking. Not only have a whole series of municipal councils been won; fifty Socialists have seats in the Chambers, and they have already overthrown three ministries and

---

[a] Friedrich II.—*Ed.*

318

a president of the republic. In Belgium last year the workers forced the adoption of the franchise, and have been victorious in a quarter of the constituencies. In Switzerland, in Italy, in Denmark, yes, even in Bulgaria and Rumania the Socialists are represented in the parliaments. In Austria all parties agree that our admission to the *Reichsrat* can no longer be withheld. We will get in, that is certain; the only question still in dispute is: by which door? And even in Russia, when the famous *Zemsky Sobor* meets—that National Assembly to which young Nicholas offers such vain resistance — even there we can reckon with certainty on being represented in it.

Of course, our foreign comrades do not thereby in the least renounce their right to revolution. The right to revolution is, after all, the only *really* "historical right", the only right on which all modern states without exception rest, Mecklenburg included, whose aristocratic revolution was ended in 1755 by the "hereditary settlement" ["Erbvergleich"], the glorious charter of feudalism[116] still valid today. The right to revolution is so incontestably recognised in the general consciousness that even General von Boguslawski derives the right to a *coup d'état*, which he vindicates for his Kaiser, solely from this popular right.

But whatever may happen in other countries, the German Social-Democracy occupies a special position and therewith, at least in the immediate future, has a special task. The two million voters whom it sends to the ballot box, together with the young men and women who stand behind them as non-voters, form the most numerous, most compact mass, the decisive "shock force" of the international proletarian army. This mass already supplies over a fourth of the votes cast; and as the by-elections to the *Reichstag*, the Diet elections in individual states, the municipal council and trades court elections demonstrate, it increases incessantly. Its growth proceeds as spontaneously, as steadily, as irresistibly, and at the same time as tranquilly as a natural process. All government intervention has proved powerless against it. We can count even today on two and a quarter million voters. If it continues in this fashion, by the end of the century we shall conquer the greater part of the middle strata of society, petty bourgeois and small peasants, and grow into the decisive power in the land, before which all other powers will have to bow, whether they like it or not. To keep this growth going without interruption until it of itself gets beyond the control of the prevailing governmental system, not to fritter away this daily increasing shock force in vanguard skirmishes, but to keep it intact until the decisive day, that is our main task. And there is only one means by which the steady rise of the socialist fighting, forces in Germany could be temporarily halted, and even thrown back for some time: a clash on a big scale with the military, a blood-letting like that of 1871 in Paris. In the long run that would also be overcome. To shoot a party which numbers millions out of existence is too much even for all the magazine rifles of Europe and America. But the normal development would be impeded, the shock force would, perhaps, not be available at the critical moment, the decisive combat would be delayed, protracted and attended by heavier sacrifices.

The irony of world history turns everything upside down. We, the "revolutionists", the "overthrowers"—we are thriving far better on legal methods than on illegal methods and overthrow. The parties of Order, as they call themselves, are perishing under the legal conditions created by themselves. They cry despairingly with Odilon Barrot: *la légalité nous tue*, legality is the death of us; whereas we, under this legality, get firm muscles and rosy cheeks and look like life eternal. And if *we* are not so crazy as to let ourselves be driven to street fighting in order to please them, then in the end there is nothing left for them to do but themselves break through this fatal legality.

Meanwhile they make new laws against overthrows. Again everything is turned upside down. These anti-overthrow fanatics of today, are they not themselves the overthrowers of yesterday? Have *we* perchance evoked the civil war of 1866? Have *we* driven the King of Hanover, the Elector of Hesse, and the Duke of Nassau from their hereditary lawful domains and annexed these hereditary domains? And these overthrowers of the German Confederation and three crowns by the grace of God complain of overthrow! *Quis tulerit Gracchos de seditione querentes?*[a] Who could allow the Bismarck worshippers to rail at overthrow?

Let them, nevertheless, put through their anti-overthrow bills, make them still worse, transform the whole penal law into india-rubber, they will gain nothing but new proof of their impotence. If they want to deal Social-Democracy a serious blow they will have to resort to quite other measures, in addition. They can cope with the Social-Democratic overthrow, which just now is doing so well by keeping the law, only by an overthrow on the part of the parties of Order, an overthrow which cannot live without breaking the law.

---

[a] Who would suffer the Gracchi to complain of sedition? (Juvenal, Satire II.)— *Ed.*

Herr Rössler, the Prussian bureaucrat, and Herr von Boguslawski, the Prussian general, have shown them the only way perhaps still possible of getting at the workers, who simply refuse to let themselves be lured into street fighting. Breach of the constitution, dictatorship, return to absolutism, *regis voluntas suprema lex*![a] Therefore, take courage, gentlemen; here half measures will not do; here you must go the whole hog!

But do not forget that the German empire, like all small states and generally all modern states, is a *product of contract*; of the contract, first, of the princes with one another and, second, of the princes with the people. If one side breaks the contract, the whole contract falls to the ground; the other side is then also no longer bound, as Bismarck demonstrated to us so beautifully in 1866. If, therefore, you break the constitution of the Reich, the Social-Democracy is free, and can do as it pleases with regard to you. But it will hardly blurt out to you today what it is going to do then.

It is now, almost to the year, sixteen centuries since a dangerous party of overthrow was likewise active in the Roman empire. It undermined religion and all the foundations of the state; it flatly denied that Caesar's will was the supreme law; it was without a fatherland, was international; it spread over all countries of the empire, from Gaul to Asia, and beyond the frontiers of the empire. It had long carried on seditious activities in secret, underground; for a considerable time, however, it had felt itself strong enough to come out into the open. This party of overthrow, which was known by the name of Christians, was also strongly represented in the army; whole legions were Christian. When they were ordered to attend the sacrificial ceremonies of the pagan established church, in order to do the honours there, the subversive soldiers had the audacity to stick peculiar emblems—crosses—on their helmets in protest. Even the wonted barrack bullying of their superior officers was fruitless. The Emperor Diocletian could no longer quietly look on while order, obedience and discipline in his army were being undermined. He interfered energetically, while there was still time. He promulgated an anti-Socialist—beg pardon, I meant to say anti-Christian—law. The meetings of the overthrowers were forbidden, their meeting halls were closed or even pulled down, the Christian emblems, crosses, etc., were, like the red handkerchiefs in Saxony, prohibited. Christians were declared incapable of holding public office; they were not to be allowed to

---

[a] The King's will is the supreme law!—*Ed.*

become even corporals. Since there were not available at that time judges so well trained in "respect of persons" as Herr von Köller's anti-overthrow bill assumes, Christians were forbidden out of hand to seek justice before a court. This exceptional law was also without effect. The Christians tore it down from the walls with scorn; they are even supposed to have burnt the Emperor's palace in Nicomedia over his head. Then the latter revenged himself by the great persecution of Christians in the year 303 of our era. It was the last of its kind. And it was so effective that seventeen years later the army consisted overwhelmingly of Christians, and the succeeding autocrat of the whole Roman empire, Constantine, called the Great by the priests, proclaimed Christianity the state religion.

London, March 6, 1895

Marx and Engels,
Selected Works in 3 vols
Vol. 1, Moscow, 1976,
pp. 186-204

Notes

[1] The *Silesian uprising*—the riot of the weavers employed in cottage industry in Silesia, in 1844 caused by brutal exploitation and extremely low earnings. The uprising was crushed by Prussian government troops and the participants subjected to savage reprisals. The Silesian uprising had a great impact on the future development of the working-class movement in Germany. p. 35

[2] In February 1845, three meetings at which communism was discussed were held in Elberfeld. Frederick Engels, who was one of the organisers of these meetings, spoke on February 8 and 15. In the "Speeches in Elberfeld" Engels for the first time set forth in public some of the conclusions reached in his work *The Condition of the Working-Class in England*, written in September 1844-March 1845. p. 40

[3] The reference is to the revolution of 1640-60 in England and the French Revolution of 1789-94. p. 41

[4] This refers to the elimination, as a result of socialist revolution, of the exploitation system based on private ownership of the means of production and the division of society into antagonistic classes. **p. 43**

[5] *The Communist Correspondence Committee* was founded by Karl Marx and Frederick Engels in Brussels early in 1846. Similar committees were founded shortly afterwards in London, Paris, Cologne and some other cities.

The aim of these committees, according to Karl Marx and Frederick Engels, was to achieve ideological and organisational unity of Communists and progressive workers and to fight against trends in the working-class movement alien to the proletariat. p. 45

[6] George Sand, *Jan Žiska*, a historical novel. Introduction. p. 47

[7] The *Principles of Communism* is the second version of the Communist League programme. It was drawn up by Frederick Engels in late October-November 1847 on the basis of the first version, the "Draft of a Communist Confession of Faith", written by him in June of the same year and approved by the Communist League First Congress of the Communist League (June 1847) as its draft programme.

323

The Communist League—the first international communist organisation of the proletariat founded by Karl Marx and Frederick Engels; it existed from 1847 to 1852. The Communist League was founded at its First Congress, held in early June 1847 in London. It took as its motto "Working Men of All Countries, Unite!" The aims of the Communist League were proclaimed in the Rules approved by its Second Congress (November 29-December 8, 1847): the overthrow of the bourgeoisie, the rule of the proletariat, the abolition of the bourgeois system and the building of a classless communist society. On the instruction of the Second Congress Karl Marx and Frederick Engels wrote the programme of the Communist League—the *Manifesto of the Communist Party*, which was published in February 1848.

After the defeat of the 1848-49 Revolution, the Communist League was reorganised and continued its activity amid mounting reaction. In the summer of 1850 a split took place in the League's Central Committee, as a result of a sectarian and adventurist policy pursued by the Willich-Schapper group. In May 1851 the League practically ceased its activity due to police persecutions and arrests of its members. Soon after the Cologne Communist trial the League officially announced its dissolution.

The Communist League was of great historical significance as a school for proletarian revolutionaries, an embryo of the proletarian party and a predecessor of the International Working Men's Association. p. 48

[8] The thesis that the victory of the socialist revolution was possible only simultaneously in all advanced capitalist countries was correct for the period of pre-monopoly capitalism. In the new historical conditions, V. I. Lenin, proceeding from the law of uneven economic and political development of capitalism in the era of imperialism, came to the conclusion that the socialist revolution could first triumph in several countries or even in a single country. Lenin also proved that at the stage of imperialism, when the capitalist system as a whole has matured sufficiently for a socialist revolution, the revolution will not necessarily win first in the most developed country; it can win in a country with a medium level of capitalist development. p. 52

[9] The *Manifesto of the Communist Party*—the first programmatic document of scientific communism, which proclaimed the fundamental principles of the scientific theory of revolutionary transformation of human society. The *Manifesto* was written by Karl Marx and Frederick Engels in December 1847-January 1848 as the Communist League programme. It was first published in London in February 1848 and in the same year translated into several European languages. "With the clarity and brilliance of genius, this work outlines a new world-conception, consistent materialism, which also embraces the realm of social life; dialectics, as the most comprehensive and profound doctrine of development; the theory of the class struggle and of the world-historical revolutionary role of the proletariat—the creator of a new, communist society" (V. I. Lenin, *Collected Works*, Vol. 21, p. 48). p. 55

[10] In their works of the 1840s and 1850s, prior to Marx having worked out the theory of surplus-value, Marx and Engels used the terms "value of labour", "price of labour", "sale of labour" which, as Engels noted in 1891 in the introduction to Marx's pamphlet *Wage Labour and Capital*, "from the point of view of the later works were inadequate and even wrong". After he had proved that the worker sells to the capitalist not his labour but his labour-power Marx used more precise terms. In later works Marx and Engels used the terms "value of labour-power", "price of labour-power", "sale of labour-power". p. 62

[11] The struggle for legislation limiting the working day to ten hours was waged in England from the end of the 18th century. In the 1830s and 1840s it was supported by broad masses of the proletariat. In June 1847, under the pressure of the Chartist movement, the Parliament passed the Ten Hour Bill, which was applicable only to juveniles and women. p. 65

[12] *Address of the Central Committee to the Communist League* was written by Karl Marx and Frederick Engels late in March 1850, when they still hoped for a new revolutionary upsurge. It summed up the results of the 1848-49 Revolution and was widely circulated as a leaflet. p. 77

[13] In March 1848, a revolution broke out in Germany. Popular uprisings flared up in Vienna, Berlin and other towns. The decisive role in the uprisings was played by the workers; however, it was the bourgeoisie who profited as a result of the revolution because of poor organisation of the proletarian masses. p. 78

[14] As a result of the March revolution, an All-German National Assembly was convened in Frankfurt-am-Main in May 1848. Its task was to eliminate the political fragmentation of Germany and draft a constitution for the whole of Germany. However, as a result of the cowardice and vacillation of its Liberal majority and indecision and inconsistency among the petty-bourgeois Left wing, the Frankfort National Assembly failed to take a firm stand on the fundamental issues of the German revolution: it did not take supreme power in the country into its hands, did nothing to improve the position of the workers and peasants and did not support the national liberation movements of the Poles and the Czechs. The Assembly did not dare to mobilise the people against the counter-revolutionary offensive and in defence of the imperial Constitution it had drawn up. In May 1849 the Assembly had to move to Stuttgart. In June 1849 it was dissolved by counter-revolutionary troops. p. 79

[15] See Karl Marx, *The Class Struggles in France, 1848 to 1850*, Chapter III (Karl Marx and Frederick Engels, *Selected Works*, Moscow, 1976, Vol. 1, pp. 256-86). p. 88

[16] On *The Eighteenth Brumaire* (November 9, 1799) Napoleon Bonaparte overthrew the government of the Directory and established a military dictatorship in France.

By the *second edition of the eighteenth Brumaire* Marx means the coup d'état carried out by Louis Bonaparte and his supporters on December 2, 1851, as a result of which he was proclaimed Emperor of the French (Napoleon III). p. 91

[17] On December 10, 1848, Louis Bonaparte was elected President of the French Republic by a general vote. p. 93

[18] *"Hic Rhodus, hic salta!"* (Here is Rhodes, leap here!)—words addressed to a swaggerer in one of Aesop's fables, who claimed that he had once made a giant leap on the island of Rhodes, to which he got the reply: "Why cite witnesses if it is true? Here is Rhodes, leap here!"

Here is the rose, here dance!—a paraphrase of the preceding quotation used by Hegel in the preface to his *Philosophy of Right* (in Greek *Rhodus*, the name of an island, also means "a rose"). p. 94

[19] In May 1852, Louis Bonaparte's term as President of the French Republic expired. According to the French Constitution of 1848, presidential elections

were to be held every four years on the second Sunday in May and no one could
be elected to the presidency for a second term.   p. 95

[20] Quoted from Goethe's *Faust*, Part I, Scene 3.   p. 95

[21] On May 15, 1848, a demonstration of the revolutionary masses took place in
Paris, led by Louis Blanqui and other revolutionaries. The demonstrators forced
their way into the hall where the Constituent Assembly was in session and
demanded that the promise of bread and work for everyone be met and a
Ministry of Labour set up. The people declared the Constituent Assembly
dissolved and formed a new Provisional Government. However, they were over-
whelmed by government troops, and the workers' leaders—Blanqui, Barbès,
Albert, Raspail and others were arrested. The bourgeoisie took advantage
of the May 15 events to carry out a number of measures against the
proletariat.   p. 97

[22] The *June Insurrection*—the heroic uprising of the Paris workers which took
place on June 23-26, 1848 and was suppressed by the French bourgeoisie with
extreme brutality. It was the first ever open civil war between the proletariat
and the bourgeoisie.   p. 97

[23] *Crapulinski*, a spendthrift Polish nobleman, is the hero of Heine's poem, *Two
Knights*. The name was formed from the French word *crapule*, which means
belly-worship, gluttony, drunkenness, and also a base scoundrel. Here Marx
alludes to Louis Bonaparte.   p. 99

[24] On *June 13, 1849* the Party of the Montagne (the petty-bourgeois party of
democratic republicans, which assumed the name of the revolutionary party in
the French Revolution) organised a peaceful demonstration as a protest against
the violation of the French Constitution by the President and the majority of the
Legislative Assembly in sending French troops to suppress the revolution in
Italy. After June 13, the government started a campaign of reprisals against the
democrats.   p. 100

[25] The *Society of December 10*—a secret Bonapartist organisation active in the
coup d'état of December 2, 1851. It was formed in 1849 primarily from *déclassé*
elements, political adventurers, representatives of the military, etc. The name
comes from December 10, 1848, the date when Louis Bonaparte was elected
President of the French Republic.   p. 100

[26] During the upsurge of the strike movement in England in 1853, the Chartists
attempted to set up a Mass Movement which was to unite the trade unions and
the broad masses of unorganised workers. The movement was to be led by a
Labour Parliament elected at mass meetings and trade union conferences. The
Labour Parliament met in session in Manchester on March 6-18, 1854. Karl
Marx was invited as an honorary delegate but failed to attend. Later on,
leadership of the Labour Parliament was seized by the trade unionists who
rejected political struggle. After 1854 it was never convened.   p. 109

[27] *The People's Paper*—a Chartist newspaper printed in London from May 1852
to June 1858. Marx and Engels contributed to it from October 1852 to
December 1856.   p. 111

[28] Engels is evidently referring to the Chartist meeting held in Manchester on October 4, 1858. Ernest Jones, a leader of revolutionary Chartism, spoke there in defence of a union with the bourgeois radicals. He intended to lead a joint fight for electoral reforms, hoping to revive the mass Chartist movement on this basis. However, for the sake of the union with the radicals Jones made important political concessions when working out a common platform and renounced every point in the People's Charter except the demand for universal manhood suffrage. Marx and Engels criticised him for this departure from revolutionary positions. p. 114

[29] On September 28, 1864, a big international workers' meeting was held in St. Martin's Hall in London, at which the International Working Men's Association, subsequently known as the First International, was founded and the Provisional Committee elected. Karl Marx became a member of the Provisional Committee and later of the commission for drawing up the Association's programme documents. p. 118

[30] *Confidential Communication* was written by Karl Marx about March 28, 1870, when the anarchists led by Bakunin intensified their struggle within the First International against the General Council, Marx, Engels and their followers. Marx, as Corresponding Secretary for Germany, sent this Communication to the Committee of German Social-Democratic Workers' Party.
p. 123

[31] This refers to the resolution of the General Council of the International Working Men's Association, adopted on November 30, 1869, "On the Policy of the British Government with Respect to the Irish Prisoners".

After the national uprisings of the Fenians (February and March 1867) were suppressed, those who had taken part were arrested and thrown into British prisons. The resolution, the draft of which was written by Karl Marx, laid emphasis on the fact that the British Government's refusal to amnesty the Irish prisoners was typical of the British bourgeoisie's colonialist policy, and expressed solidarity with the Irish people fighting for the liberation of their imprisoned comrades. p. 123

[32] Reference is to the 1801 Act of Union imposed on Ireland by Britain after the suppression of the 1798 uprising. The Act of Union destroyed the last vestiges of Ireland's autonomy, dissolved the Irish Parliament and led to the complete enslavement of Ireland, turning in into a British colony. p. 123

[33] *Asiento*—the name of the treaties, under which, in the 16th-18th centuries, Spain granted an exclusive right to foreign states or private individuals to sell Negro slaves to her colonies in America. p. 135

[34] *Tantae molis erat* (it was worth the effort)—a phrase from Virgil's *Aeneid*, Book One, Verse 33. p. 135

[35] *The Paris Commune* was the first attempt to set up a dictatorship of the proletariat; it lasted from March 18 to May 28, 1871. The Paris Commune separated the church from the state and the school from the church, replacing the standing army by the universal arming of the citizens, introduced the principle that judges and officials should be elected by the people, establishing that the highest salary of the employé was not to exceed the worker's wage and took a number of measures to improve the condition of the workers and the

327

urban poor. On May 21, 1871, the troops of Thiers' counter-revolutionary government broke into Paris and drowned it in blood: about 30,000 people were killed, 50,000 arrested and many thousands condemned to penal servitude. p. 140

[36] *The Civil War in France* by Karl Marx is an outstanding programme document of scientific communism. It was written as an address of the General Council of the First International to all the members of the International Working Men's Association in Europe and the United States of America in April-May when the Paris Commune was waging its heroic struggle against the armed forces of counter-revolution. p. 143

[37] See Karl Marx, "Second Address of the General Council of the International Working Men's Association on the Franco-Prussian War" (Karl Marx and Frederick Engels, *Selected Works*, Vol. 2, Moscow, 1976, pp. 195-201). p. 143

[38] *Legitimists*—supporters of the "legitimate" Bourbon dynasty overthrown in France in 1792; they represented the interests of the large hereditary landowners and the upper clergy. In 1830, following the July revolution and the second overthrow of the Bourbons, the Legitimists formed a political party.
Orleanists—supporters of the House of Orleans, the younger branch of the Bourbons which was in power during the July monarchy (1830-48) and was toppled by the revolution in February 1848; the party represented the interests of the financial aristocracy and the big bourgeoisie.
In 1848, after the February revolution, both monarchist parties formed a bloc under the name of the *Party of Order*. p. 145

[39] *Chambre introuvable*—Chamber of Deputies in France during the early years of Restoration (1815 and 1816), made up of extreme reactionaries. p. 145

[40] On March 10, 1871, the National Assembly passed a law on the deferred payment of debts, which was a heavy blow to the workers and other poor strata of the population and also led to the bankruptcy of many small entrepreneurs and traders. p. 146

[41] *Décembriseur*—participant in the Bonapartist *coup d'état* of December 2, 1851. General Vinoy personally participated in it, commanding the troops which suppressed the attempt of the Republicans to raise a rebellion in one of the *départements*. p. 146

[42] According to the newspapers, Thiers and his ministers intended to pocket over 3,000 thousand francs as "Commission" from the Internal loan which the Thiers Government had decided to raise. Thiers confessed later that the financial circles with which negotiations on the loan had been conducted had demanded a speedy suppression of the revolution in Paris. The law on the loan was passed on June 20, 1871, after the crushing of the Paris Commune. p. 146

[43] *Capitulards*—a contemptuous nick name given to the advocates of capitulation during the siege of Paris by the Prussian troops in 1870-71. p. 147

[44] On October 31, 1870, an attempt was made in Paris to revolt against the Government of National Defence. On learning that the government had decided

to begin talks with the Prussians, the workers and revolutionary National Guards captured the town hall and set up an organ of revolutionary power—the Committee of Public Safety—with Louis Blanqui at the head. The members of the Government of National Defence detained in the hall were forced to promise to hold elections on November 1, hand over the power to the Commune and resign. However, taking advantage of the poor organisation of the insurgents and discord among their leaders, the government managed to recapture the town hall with those National Guard units which remained loyal to it and regain power.   p. 150

[45] On *January 22, 1871*, a revolutionary demonstration of the proletarians and the National Guard took place in Paris on the initiative of the Blanquists. The demonstrators demanded the overthrow of the Government of National Defence and the formation of a Commune. The troops guarding the town hall fired on the demonstrators at the orders of the government; many of the participants were arrested and decrees issued closing all Paris clubs and banning people's gatherings and the publication of a number of newspapers. After stifling the revolutionary movement the Government of National Defence began preparations for the capitulation of Paris.   p. 150

[46] *Sommations* (a preliminary demand to disperse)—a warning before dispersing a demonstration, gathering or meeting by force. By the 1831 law, the warning was repeated three times, after which force could be used.   p. 151

[47] During the events of October 31, 1870, when the members of the Government of National Defence were detained in the town hall, some insurgents demanded that they be shot, but Gustave Flourens prevented this.   p. 152

[48] Voltaire, *Candide*, Chapter 22.   p. 152

[49] *The Civil War in France* by Karl Marx was printed with a supplement containing documents which testified to the atrocities committed by the Versailles counter-revolutionary clique headed by Thiers.   p. 152

[50] *Girondins*—the party of the big commercial, industrial and landowning bourgeoisie during the period of the French Revolution. When in power (August 1792-May 1793), they opposed immediate proclamation of a republic, hindered the progress of the revolution and eventually sided with the counter-revolution. During the Jacobin dictatorship (June 1793-July 1794) they opposed the Jacobin government and the revolutionary masses supporting it under the pretense of defending the *départements*' right to autonomy and federation.   p. 158

[51] The reference is to the Paris Commune's decree of April 16, 1871 deferring all debt payments for three years and abolishing all interest on them. The decree substantially improved the financial position of the petty bourgeoisie.   p. 161

[52] Marx refers to the rejection by the French Constituent Assembly of the draft bill on *concordats à l'amiable* aimed at deferring debt payments. As a result, a considerable section of the petty bourgeoisie were utterly ruined and found themselves at the mercy of their creditors, the rich bourgeoisie.   p. 161

[53] *Frères Ignorantins* (Ignorant Brothers)—nickname given to the religious order founded in the 17th century whose members educated the children of the

poor. Pupils as the Order's schools were given an essentially religious education with very limited general instruction. By using these words Marx stresses the poor quality and clerical character of primary education in France.   p. 162

[54] *Alliance républicaine des Départements* (Republican Union of the Departments)—a political association of Paris residents who came from different departments of France. The Alliance supported the Paris Commune and called for struggle against the Versailles government and the monarchist National Assembly.   p. 162

[55] This evidently refers to the Paris Commune's appeal "Aux travailleurs des campagnes" (To the working people of the villages) printed in April-early May 1871 in newspapers and as a separate leaflet.   p. 162

[56] The allusion is to the law of April 27, 1825, passed by the reactionary government of Charles X, on paying compensation to former émigrés for the confiscation of their estates during the French Revolution. The greater part of the sum, which amounted to about 1,000 million francs and was paid as a 3 per cent state rent, went to court aristocracy and big landowners.   p. 162

[57] See Note 38.   p. 163

[58] This refers to a number of laws which Marx aptly described in his work *The Class Struggles in France*: the decree under which France was divided into military districts where the commanders enjoyed wide powers and the President of the Republic was given the right to appoint and replace mayors; the law placing village teachers under the prefect's control; and the law enhancing clerical influence on public education.   p. 163

[59] The *Vendôme column*, made of bronze from captured enemy guns and crowned with the statue of Napoleon, was erected in Paris in 1806-10 to commemorate the victories of Napoleonic France. On May 16, 1871, it was pulled down by order of the Paris Commune, but was re-erected in 1875.   p. 164

[60] A search of the Picpus nunnery brought to light instruments of torture and cases of nuns being incarcerated in cells for many years; in the Church of Saint Laurent a cemetery for the victims of secret murders committed there was discovered. The Commune made public these facts in its newspaper *Mot d'Ordre* on May 5, 1871 and also in the pamphlet *Les Crimes des congrégations religieuses.*   p. 165

[61] *Wilhelmshöhe*—a castle of the Prussian kings near Cassel where Emperor Louis Napoleon Bonaparte and the commanders of the French army captured at Sedan were imprisoned. Their chief occupation there was making cigarettes for their own use.   p. 165

[62] *Absentees*—rich landowners who did not as a rule live on their estates.   p. 166

[63] *Francs-fileurs* (literally: "free absconders")—the nickname given to the Paris bourgeois who fled from the besieged city. The name sounded all the more ironical because of its similarity to the word *"francs-tireurs"* ("free sharp-shooters"), French guerillas who actively fought against the Prussians.   p. 167

⁶⁴ *Coblenz*—a city in western Germany; during the French Revolution it was the centre from which French landlord-monarchist émigrés organised plots and made preparations for intervention against revolutionary France. Coblenz was the seat of the émigré government headed by the rabid reactionary de Calonne, former Finance Minister of Louis XVI.   p. 167

⁶⁵ *Chouans*—participants in counter-revolutionary riots in Brittany and adjoining areas at the time of the French Revolution. During the Paris Commune the name was given by analogy to monarchist detachments recruited in Brittany by the Versailles Government.   p. 168

⁶⁶ Under the impact of the proletarian revolution in Paris, mass revolutionary actions took place in Lyons, Marseilles and several other towns of France in late March-early April 1871. On March 22, the National Guard and the working people of Lyons captured the town hall and on March 26 proclaimed the Commune. In Marseilles the insurgents captured the town hall, arrested the prefect, formed a *département* commission and fixed April 5 as the date for elections to the Commune. The revolutionary actions of the Lyons and Marseilles working people were brutally suppressed. The town of Marseilles was shelled.   p. 169

⁶⁷ Karl Marx cites the appeal of the National Guard Central Committee to the citizens of Paris of March 22, 1871. The appeal was issued as a poster and also printed in the *Journal Officiel de la République Française* No. 84, March 25, 1871.   p. 180

⁶⁸ In this sentence Karl Marx sums up the content of the article which described the stand taken by the National Guard Central Committee on the payment of the indemnity. The article was printed in the *Journal Officiel de la République Française* No. 83, March 24, 1871.   p. 183

⁶⁹ An additional tax of 45 centimes per franc of direct taxation was introduced by the Provisional Government of the Second Republic on March 16, 1848, the full burden of which was borne by the peasants and caused deep resentment among them. The big landowners and the Catholic clergy made use of it to set the peasants against the democrats and the Paris workers.   p. 184

⁷⁰ *Phalanstères*—palaces where members of producer and consumer associations of the ideal socialist society were to live, according to the French utopian Socialist Charles Fourier.

Icarie—an imaginary communist country depicted in the philosophic and social novel *Voyage en Icarie* by the French utopian Communist Étienne Cabet.
                                                  p. 188

⁷¹ This refers to a provocative rumour, spread by the reactionary newspaper *Paris-Journal*, that the Paris members of the First International, acting in the spirit of the Anti-German League, had expelled all the Germans from its sections. The provocation was exposed by the Paris Federal Council of the International Working Men's Association in a special letter to the General Council, and also in a declaration by the General Council, written by Karl Marx and printed in the *Times*.

The *Anti-German League* was set up in Paris and financed by the aristocrats and the bourgeoisie; the workers had nothing to do with this organisation. p. 189

[72] The reference is to the anarchists, followers of Bakunin, who rejected the principle of authority in the revolutionary struggle and denied the necessity of a working-class party and a proletarian state.   p. 195

[73] Engels paraphrases the inscription made over the entrance to Hell in Dante's *Divina Commedia*.   p. 196

[74] *L'Alliance de la Democratie Socialiste* (the Alliance of Socialist Democracy) — an international anarchist league founded by Bakunin. In 1869, the members of the Alliance joined the International Working Men's Association (the First International), where they led an overt and covert struggle against the General Council headed by Karl Marx and Frederick Engels with the aim of splitting the international working-class movement and subordinating it to the anarchists. Their rejection of the class struggle and opposition to the formation of mass political parties of the working class were bound to lead to the subordination of the working-class movement to the bourgeoisie. At the Hague Congress of the First International (1872) the anarchists' ideas were denounced and Bakunin and Guillaume, the Alliance leaders, expelled from the International.   p. 200

[75] A series of articles under the general heading of "El Cagliostro Bakunin" were printed in the newspaper *Der Volkstaat* Nos. 87, 88, 89 and 90 of September 19, 21, 24 and 26, 1873. The articles, by Frederick Engels, were a brief summary in German of his work "The Alliance of Socialist Democracy and the International Working Men's Association." In the 1894 edition Engels referred the reader to the full German translation of the work, which appeared in 1874.   p. 200

[76] The reference is to the constitutional monarchists who supported King Amadeo of Spain, a protégé of the European powers.   p. 202

[77] The *Alfonsists*—a group associated with Spanish reactionary circles of large landowners, the clergy and the upper bourgeoisie. They supported the claims to the Spanish crown of a representative of the Bourbon dynasty, who was proclaimed King of Spain (Alfonso XII) in 1874.   p. 202

[78] The *Carlists*—a reactionary clerical-absolutist group who in the first half of the 19th century supported the pretender to the Spanish throne—Don Carlos, brother of King Ferdinand VII. Backed by the military, the Catholic clergy and the backward peasantry in some Spanish provinces, the Carlists unleashed a civil war (1833-40), which actually turned into a fight between the feudal and Catholic elements on the one hand and bourgeois liberals on the other. Following Don Carlos' death in 1855, the Carlists supported his grandson, Don Carlos the Younger. In 1872, amid political crisis and an acute class struggle, the Carlists intensified their activity and began another civil war that ended only in 1876.   p. 202

[79] See Karl Marx and Frederick Engels, *Collected Works*, Vol. 4, p. 518. p. 203

[80] See Karl Marx and Frederick Engels, "The Alliance of Socialist Democracy and the International Working Men's Association".   p. 205

[81] William Shakespeare, *King Henry IV*, Part I, Act V, Scene 4.   p. 206

[82] *The Republican-Intransigents*—a bourgeois Republican party.   p. 215

[83] *Critique of the Gotha Programme*, written by Karl Marx in April-May 1875, contains critical remarks on the draft programme of a United Socialist Workers' Party of Germany which was published in connection with the unification congress to be held in Gotha on May 22-27, 1875. The two German workers' organisations—the Social-Democratic Workers' Party (Eisenachers) and the General Association of German Workers (Lassalleans)—were to merge into a united Socialist Workers' Party of Germany. Though Marx and Engels were in favour of mending the split in the German working-class movement, they were resolutely opposed to ideological compromise and concessions to the Lassalleans on questions of principle. They sharply criticised the erroneous theses of the draft programme, which was nevertheless adopted by the Congress with minor amendments. p. 217

[84] This refers to the Social-Democratic Workers' Party, founded at a Congress of German, Austrian and Swiss Social-Democrats held in Eisenach on August 7-9, 1869, and later known as the Eisenachers. The party's programme (the Eisenach programme of 1869) corresponded in the main to the principles of the First International. p. 217

[85] The German *People's Party* was founded in 1865; it was made up of democratic elements from among the petty and middle bourgeoisie, mainly in the South-German lands. The party opposed Germany's unification as a centralised democratic republic under Prussian hegemony and advocated the idea of a federative German state, the so-called "Greater Germany" including both Prussia and Austria. The left wing of the People's Party, formed by the Saxonian Workers' Party which joined it in 1866, was close to the First International; it subsequently left the People's Party and took part in founding the Social-Democratic Workers' Party (Eisenachers) in 1869. p. 217

[86] *Lassalleans, Lassalleanism*—an opportunist trend in the German working-class movement in the 1860s-1870s, named after Ferdinand Lassalle, a petty-bourgeois Socialist, president of the General Association of German Workers' Union (1863). The Lassalleans spread reformist illusions on the possibility of advancing towards socialism by means of legal propaganda, universal suffrage and producers' associations subsidised by the reactionary bourgeois-junker Prussian state. They regarded the state as a supra-class institution and maintained that it could be gradually transformed into a so-called "free people's state". The Lassalleans also rejected the necessity for economic struggle by the working class and the trade unions, basing themselves on the pseudo-scientific "iron law of wages" conceived by Lassalle, according to which the workers could not win even a slight increase of wages under capitalism. p. 218

[87] The "Marat of Berlin" is obviously an ironical reference to Hasselmann, editor-in-chief of the *Neuer Social-Demokrat*, the organ of the Lassallean General Association of German Workers. p. 227

[88] *The League of Peace and Freedom*—a bourgeois pacifist organisation set up by petty-bourgeois republicans and liberals in Switzerland in 1867. The League spread false ideas among the masses and diverted the proletariat from the class struggle, asserting that it was possible to prevent wars by creating "the United States of Europe". p. 228

[89] Quoted from Goethe's poem, "Das Gottliche". p. 229

[90] The reactionary *population theory* of the British economist and clergyman Thomas Robert Malthus (1766-1834) denied the existence of capitalist exploitation and held that the plight and destitution of the workers in capitalist society was caused by an excessively high birth-rate among workers' families. Malthus based himself on the false thesis that population growth always runs ahead of the production of the means of consumption and insisted on measures to reduce the birth-rate among the working classes. p. 229

[91] *Kulturkampf*—the name given by bourgeois liberals to a system of reforms carried out by Bismarck's government in the seventies of the 19th century under the banner of a campaign for secular culture. The reforms were directed against the Catholic Church and the Centre Party which supported the separatist and anti-Prussian trends of the landowners, the bourgeoisie and part of the peasantry in the Catholic regions of Germany. Bismarck's policy was aimed at diverting the workers from the class struggle by fanning religious differences. In the early eighties, when the workers' movement was on the upsurge, the greater part of these reforms was repealed. p. 235

[92] Marx's letter to the editorial board of the *Otechestvenniye Zapiski* was written soon after the publication in that journal in October 1877 of the article "Karl Marx before the Tribunal of Mr. Zhukovsky" by N. K. Mikhailovsky, an ideologist of Russian Narodism. The article contained false interpretations of a number of theses from Marx's *Capital*. The letter was never sent and was found by Engels after Marx's death among his papers.
Otechestvenniye Zapiski—a literary-political journal printed in St. Petersburg in 1820-84. p. 237

[93] The reference is to the book by August Haxthausen, *Studien über die innern Zustände, das Volksleben und insbesondere die ländlichen Einrichtungen Russlands* (Studies of the Domestic Conditions, the Life of the People and Especially the Rural Institutions in Russia), Parts I-III, Hannover-Berlin, 1847-52. p. 237

[94] *The Anti-Socialist Law* was introduced in Germany on October 21, 1878. The law banned all Social-Democratic and mass workers' organisations and the labour press; socialist literature was confiscated and Social-Democrats subjected to reprisals. The law was repealed on October 1, 1890, under pressure from the mass working-class movement. p. 241

[95] The words are from the answer by Count Eulenburg, the German Minister of the Interior, to August Bebel's speech, delivered in the Reichstag on September 16, 1878. p. 241

[96] An allusion to the American Civil War (1861-65). p. 241

[97] Quoted from a poem in Heine's "Buch der Lieder" beginning with the words *"Ein Jungling liebt ein Mädchen..."*. p. 242

[98] The *Programme of the French Workers' Party*, which was founded in 1879, was drawn up in May 1880. It contained a theoretical part—the Introduction, written by Karl Marx and a practical part—the minimum programme, drafted by Jules Guesde and Paul Lafargue. In Engels' words, the theoretical Introduction formed a communist substantiation of the tasks facing the French

Workers' Party. The programme was adopted at the party congress held in November 1880.   p. 252

99 The reference is to the Reform Bill adopted by the British House of Commons in 1831 and finally approved by the House of Lords in June 1832. It was directed against the political monopoly of the landowning and financial aristocracy and gave representatives of the industrial bourgeoisie access to Parliament. The proletariat and the petty bourgeoisie who were the main force in the struggle did not receive the right to vote.   p. 257

100 In mentioning the year 1845 Engels has in mind the exposition of Marx's and his own views presented in their joint work, *The German Ideology*, written in 1845-46.   p. 262

101 *The question of the "republic"* was raised in the pages of the *Sozialdemokrat*, the central organ of German Social-Democracy, in the articles "From the Defence Speech of Louise Michel" and "Republic or Monarchy? On the Anniversary of the Storming of Bastille", published in the issues No. 27 and No. 28, June 28 and July 5, 1883.   p. 264

102 The *German Progressive Party*, was founded in 1861 and was supported by the commercial bourgeoisie, small industrialists and some craftsmen. The Progressives supported the unification of Germany under Prussia's hegemony, the convening of an all-German parliament and the establishment of a liberal ministry responsible to the parliament. After the unification of Germany (1871), the Progressive Party, out of fear of the working class and hatred of the socialist movement, tolerated the domination of Prussian Junkerdom in semi-absolutist Germany. In 1884 the Progressives merged with the Left wing of the National-Liberal Party, forming the German Free-thinking Party.   p. 265

103 The reference is to the counter-revolutionary rebellion. In *The Civil War in France* Marx refers to the counter-revolutionary mutiny of the Versailles against the Paris Commune as the "slaveholders' rebellion" and "slaveholders' conspiracy" by analogy with the revolt of the slave-owners in the South which led to the American Civil War of 1861-65.   p. 271

104 *Possibilists*—an opportunist trend in the French socialist movement led by Bruce, Malon and others. The leaders of the Possibilists proclaimed the reformist principle of fighting only for that which is "possible", hence the name.
p. 277

105 *The constitutional conflict* between the Prussian government and the bourgeois-liberal majority in the Diet broke up in the early 1860s. In February 1860 the Diet rejected the bill on the reorganisation of the army submitted by War Minister von Roon. However, the government soon secured approval for budgetary allocations to maintain the "fighting spirit of the army" which actually meant the beginning of reorganisation. In March 1862, when the liberal majority refused to approve the military budget and demanded a responsible ministry, the government dissolved the Diet and called new elections. In September 1862, a reactionary ministry under Bismarck was set up, which again dissolved the Diet in October of the same year and initiated a military reform, spending on it funds without the Diet's approval. The conflict was resolved only in 1866 when the Prussian bourgeoisie capitulated to Bismarck following Prussia's victory over Austria.   p. 281

[106] Frederick Engels ironically joins together the names of the two dwarfish "sovereign" states incorporated in the German Empire in 1871—Reuss-Greiz and Reuss-Gera-Schleiz-Lobenstein-Ebersdorf. p. 281

[107] *Manchesterism, or Freetradism*—a trend in the economic policy of the first half of the 19th century. The Free-Traders represented the interests of the industrial bourgeoisie, above all the British, and defended the principles of free trade and non-interference by the state in economic affairs. In the 1840s and 1850s the British Free-Traders were an independent political group which joined the Liberal Party in the 1860s. The so-called Manchester School led by the textile manufacturers Cobden and Bright expressed Free-Tradism as a trend in economic thinking. p. 282

[108] The south-German states, Bavaria and Württemberg, enjoyed special rights laid down in the treaties on their incorporation in the North-German Confederation (1870) and in the Constitution of the German Empire (1871). They retained, for example, the right to levy a special tax on brandy and beer, and control over posts and telegraphs. Bavaria also retained independent control of its army and railways. In the Federal Council the representatives of Bavaria, Württemberg and Saxony formed a special commission on questions of foreign policy which had the right of veto. p. 283

[109] The reference is to the dictatorship of Napoleon Bonaparte who proclaimed himself first consul following the *coup d'état* of the eighteenth Brumaire (November 9) 1799. This *coup d'état* completed the bourgeois counter-revolution in France. In 1804 France was officially proclaimed an Empire and Napoleon, the Emperor of the French. Many bureaucratic institutions of the First Empire (1804-15) were retained in France even during the Third Republic (1870-1940), despite changes of régime. p. 284

[10] This article was written as an answer to criticism by Giovanni Bovio, an Italian bourgeois philosopher and political figure, of the first part of Engels' "Socialism in Germany", which appeared in the Italian Magazine *Critica Soziale* on January 16, 1892. The editor, F. Turati, sent Engels Bovio's article on February 2, 1892, with a request that Engels reply to the criticism. On February 6, 1892, Engels sent Turati a letter which was published in the *Critica Soziale* on February 16, 1892 as an article under the heading "Frederick Engels to Giovanni Bovio" and was later reprinted by several Italian newspapers. p. 286

[111] The greeting was written in connection with an invitation sent to Frederick Engels to participate in the work of the International Congress of Socialist-Minded Students in Geneva (December 22-25, 1893) at which Armenian, Belgian, Bulgarian, Italian, German, Polish, Rumanian, Russian, French and Swiss student organisations were represented. The congress discussed the questions of participation by brain-workers in the socialist movement, anti-Semitism, anarchism, "state socialism", etc. The congress adopted resolutions in the spirit of the Brussels (1891) and Zurich (1893) congresses of the Second International. p. 290

[12] The Introduction to Marx's work *The Class Struggles in France, 1848 to 1850* was written by Engels for a separate edition of this work (Berlin, 1895).

336

In 1895, when the Introduction was printed in *Vorwärts*, the central organ of the German Social-Democratic Party, the most important formulations of the proletariat's class struggle were left out without Engels' knowledge and the text was distorted (see Engels' letters to Karl Kautsky of April 1, 1895 and to Paul Lafargue, of April 3, 1895). At Engels' insistence the Introduction was immediately published in the magazine *Die Neue Zeit*, the theoretical organ of the German Social-Democratic Party, and in the separate edition of Karl Marx's work mentioned above. Howeyer, as a result of the political situation in Germany at that time, Engels had to agree to certain changes in the text, including deletions. The unabridged text of the Introduction was published for the first time in 1930 in the Soviet Union. p. 304

[113] The reference is to governmental grants which Engels named after the Sachsenwald estate, presented as a gift to Bismarck by William I. p. 307

[114] Engels uses here a term denoting one of the foreign-policy principles of the Bonapartist Second Empire (1851-70). The Bonapartist "nationality principle" contained the demand, concealed by demagogic wording, for reconsideration of historic state borders and was aimed at kindling national strife and using national movements for aggressive purposes. p. 311

[115] The reference is to the 5,000 million francs paid by France as an indemnity to the German Empire after the Franco-Prussian War of 1870-71. p. 312

[116] This refers to the prolonged struggle waged between the Dukes and the nobility in Mecklenburg-Schwerin and Mecklenburg-Strelitz. The struggle was concluded by the signing of the Constitutional Treaty on hereditary rights of the nobility (1755), whereby the former rights and privileges of the Mecklenburg nobility were confirmed. It also exempted half of their land taxes and trade and crafts from taxes and secured their dominant position in the estate Provincial Diets and their standing bodies. p. 319

NAME INDEX

A

Affre, Denis Auguste (1793-1848)—Archbishop of Paris (1840-48).—176

Aikin, John (1747-1882)—English physician, historian and radical writer.—126, 134, 135

Albarracin, Severino—Spanish anarchist, member of the Spanish Federal Council (1872-73), an organiser of the insurrection in Alcoy (1873).—207

Alerini, Charles (b. 1842)—French anarchist, an organiser of the Commune in Marseilles in April 1871; after its suppression emigrated to Italy and then to Spain, where he propagandised anarchism; expelled from the International on May 30, 1873.—204, 205

Amadeo (1845-1890)—King of Spain (1870-73), son of King Victor Emmanuel II.—202

Anderson, Adam (c. 1692-1765)—Scottish economist, author of a book on the history of commerce.—135

Auer, Ignatz (1846-1907)—a leader of the German Social-Democratic Party.—217

Augier, Marie—French journalist, author of a number of articles on economics.—136

Aurelle de Paladines, Louis Jean Baptiste d' (1804-1877)—French

Jesuit general, commander-in-chief of the National Guard in Paris (March 1871).—146, 147, 149

B

Bailly, Jean Sylvain (1736-1793)—French astronomer, a leading figure in the French Revolution, one of the leaders of the liberal constitutional bourgeoisie.—93

Bakunin, Mikhail Alexandrovich (1814-1876)—Russian revolutionary and writer, one of the founders and ideologists of anarchism.—200, 210, 211, 213, 217, 263

Barbès, Armand (1809-1870)—French petty-bourgeois democrat, a leading figure in the 1848 Revolution, deputy to the Constituent Assembly.—111

Barrot, Odilon (1791-1873)—French bourgeois politician; head of a ministry supported by the counter-revolutionary bloc of monarchist factions (December 1848-October 1849).—320

Bauer, Bruno (1809-1882)—German idealist philosopher, Young Hegelian.—38

Bebel, August (1840-1913)—one of the founders and leaders of German Social-Democracy; friend and comrade-in-arms of Marx and Engels.—217, 314

339

the Paris Commune; on April 4, 1871 was taken prisoner and shot by Versailles troops.—152

E

Eden, Frederick Morton (1766-1809)—English economist, disciple of Adam Smith.—133, 136

Engels, Frederick (1820-1895)—40, 56, 179, 217, 260, 262

Estrup, Jacob Brönnium Scavenius (1825-1913)—Danish conservative statesman, Finance Minister and Prime Minister (1875-94).—274

Eulenburg, Wendt August Botho, Count (1831-1912)—Minister of the Interior of the German Empire.—241

F

Favre, Jules (1809-1880)—French lawyer and statesman, Foreign Minister in the National Defence government and Thiers' Cabinet (1870-71), executioner of the Paris Commune.—144, 146, 149, 152, 165, 171, 191

Feuerbach, Ludwig (1804-1872)—German materialist philosopher of the pre-Marxian period.—43

Fielden, John (1784-1849)—English manufacturer, philanthropist, proponent of factory legislation.—133-34

Flocon, Ferdinand (1800-1866)—French politician and writer; and editor of the newspaper *Réforme*, member of the Provisional Government (1848).—295

Flourens, Gustave (1838-1871)—French revolutionary and naturalist; Blanquist, member of the Paris Commune; brutally murdered by the Versaillese in April 1871.—146, 150, 152

Fourier, Charles (1772-1837)—French utopian Socialist.—41

Frankel, Leo (1844-1896)—prominent figure in the Hungarian and international working-class movement, Paris Commune member, comrade-in-arms of Marx and Engels.—164, 190

Frederick II (1712-1786)—King of Prussia (1740-1786).—303, 317

G

Galliffet, Gaston Alexandre Auguste, Marquis de (1830-1909)—French general, a hangman of the Paris Commune.—152, 153

Ganesco, Grégori (c. 1830-1877)—French journalist, Bonapartist, subsequently a supporter of Thiers' government.—163

Geib, August (1842-1879)—German Social-Democrat.—217

George Sand (Aurore Dudevant) (1804-1876)—French writer.—47

Giffen, Robert (1837-1910)—English economist and statistician, finance expert.—247

Gladstone, William Ewart (1809-1898)—British statesman, leader of the Liberal Party, Prime Minister (1868-74; 1880-85; 1886; 1892-94).—234

Gracchus Gaius Sempronius (153-121 B.C.)—tribune of the people in ancient Rome (123-122).—92, 319

Gracchus Tiberius Sempronius (163-133 B.C.)—tribune in ancient Rome (133 B.C.).—92, 320

Guizot, François Pierre Guillaume (1787-1874)—French historian and reactionary statesman.—55, 92, 101, 116

Gülich, Gustave (1791-1847)—German economist and historian, author of works on the history of the national economy.—129

H

Hasselman, Wilhelm (b. 1844)—a leading figure in the Lassallean General Association of German Workers, editor of the *Neuer Social-Democrat* (1871-75); in 1880 was expelled from the German Social-Democratic Party for his anarchist leanings.—227

Hastings, Warren (1732-1818)—first British Governor-General of India (1774-85), pursued brutal colonial policy; in 1788 was brought to trial for abuse of power, was later acquitted.—128

Haussmann, Georges Eugène (1809-1891)—French politician, Bonapartist; participated in the *coup d'état* on December 2, 1851; directed work on the reconstruction of Paris.—174

Haxthausen, August (1792-1866)—Prussian official and writer, travelled in Russia and wrote a book on land relations there.—56, 237

Heeckeren, George Charles d'Anthès, Baron de (1812-1895)—French politician, Bonapartist.—151

Hegel, Georg Wilhelm Friedrich (1770-1831)—German idealist philosopher, prominent for his dialectics. —38, 116

Heinzen, Karl (1809-1880)—German writer, petty-bourgeois republican.—104

Hervé, Edouard (1835-1899)—French writer, bourgeois liberal.—173

Herzen, Alexander Ivanovich (1812-1870)—Russian revolutionary democrat, materialist philosopher and writer.—221

Hodgskin, Thomas (1787-1869)—English economist and writer who championed the interests of the proletariat and criticised capitalism from the standpoint of utopian socialism.—126

Horner, Francis (1778-1817)—English economist and politician.—134

Huxley, Thomas Henry (1825-1895)—English naturalist, follower of Darwin.—161

J

Jacquement—Vicar-General of the Archbishop of Paris.—158

Jaubert, Hippolyte-François, Count (1798-1874)—French statesman, monarchist, Minister of Public Works in Thiers' government (1840), deputy to the National Assembly (1871).—178

Jones, Ernest Charles (1819-1869)—one of the leaders of revolutionary Chartism.—114

Juvenal (Decimus Junius Juvenalis) (born c. 60-died after 127)—Roman poet and satirist.—320

K

Kautsky, Karl (1854-1938)—German Social-Democrat, initially a Marxist theoretician, subsequently an opportunist and ideologist of Centrism.—260

Köller, Ernst Matthias (1841-1928)—German statesman, Prussian Minister of the Interior (1894-1895); persecuted the Social-Democratic Party.—321

Kugelmann, Ludwig (1830-1902)—German Social-Democrat; took part in the 1848-49 Revolution in Germany; member of the First International, friend of Marx and Engels.—140-42

L

Lafargue, Paul (1842-1911)—prominent figure in the French and international working-class movement, an outstanding propagandist of Marxism, writer; one of the founders of the French Workers' Party (1879), disciple and comrade-in-arms of Marx and Engels.—289, 296, 300

Lange, Friedrich Albert (1828-1875)—German philosopher, neo-Kantian.—229

Lassalle, Ferdinand (1825-1864)—German Socialist, founder of the General Association of German Workers (1863); advocated unification of Germany from "above", under the supremacy of Prussia; with his followers, he constituted an opportunist wing of the German working-class movement.—221, 227, 229-30, 313

Lecomte, Claude Martin (1817-1871)—French general, killed by the insurgent soldiers on March 18, 1871.—149, 150, 153, 170, 172

prominent Jacobin leader of the French Revolution, head of the revolutionary government (1793-94).— 91, 92

Robinet, Jean François Eugène (1825-1899)—French physician and historian, republican, Mayor of a Paris department during the siege of the city in 1870-71.—178

Rössler, Konstantin (1820-1896)—German writer, supporter of Bismarck.—320

Royer-Collard, Pierre Paul (1763-1845)—French philosopher and politician, supporter of constitutional monarchy.—92

Ruge, Arnold (1802-1888)—German writer, Left Hegelian, bourgeois radical.— 35, 36

Rousseau, Jean Jacques (1712-1778)—French Enlightener and democrat.— 220

S

Sagasta, Praxedes Mateo (1825-1903)—Spanish statesman, leader of the Liberal Party.—214

Saint-Just, Louis Antoine (1767-1794)—prominent Jacobin, leader of the French Revolution.—92

Saisset, Jean (1810-1879)—French admiral and politician, monarchist.— 151

Saltykov, Alexei Dmitrievich, Prince (1806-1859)—Russian traveller, writer and artist; travelled in India (1841-43 and 1845-46).—106

Say, Jean Baptiste (1767-1832)—French economist, representative of vulgar political economy.—92

Scheffer—member of the National Guard and of the Paris Commune.— 153

Simon, Jules (1814-1896)—French statesman, Minister of Public Education in the National Defence Government and Thiers' Cabinet (1870-73); an instigator of the struggle against the Commune.—146

Smith, Adam (1723-1790)—Scottish economist, prominent representative of classical political economy.— 136

Soria Santa Cruz, Frederico (1815-1891)—Spanish general, suppressed the Andalusian uprising in 1872.— 208

Sulla (Lucius Cornelius Sulla) (138-78 B.C.)—Roman general and statesman, Consul (88 B.C.), dictator (82-79 B.C.).—144

T

Tacitus (Publius Cornelius Tacitus) (c. 55-c. 120)—Roman historian.— 173

Tamerlane—see *Timur*

Tamisier, François Laurent Alphonse (1809-1880)—French general and politician, Republican; Commander-in-Chief of the Paris National Guard (September-November 1870).—150

Thiers, Louis Adolphe (1797-1877)—French historian and statesman, President of the Republic (1871-73), executioner of the Paris Commune.—140, 143, 144-48, 150, 151, 152, 155, 163-64, 165, 167-72, 175-76, 184, 311

Thomas, Clément (1809-1871)—French general and politician, bourgeois republican; took part in suppressing the June 1848 uprising in Paris; commander of the Paris National Guard (November 1870-February 1871); was shot by insurgent soldiers on March 18, 1871.—149, 150, 153, 170, 172

Timur (Tamerlane) (1336-1405)—Central Asian general and conqueror.—152

Tolain, Henri Louis (1828-1897)—French engraver, Right-wing Proudhonist; during the Paris Commune went over to the side of the Versaillese; subsequently expelled from the International.—153

Tomas, Francisco (c.1850-1903)—member of the Spanish Federal Council of the International (1872-73), a leader of the anarchist organisation in Spain; expelled from the International in 1873.—208

Trier, Garcon (b. 1851)—Danish Social-Democrat, a Left-wing leader of the Social-Democratic Party of Denmark.—273

Trochu, Louis Jules (1815-1896)— French general and statesman, head of the National Defence Government, Commander-in-Chief of the armed forces of Paris (September 1870-January 1871); treacherously sabotaged the city's defence.—143, 144, 148, 150, 175

Tucker, Joshua (1712-1799)—English parson and economist.—136

V

Vaillant, Edouard Marie (1840-1915)— French Socialist, a founder of the Socialist Party of France.—276

Valentin, Louis Ernest—French general, Bonapartist, Prefect of Paris police on the eve of the March 18, 1871 uprising.—146, 147

Velarde, José Marie—Spanish general, captain-general of Catalonia (April-September 1873).—207

Viñas, Garcia Jose—Spanish medical student, anarchist; an organiser of the Spanish Alliance (1868); took part in revolutionary actions in 1873.—204

Vinoy, Joseph (1800-1880)—French Bonapartist general, participant in the *coup d'état* of December 2, 1851; Governor of Paris from January 22, 1871; one of the butchers of the Paris Commune.—140, 146, 147, 148, 151, 152

Voltaire, François Marie Arouet (1694-1778)—French deist philosopher, satirist and historian, prominent Enlightener.—152

W

Weitling, Wilhelm (1808-1871)—prominent figure in the German working-class movement in its initial stages, a theoretician of utopian egalitarian communism.—286, 287

Weydemeyer, Joseph (1818-1866)—prominent figure in the German and American working-class movement, first propagandist of Marxism in the U.S.A., friend and comrade-in-arms of Marx and Engels.—104

William I (1797-1888)—King of Prussia (1861-88), Emperor of Germany (1871-88).—171, 322

Witt, Jan de (1625-1672)—Dutch statesman who championed the interests of the big merchant bourgeoisie.—132

Wróblewski, Walery (1836-1908)— Polish revolutionary democrat, a leader in the Polish insurrection 1863-64; general of the Paris Commune; member of the General Council of the International.—164

SUBJECT INDEX

348

154, 155, 156, 177, 178, 228, 250, 264-65, 289, 307, 310-11, 314, 316
— loss of its revolutionary spirit in bourgeois-democratic revolutions— 78-79, 98, 99, 100, 101, 102, 211, 307
See also *Capitalism, Classes and class struggle, Revolution, bourgeois, Working class*

C

Capitalism
— as a mode of production—49, 58-67, 106-07, 116-17, 125-39, 226, 229, 238-39, 243, 245-51, 257-59.
— its contradictions—57-66, 112, 138-39, 160, 248, 250
— inevitability of its collapse—39, 48-49, 62-67, 104, 107, 111, 115, 117, 138-39, 161, 177-78, 239, 243, 246-47, 250, 255, 258, 269
See also *Anarchy of capitalist production, Bourgeoisie*
Capitalist class—see *Bourgeoisie*
Chartism—203
Chauvinism—189-90
Classes and class struggle—4, 46-47, 48-49, 52, 65, 74, 98, 104, 159-60, 177, 182, 247, 248, 256-59
— in bourgeois society—40-41, 43, 52, 56-76, 104, 109, 160-61, 177, 226-28, 246-47, 256-59, 264, 265, 293, 304-22
— essence of the Marxist theory of classes and class struggle—104
See also *Bourgeoisie, Communism (socio-economic formation), Dictatorship of the proletariat, Historical materialism, Peasantry, Petty bourgeoisie, Revolution, socialist, State, Working class*
Colonies
— colonial policy—107, 126-29, 132, 135, 260
— national liberation struggle in the colonies and the revolutionary movement of the working class—104, 261
See also *National question, national liberation movement*
Commune—see *Paris Commune of 1871*
Communism, scientific—see *Socialism, scientific*

Communism (socio-economic formation)—41, 46-47, 48, 52-54, 70, 71, 73-76, 81, 88, 223-25, 245, 248-49, 251, 269
— conditions for the building of— 44, 46-47, 50-52, 54, 291
— two phases of communist society—223-25
— transitional period between capitalism and socialism—88, 104, 232
— and the national question—73-74
— its basic principles—48, 52-54, 69, 75, 81, 223-25, 226, 245-46, 248-49, 269, 291
— abolition of classes and class distinctions, society without classes— 43, 46-47, 53-54, 75-76, 81, 88, 104, 191, 230, 246-47, 251, 268
— as association in which the free development of each is a condition for the free development of all—76
— and withering away of the state— see *State*
See also *Dictatorship of the proletariat, Means of production, Revolution, socialist*
Communism, utopian—see *Socialism, utopian*
Communist League, the—77-87
Communist movement, Communist— 45, 48-50, 55, 68-76, 293
See also *Communist League, Party, proletarian*
Conspiracies, revolutionary conspiracy—49, 277
See also *Bakuninism, Blanquism*
Contradictions, antagonistic—46-47, 56, 57, 67, 69, 74, 76, 112, 116-17, 243, 250
See also *Classes and class struggle*
Co-operation, co-operative movement— 119, 160, 230-31, 298-99, 301-02
Counter-revolution—98, 145-53, 155, 164, 166-69, 171-74, 176-77, 211, 212, 242, 286, 311, 320
Crises of over-production—see *Economic crises*

D

Democracy
— bourgeois—70, 143-57, 165, 166,

H

Historical materialism
— materialist conception of history as the philosophical foundation for theory of scientific communism— 43-44, 48-76, 91, 104, 105, 116-17, 126, 137-39, 142, 188, 237-39, 240, 245-51, 254-55, 304-22
See also *Basis and superstructure, Classes and class struggle, Communism (socio-economic formation), Masses, their role in history, Mode of production, Productive forces and production relations, Revolution, socialist, Socialism (communism), scientific, Socio-economic formation, State*
Historical tendency of capitalist accumulation—137-39, 237-39

I

India—56, 106, 107, 128, 260
See also *National question, national liberation movement*
Industrial revolution—57, 59-60, 110, 112, 310
Initiative, revolutionary—69, 89, 140, 161, 187
Insurrection of the Paris proletariat of June 1848—97-98, 150, 155, 161, 316
Insurrection, uprising—36, 40-41, 47, 64, 84, 89, 97, 140, 156, 187, 204-14, 215-16, 254, 307, 311, 315-19
— as an art—89, 210, 315-19
Internationalism, proletarian—55, 67, 68, 73, 105, 119-22, 123-24, 178, 189, 190, 228, 243, 310, 312, 320
International, the First—118-19, 121-22, 124, 177-78, 188, 200, 201, 212, 213, 214, 215, 221, 227-28, 262, 311
International Working Men's Association—see *International, the First*
Ireland—56, 123-24, 132
See also *National question, national liberation movement*
Italy
— working-class and revolutionary movement—119, 294-95

— prospects for socialist revolution—244, 295

L

Labour
— under capitalism—39, 54, 56, 59, 63-64, 67, 69-71, 118, 125, 133, 134, 135, 160, 182-83, 186, 229, 301
— under communism—53-54, 70, 71, 118, 186, 223-24, 225
Lassalleanism, Lassalleans—218-23, 225-36
Law, right, legislation
— as a superstructure—71, 117, 222, 225
See also *Basis and superstructure*

M

Marxism—see *Communism scientific; Historical materialism, Political economy (Marxist)*
Masses, their role in history—30, 66-67, 139, 187, 244, 265, 308-10, 318
Materialist conception of history—see *Historical materialism*
Means of production, the
— expropriation of the petty producers under capitalism—46, 126, 132, 137-38, 139, 161, 163, 186, 238
— expropriation of expropriators— 50-53, 69, 75, 87, 138, 139, 160, 246, 247-49, 291, 302, 307
— socialisation of the means of production—48, 51-53, 70, 139, 160, 186, 223, 239, 246, 247-49, 252, 287, 291, 302, 306
— possibility for the means of production to be purchased from their owners under the dictatorship of the proletariat—51, 304
See also *Productive forces and production relations*
Mode of production—49, 58-64, 75, 116-17, 137-39, 226, 245-51
See also *Capitalism, Communism (socio-economic formation), Productive forces and production relations, Socio-economic formation*

351

REQUEST TO READERS

Progress Publishers would be glad to have your opinion of this book, its translation and design and any suggestions you may have for future publications.

Please send all your comments to 17, Zubovsky Boulevard, Moscow, U.S.S.R.

MARX K. *Critique of the Gotha Programme.*
New edition

This work written in 1875 deals with some
major problems of Marxist theory.

Marx describes the basic features of communist society and reveals the difference
between socialism, its first phase, and communism, its higher phase, which will see
the implementation of the principle "From
each according to his ability, to each according to his needs".

Critique of the Gotha Programme is a
model of the scientific elaboration of
working-class party's tasks, a model of an
irreconcilable attitude to all opportunism.

The book is annotated and has a name
index.

**Progress Publishers
will soon publish**

MARX K., ENGELS F. *Manifesto of the Communist Party.* New edition

This work is the first programme document of Marxism.

It expounds with brilliant clarity and vividness the fundamentals of Marxism and sets forth the aims of the struggle of the proletariat and of its vanguard—the Communist Party. The Manifesto scientifically outlines the paths of the development of society and reveals the historic role of the proletariat. The book elucidates the basic problems of the strategy and tactics of the working class and its Party.

The book is supplied with notes.